For Lucy & Bob —

Hope you like it —

Robert van Gulik "Kore"

From Lion to Eagle

*A true story of an immigrant
and what is still possible in America*

Robert van Luyn

Pocahontas Press, Inc., Blacksburg, Virginia

From Lion to Eagle, by Robert van Luyn
     Cover Art by Arthur Calvin McCash and Robert van Luyn
     Book Design by William Babboni

Published by Pocahontas Press, Blacksburg, Virginia
Printed and bound in the United States of America
          by Taylor Specialty Books, Dallas, Texas

Copyright©2008 by Robert van Luyn
     ISBN 978-0-926487-45-1
     ISBN 0-926487-45-0

For Trudy,
who listened to these stories
dozens of times
for more than forty years
and never discouraged me
from telling them one more time
to someone else

Acknowledgments

How does one acknowledge all the people who helped, encouraged, and supported me and made possible the experiences that made my journey in this wonderful country so unbelievable? They are too many to mention, almost too many to remember, but all deserving credit for the influence they had on my life. Too often situations present themselves that need explanation. How could I possibly explain all the people who came into my life with their determination to change the path I had taken; or those who unintentionally changed the direction in a positive way by their example? How do I do justice in recognizing them and the influence they have had on every step I took?

I hope that my memories will shed some light on the continuing possibilities that are still available to all inhabitants of this fantastic country. Just think — all those born in America start life at such a fantastic advantage over anyone else in the world. Americans' desire and drive are the only limits that determine their future. In this country we all are able, if we are not satisfied with our present situation, to change it, even in midstream, and undertake a new course of action.

Many thanks go to the friends who for years encouraged me to record all the fantastic happenings that seemed to have been following (or guiding?) my life. A mere heartfelt "thank you" does not begin to do it justice. I owe a great deal to my dear wife Trudy, who eliminated an overabundance of dangling participles; and to Susannah Masten Wilson, who checked my writings and gave me valuable advice on how to bring this effort to fruition; and to Arthur Calvin McCash, whose original art work was used on the favors for my 50th arrival anniversary party and was slightly modified for this book.

To all who made this fantastic journey possible, my heartfelt thanks.

— Robert van Luyn

Contents

1

Perhaps Not Quite Wanted

My birth certificate states that I was born on March 30, 1933, in Rotterdam, the Netherlands. I had two older sisters, Thea, who was twelve, and Tine, who was two-and-a-half years old. Since I was the first of the family born in a hospital, my family was proud to say that I was born on the Henegouwelaan, where the Mother and Child Hospital was. I was told that I cried a lot and had some terrific lungs, with the result that my cradle was parked in the bathroom so that whenever I cried I would not keep other babies awake. A popular Dutch crooner at that time was named Bob Scholte. All the nurses called me Bob Scholte whenever I cried, and I would be transferred immediately to the bathroom.

I was born on a Thursday evening at 7:00 o'clock. Late that afternoon, Mamma had walked perhaps three miles to the market at the Noordplein, bought some fish, proceeded to walk home, fried the fish, and then decided that it was time to deliver. She called her sister Rie, and the two took a taxi to the hospital. Pappa was at work and was notified that Mamma was on her way to the hospital, but by the time he had made it to the hospital, I had already been born.

The first two children were girls. Pappa was looking forward to a third girl and was not terribly pleased when he was told that he was the father of a healthy boy. He made that very clear the next day when he went to the City Hall to register his newborn son. All newborn Dutch children had to be registered at the City Hall. The clerk at City Hall was ready with his book to check if the name selected was an allowable name. At that time in Holland, the law did not allow surnames as a middle name because a double last name would denote nobility, and one could "sneak in" a little touch of nobility at a later time by using the middle name more prominently. Well, Pappa, still being perturbed about what had happened the night before, responded when the clerk asked for the name of his newborn son with: "Bob."

The clerk asked, "What else?" Again, in Holland it is not unusual to have two or three middle names.

"Nothing else, just Bob."

"Come on, you can do better than that."

"No, just Bob."

"Well, let's at least make it Robert."

"All right, Robert then."

Back at the hospital, grandmother Uitenbroek said to Pappa, "I've seen the baby."

Pappa said, "Yes, what an ugly thing, isn't he?"

Grandmother Uitenbroek, a bit hard of hearing, misunderstood what Papa said and innocently responded with "Yes, I think so too, just like you."

This story was told to me many times, and we all laughed about it. My two sisters always said that I was Pappa's favorite in spite of that less-than-warm welcome into this world.

The first thing that I can remember clearly is taking my first steps. It happened at the beach in Scheveningen in June or July 1934. Apparently, I was slow in starting to walk. The whole family would have a week of vacation at a bed and breakfast, and I clearly remember that Mamma, my sisters

Thea and Tine, and my *Tante* (aunt) Rie went for a stroll on the beach. I was left with *Oom* (uncle) Jan, Tante Rie's husband, who was the "he-man" in the family. He was strong and athletic and could swim like the best. We played a little, and Oom Jan encouraged me to try to walk a few steps in the sand. And sure enough, my first steps were taken right then and there. I remember feeling good because he praised me.

When everyone came back from their stroll, Oom Jan said: "Guess what happened?" And we showed what had occurred. Tante Rie, Mamma's sister said, "Oh, he dared to walk because he knew that he could not hurt himself in the sand if he fell." Rather than praising me for my proud accomplishment, I was criticized for something that was not even true. That comment has always stuck with me because, as young as I was, I felt good about my accomplishment, and I had not given it a thought that I could have hurt myself if not surrounded by soft beach sand. Later in life, I've always been careful around young children because they can hear and understand a great deal more than we adults tend to think they do.

When I was three years old, the family moved from the Dahliastraat to the Jasmijnstraat, which was later renamed the Malvastraat, after the village of Hillegersberg was annexed by Rotterdam. After convincing Pappa that I could carry a small potted plant safely from one house to the next, a couple of streets away, without dropping it, like my sister Tine and cousin Annie were allowed to do, I was allowed to do so and was so proud of myself.

That same year I went to nursery school. I enjoyed it, but what sticks in my mind is that dumb routine in which parents participate — comparing the progress of their child with that of another child. Tante Rie and Oom Jan had two daughters; Annie was three years older than I was, and Riet was a little less than a year younger. Mamma was an easygoing type of person who would avoid conflicts if possible, but Tante Rie was domineering and insisted that, come hell or

Kindergarten, 1937 "From My Toddler Time," says sign

high water, she would voice her opinion and that she, of course, was always right! I was constantly compared to Riet, my younger cousin. In kindergarten, Riet could tie her shoes, and I could not. Riet had no fear of water, and I was petrified by the mere sound of the word "water." Every time we saw Tante Rie, she had to tell Mamma how fantastic my younger cousin Riet was.

So on one spring day, I, a very shy boy, asked my teacher if she could teach me how to tie my laces. I did not think that it was a good idea to let her know about my shortcomings because if she knew she might actually laugh about it, I reasoned, and that was the last thing I would want. So I got up the courage to ask her, so that perhaps I could show my Tante Rie that I had learned to lace my shoes "without any help from anybody." In Dutch, the word for "to tie" is *"strikken,"* which happens to be the same name for the plural of "bows." Several days went by, and the teacher did not do anything for me, so I timidly asked her again, and she appeared to be slightly annoyed because she had forgotten to do it for me. At the end of the day, at about 3:15 p.m., she had made me a pair of brightly colored crepe paper bows and had tied them to the tops of my shoes. I thought that it made me look like a little girl, and that was, of course, the last thing that I wanted. As soon as I walked around the corner of the street on which the school was located, I started to tear off the crepe paper bows from my shoes. Papa came to meet me and saw one of the bows and made some comment. However, I never said anything to anybody about the incident or why I wanted and needed the help. Sometime later, I learned to tie my shoes and, when I did, nobody cared nor noticed that I had reached another milestone.

At six years of age, I went to elementary school. I honestly enjoyed school even though I was an average student. In the first grade, we learned to write, and right away we started to write with pen and ink. The school desk had an inkwell built into the desk at the upper right corner, and we had little nibs that we could slip into the penholder. The teacher, *Juffrouw* (Miss) Wapenaar, instructed us that we were to dip the nib of the pen into the inkwell to a depth of about a quarter of an inch. The nib was made out of curved split steel with a small hole in it. If the pen was dipped into the inkwell more than the instructed depth, the hole would be covered with ink. Well, my coordination not being fully developed caused me to go past that hole. I knew that I would get criticized for doing it wrong, so I decided to correct that by holding the pen over the inkwell and blowing the ink from the pen into the inkwell. Of course, the result was that I blew the ink out of the inkwell and into my face.

Luckily, Juffrouw Wapenaar did not see the incident, but a little later, to my surprise, she asked me what had happened. I could not figure out how she could have known about my little mishap, until I got home and Mamma told me to look in the mirror. When I did, I saw that my face was speckled with blue ink.

As I was learning to write, I faced a problem with writing the numeral "two." For some reason or other, my brain was not able to tell me how to control my fingers, with the result that Juffrouw Wapenaar "bled" all over my paperwork with her red ink. After a few days of not being able to put the little "wave" on the bottom of the "two," instead just finishing it off with a straight line, I told Tine about my problem. Tine told me to finish the writing of the number two the same way as I started writing the letter "z" longhand. Problem fixed, my sister knew how to help me! We were close because of the age difference between Thea and the two of us; Tine and I seemed to depend on each other more. Thea substituted as babysitter when Mamma had to go somewhere and ended up as somewhat of a disciplinarian.

Less than a year later, our entire family would have to depend on each other more than we ever had before.

2

War

Near the end of my first school year, I woke up one morning with the radio blasting downstairs; it was May 10, 1940, and I could not figure out what was happening. I remember the radio reporter announcing that German paratroopers were jumping near Waalhaven, a small military airport in the southern part of Rotterdam. Nobody was home. Something strange was at hand! I checked under all the beds because I thought that my sisters had pulled a trick on me. I got out on the street after I had dressed and saw our neighbor's boy, Frans Berggren. I told him that I had dressed and had not even washed my face that morning because of all the confusion. Frans told me that we were at war with Germany, and that statement did not mean a thing to me.

I decided to go a block away to Tante Rie's house and see if she knew what was happening and if she had seen my mother and sisters. When I arrived at my aunt's, my mother and sisters were there and some other people. No one could figure out why I was rather puzzled, waking up in a house with the radio blasting away with nobody at home. So much for what I thought.

I went outside and mingled among the Dutch soldiers who were aiming their rifles at the German planes. I was standing next to one soldier, and he said, "Captain, I think I can hit that one."

The captain replied, "You had better save your ammunition; we may need it later." It was crazy to think that they let children walk around them and did not tell the children to leave.

The fact, of course, was that Holland had not been at war for a long time. Holland was left out of the conflict of World War I because we had declared ourselves neutral. Not having been involved during 1914–1918, the Dutch figured that they would do the same in what turned out to be World War II.

Hitler, however, had different ideas and did not care much for neutrality. Even though the Dutch soldiers did not know too much about war, they were, much to their sorrow, soon to find out much more. Tine and I went to our elementary school, where there was a notice posted on the door stating that there was not going to be school that day due to the fact that war had broken out. I said to Tine, "Oh, great, we have a day off today." I saw the frown on the principal's face. I quickly made my way home and did not think about the incident for a number of years.

May 14 came and marked the end of the open resistance by the Dutch army against the German armed forces.
I remember the day as if it were yesterday. It was a beautiful May day, and the street makers were working in our street. The soil in Holland is so soft that the streets settle about three inches each year, so that, each four-year period, the paving stones are taken up in the street, as well as the sidewalk and the curbs. Sand is brought in and the entire street is elevated about twelve inches. The street is then paved again, removing all the bumps and potholes.

Mamma would always warn: "If you do not behave and do not work hard in school and get good grades on your report card, you'll end up being a street paver." Obviously, she did not think that that job was very high on the social scale.

Well, the bombing of Rotterdam began around noon that day, while the pavers were on their lunch break. After they had eaten their lunch, they proceeded to lie in the back of the horse-drawn sand wagon to take a sunbath. The wagon had about three or four cubic yards of sand in it. It was clean river sand and, weather permitting, it was normal for the pavers to use their lunch break in that manner. Due to the intense bombing, the center of Rotterdam was completely destroyed in a couple of hours. When the bombs fell close to our street, perhaps four or five city blocks away from us, the pavers knocked on the door and asked if they could take shelter in our neighbor's house. We were also there because Mamma had decided that we would be safer next door with the Berggrens, so we proceeded to sit on their staircase; I guess misery likes company.

Mevrouw Berggren, who had not struck me as a very religious person, was continuously praying out loud and literally scared the hell out of me. I figured if an adult was that scared, what was this seven-year-old boy supposed to feel? Certainly the bombing made a horrible racket, but that lamenting really made it unbearable. The three of us (Mamma, Tine, and I) were there, and I felt that we would have been more at ease had we stayed in our own house.

Pappa and Thea were both at work, and we had no idea in what kind of situation they had found themselves. When the bombing was over, we went outside and saw the red sky over Rotterdam. An acrid smell permeated the air, and we started to get worried about Pappa and Thea.

An hour later, Pappa came home and told us that the entire center of Rotterdam had been completely destroyed. Pappa was a manager in Rotterdam's biggest hotel-restaurant, named "Atlanta." It was in the center of town, and he had witnessed the bombing. He assured Mamma, Tine, and me that Thea was all right because it was the center of the town that had been hit, and Thea was working in the eastern

part of town that hadn't been hit. Thea had graduated from
the Home Economics High School and, at nineteen years of
age, was the youngest branch manager of the van Buren
chain of confectionary stores.

Pappa had seen the bombing from a tremendous vantage
point. In order to get a better look at what was happening,
Mr. Dirk Reese, the owner of Atlanta Hotel-Restaurant-Café,
and Pappa had decided to go to the hotel's roof terrace to get
a better view of the city and of the situation. Observing the
bombing from a "front row seat," they saw the German Stuka
bombers go down and thought that the Dutch anti-aircraft
soldiers had shot them down. Mr. Reese and Pappa were

View from Hotel Atlanta's roof terrace. Taken in 2006
(Town hall with clock; post office to right)

jumping up and down for what they thought was a success-ful hit. However, curiously, the damned things were pulling out of their "crashes" and were flying away. None of us had heard of dive bombers, at least civilians had not; however, we learned quickly how deadly they were.

The craziest thing happened while Pappa and Mr. Reese were on the roof terrace, which was five or six stories high. Since the terrace was used by hotel guests in the summer, there was an opportunity to sit in the sun and enjoy views of a bustling Rotterdam while having an afternoon drink. Of course, there were bathroom facilities, and Mr. Reese had to use the bathroom. Just as he was leaving the bathroom, a bomb hit a corner of the main post office directly across the street from the Hotel-Restaurant Atlanta. "It's getting a little dangerous," he said to Pappa, so they decided to leave the roof terrace and, of all things, rode the elevator down to the main floor. The wind had blown some burning material across the street, and the restaurant was starting to burn.

Arriving downstairs, Mr. Reese realized that the sound of the direct hit at the post office had scared him so much that he had forgotten to flush the toilet. In spite of the fact that all the windows had been blown out of the restaurant and things were starting to burn, he summoned a bellhop and told him to go to the roof terrace and flush the toilet. The bellhop completed the task, riding the elevator up to the roof terrace and back down again, and, lo and behold, the boy made it safely up and down. People do strange things when they are in stressful situations.

The hotel and restaurant burned completely, but because the building inspectors were too busy checking all the dam-age elsewhere in town after the bombing, Mr. Reese was able to hide much of the structural damage. The building was deemed repairable and was not condemned. (Today the restaurant has been converted and now houses an upscale men's clothing store, but the hotel, including the roof ter-race, is still there and celebrated its 75th birthday in 2006.)

The fact that Thea was still not home started to worry Mamma. Pappa's reassurances did not seem to do any good, but around 3:30 that afternoon, Thea came running down the street, screaming on the top of her lungs. She ran into the house, and Mamma put her on the couch, but she could not be calmed down.

I was terribly embarrassed by the whole situation because I knew that my friends were going to tease me about my big sister's behavior. Later that day, we found out what Thea had experienced. The section of town where her candy store was located had been completely destroyed during the bombing. It was a pure miracle that she had survived it. When the bombing got heavy, Thea decided to lock the store and leave for home. Before leaving the store, she took the cash out of the register and locked the door, but forgot to change back into her street shoes - a brand new pair she had just gotten for her birthday less than a week before. As she crossed the street, the store was destroyed by a direct hit.

Thea ran from building to building, and on several occasions she had been pulled by police and first aid personnel into shelters because they deemed it too dangerous to be outside. Each time, she managed to move on because she thought it better to get out of the area altogether and try to get home.

A walk that would normally take her twenty minutes took her — stretched into dash, run, and hide — almost two hours. Her nerves were shot, and it took several months before she stopped screaming every time she heard a car backfire or any kind of loud noise. When everything sort of settled down, Mamma was quite upset that Thea had taken time to take the boss's cash from the register and had not saved her brand new shoes! I must admit that Mamma hinted that Thea should take the cost of the shoes out of the cash she had. The fact that we were brought up to be honest flew in Thea's face, and she was not about to do that.

A couple of days later, Frans Bergren and I went into the downtown area, and the devastation was unimaginable. A horrible acrid smell was very strong and, if we had stayed long enough in the area, our clothes would certainly have absorbed the smell.

We heard all sorts of crazy stories from people. One of Mamma's brothers, Oom Willem, was living in the heart of Rotterdam. While bombs were falling all around him, he went back into his burning house to save his radio. In those days, a radio was an expensive piece of furniture and worth saving. A nearby explosion caused him to grab his radio and a bottle of vinegar. As he got out of the burning house, he handed his prized possession — the radio — to a stranger who was passing by and offered to help. When there was a lull in the air attack, Oom Willem found himself with a bottle of vinegar and no helpful stranger, who in his consternation had run somewhere else. The stranger had not necessarily stolen the radio but probably took shelter somewhere in a panic, and my uncle did not have time to look for him. In disgust, he threw the bottle of vinegar away and ended up losing all his belongings.

The war and the subsequent occupation by the German troops was gradually changing life as we knew it. The first thing that happened was that we went to Berlin-time. Berlin-time was not like going on daylight saving time because Berlin was one hour and forty minutes ahead of Amsterdam. The Germans decided that it was much easier to set the Dutch clock to the same time zone as Germany and, since they were the conquerors, they could do as they pleased. The result was that it was light very late in the summer evenings.

Everybody was issued a ration card. To begin with, it was a "general card" and, each week or month, certain numbers were assigned to be good for a pound of sugar, or a pound of meat, or so many points of textile.

One needed a certain number of points for a pair of socks and a different number for a shirt. Those were the days when certain items might be scarce; however, with some effort they could still be found in a store. With scarcity, prices went up. We lost our currency because it was made of silver, nickel, and copper. It was replaced by zinc coins and paper money. The *guilder*, the 2½ *guilder*, and some smaller coins were made of silver and bore the likeness of our Queen Wilhelmina, so the Germans declared it illegal to have a photograph of the royal family or any likeness of them. There was one place where one could see the silver coins throughout the war, and that was in Volendam, where until today native citizens still wear their particularly fancy traditional clothes. The men's two top pants buttons placed horizontally next to each other were made of 2½ *guilder* pieces. For some reason, the Germans did not insist on that custom being stopped.

The insult added to injury came when the edict went out that all the Jews had to wear a yellow Star of David on their outer garments. To obtain the cloth stars, they had to buy them in a notions store and had to surrender half a textile point for each cloth star, in addition to paying for the star. They had to purchase one star for each garment.

For children, the occupation was not too noticeable, but parents taught their children to keep their mouths closed, to avoid looking at Germans, and to suspect everyone for being a collaborator. One could expect collaborators anywhere and everywhere, and a simple statement such as "That rotten Kraut" would land you in jail without a trial. At night, at about eight o'clock, we would all listen to a Dutch radio broadcast from the BBC (British Broadcasting Corporation). It was strictly forbidden to listen to the BBC, and collaborators would sneak around the neighborhoods and try to find someone who had his radio on too loud. If he was caught, he would lose his radio and spend time in jail.

The Dutch news program on the BBC would start with a signature tune, a patriotic melody that was outlawed by the German occupiers. Hence, it could not be sung in school any longer. The song was "In the name of Orange open the gate...." It was a song that celebrated the Eighty-Years War in the later 16th century against the Spanish. Some of the collaborators would go around to the schools and play the tune on a portable crank-type record player and ask if any of the children had heard the song recently. I was warned that someone might come around to our classroom and ask if my parents had listened to that program. I was told by my parents not to raise my hand if such a question was asked. If a child admitted that he or she had heard the song recently, the father of the household would be arrested. My parents did not realize that I was petrified, thinking about what could happen if I were asked that question. Could I say no, if asked, and stop myself from blushing because I knew that I was lying and thereby give away the fact that Pappa listened to the BBC every night?

There is no way that anyone can imagine what you go through when you are stripped of all liberties. Despite all the miserable things we had to face day after day, school went on as normally as could be for the first three years of the war. We learned about our Dutch history and, in particular, the Eighty-Years War the Dutch had fought against the Spaniards. We were taught that the Spaniards were bad people, but that Charles V was a good and benevolent emperor and that the Dutch people did not dislike him. His son Philip II, now, that was a different story altogether. He was a devoted Catholic, did not approve of Luther's reformation, did not like the mostly Protestant Dutch people, and was not about to visit the Netherlands because it was too cold there.

In the latter part of the sixteenth century, big riots broke out in Holland, referred to as the Statues Storm. The Dutch Protestants went into the Catholic churches and broke all the statues because it says in the Bible: "You shall not make a graven image...." Well, Lord Alva was sent to Holland by Philip II to straighten out the trouble. When Lord Alva arrived, he could not tell the difference between the Protestants and the Catholics. He took care of that situation rather easily. The Protestants had destroyed the statues, and the Catholics had allowed it to happen. Therefore, all the Dutch were guilty, and Alva persecuted the entire population of Holland.

I digress with this story because I want to point out that we were taught in school to dislike things and people based on situations that had happened 300 years or more ago. Here in the United States, we think that situations ought to progress much faster. A couple of "used-to-be-Dutch eyes" look at things slightly differently and cannot help being excited because of the speed with which things change in this country and how flexible the people are.

There were new edicts in the war. Since metals were getting scarce, the Germans confiscated all copper items. The first to fall victim to their disgusting thievery were the bells from all the church steeples. Then the Dutch population had to turn in all the copper containers, spoons, and other utensils made of copper. Pappa had a few items with which he did not want to part, so Mamma made a token delivery of some copper items and our name was duly registered as having complied with the order. Pappa removed some boards on the third floor in the small bathroom and hid a number of small copper and brass items. "So those are a few items we will retrieve when the war is over," Pappa said.

As time went on, the occupation by the Germans went from bad to worse. In spite of this, or perhaps because of it, Pappa and Mamma made a point of taking the family on "normal" summer vacations. Soon we could not go to the beach any longer. It was off limits because the Germans did not want to give any young men a chance to escape and row or sail to England across the North Sea, and they also expected an invasion to begin on the beaches of Holland. Thus our vacations were spent at bed-and-breakfasts within Holland.

Since the occupying German forces had to be billeted somewhere, the Germans decided that the most logical places were the neighborhood schools. There were many

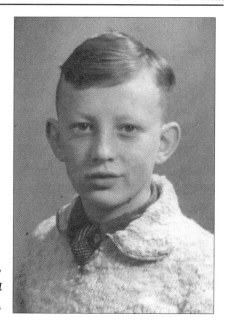

Wool was getting scarce, so Thea knitted a sheep's-wool sweater for me.

neighborhood elementary schools in Rotterdam with only six classrooms, so the Germans took over a number of schools. The children had to double up somewhere else, and we could only go half-days to school.

Then they instituted the curfew. No one without an *ausweis* (permit) was allowed outside after 8:00 at night nor before 7:00 the following morning. If you were caught outside, you would be hauled off to jail, and if you did not stop when ordered, you could be shot at or seriously hurt, to say the least. If you were not hit, it would scare the daylights out of you so you would not chance even crossing the street during curfew.

* * * *

Pappa told us stories about America and all the things that were going on there, such as what a terrific president Mr. Roosevelt was, and all the opportunities that were available to U.S. citizens. The reason why Pappa was so well informed was that he had lived in the U.S. for two-and-a-half years in the New York City area. In 1927, the depression had hit Holland a bit earlier than in the U.S. Obviously the first affected were restaurant-type businesses, including the café where Pappa worked at that time. Pappa as a young boy had made some trips working on some freighters sailing to the Middle East, so he reasoned that he could sign with the Holland America Line and work as a steward. Applicants agreed to work on a round trip, so a contract ended the moment the ship returned to Rotterdam. Well, Pappa had different plans: he worked the trip to America, got off the ship in Hoboken, and did not return when the ship departed for Rotterdam. He went to work in New York City, in the restaurant business. Each week, he sent half of his salary to Mamma who, with their six-year-old daughter Thea, was living with her parents. The reason both Pappa and Mamma could live relatively well was that the dollar's value was high compared with the Dutch guilder. Pappa did not dare to give his return address on his letters because he was considered a deserter and could be arrested in the U.S. and be returned immediately. Mamma, of course, had no intention of giving his address to the authorities, but without a return address she couldn't write back to him.

Mamma's oldest brother, Willem, a waiter in one of the restaurants in Rotterdam, said, "Sis, I'll take care of that."

"How can you? America is a large country; you'll never find him," was Mamma's response.

"I'll sign up for a round trip, and I know from previous trips a pub where the Dutch people hang out!"

Sure enough, after arriving in New York, *Oom* Willem walked into the pub he had mentioned to Mamma, and there was Pappa.

"What are you doing here?" were Pappa's first words.

"Finding you. Sis is worried to death and can't write to you!"

Pappa sent his return address in his next letter. The short and the long of it is that Pappa stayed in the New York area for two-and-a-half years, never missing sending half his week's salary to Holland. He was not able to get Mamma and

Thea to the U.S. because, everywhere she went, even in Belgium, the authorities knew that Pappa was illegally in America. Even when Mamma took a job as a governess with a well-to-do family, accompanied by Thea, the authorities did not allow Mamma to get on board a ship. Near Christmas 1929, Pappa decided to go back to Holland and sailed back to Rotterdam.

So Pappa had always been full of stories about America, and there were books around the house and a trunk in the attic with all sorts of interesting things from America. We were literally spoon-fed America from the moment we could remember.

On December 7, 1941, Pearl Harbor was attacked, and the United States entered the war. Pappa said, "It will be over now very soon because America is joining the fight and, with their industrial might, the Americans will crush Germany in a few months." Let's face it, Pappa had lived in America for more than two years, and he knew! When President Roosevelt (lucky for us, because he was of Dutch descent, as Pappa said) came on the BBC and said that the conflict could last a few more years, Pappa said he was crazy. That really scared me because Pappa, with his pro-American attitude, calling the man who was going to bring this mess to an end "crazy" was a little more than I could handle.

✳   ✳   ✳   ✳

Queen Wilhelmina, who had escaped to England at the beginning of the war, came on the BBC Dutch program and said something to the effect that Holland, although occupied by the Germans, was in pretty good shape because "We still have our 1940 army." As a result, all of the Dutch army, navy and marine corps — who had been returned to civilian life by the German occupying forces — were called up, this time not for active duty, but to be sent to Germany to be interned as prisoners of war.

That took a large number of teachers out of the school system, besides all the other positions those men had filled. My first cousin, Wim van Luijn, was a sergeant in the Dutch army and had to give up his job as a bank branch manager and was interned for the rest of the war in Germany. His *lager* (POW camp) was 60 kilometers from Dresden, and he saw the phosphor bombing of that city, and all his fellow POWs did not feel the slightest bit sorry for those civilians.

Wim told me later that the Russian POWs in the camp were treated terribly. The camp guards would just throw soup and other food on the ground and let them fend for themselves, as if they were hogs.

Some Dutch soldiers did not report to be imprisoned in Germany. These men hid from the Germans, but, since Holland is a relatively small country, it was very difficult to hide and not be caught. Once a person was hiding from the Germans, his ration card was revoked, making food much more difficult to get. In addition, the German soldiers were constantly looking for them.

One day, it was announced that everyone had to turn in their radios. It was easy for the Germans to expect to get all the radios in the country because the Dutch government had decided, before the war, that all radios had to be taxed and registered. A radio had to be registered in the same manner that a car is registered. Dutch citizens had to buy radio stamps at the post office and stick them, every month, on a special radio card that was supposed to hang on the wall next to the radio. If one did not turn in his radio, the Germans would know, and the head of the family would go to jail. Pappa said that he was not going to do it, but I begged him to because I was scared to death of the consequences.

Even before the outbreak of the war, we had no hot running water in our houses. If one wanted to take a bath, one would boil water on the stove or buy hot water. The person who sold hot water was a *waterstoker* (waterboiler). For two cents, one could buy a five-gallon bucket of hot boiling water and carry that for a couple of city blocks home and take a bath. That was a regular Friday night routine. In the latter part of March, when Mamma was walking home with two buckets of hot water, she turned her ankle in our street. Somehow she spilled both buckets of water over herself and had severe burns on her face, chest, thighs, and legs. She was in agonizing pain for a couple of days. When the doctor finished bandaging her, she looked like a mummy. The day after my birthday on March 30, 1943, there was a heavy bombing attack by the U. S. on the harbor in Rotterdam. What made it especially scary for us was that Mamma's bandages caused her great difficulty in walking, and she could not easily have gotten to the stairs if the bombing had come nearer to our neighborhood. Even though bombs were falling in the "target area," none hit the actual harbor installations, but instead hit civilian houses near the harbor. Over 300 people were killed in the bombing. I never heard an ugly word uttered toward the Americans who did the bombing. Those boys were going to liberate us from the Germans, and this was war; therefore, things like that happened. That was the general attitude.

In the summer of 1943, the Germans issued an order to all male citizens in Rotterdam ages 18 to 50 to report for one week of work in the fields around Rotterdam. The men had to dig three-foot-deep holes into which they had to place poles (similar to telephone poles). The placing was in a matrix of approximately 30 feet by 30 feet. Hundreds of poles were placed in the field, and barbed wire was fastened to them so that airplanes could not land in the fields. If one refused to report for work or was obviously not working hard enough, the person was assigned to work for a longer period at the North Sea coast. There, difficult work involved placing obstacles in the sea to hinder a possible invasion from the United Kingdom by the Allies. Supervision of all this slave labor was conducted by armed German army personnel, who would not hesitate to use their rifles for effect.

Since the Germans had ordered all the Jews in Holland to be clearly identified by wearing the yellow star of David, it was easy for the Germans to spot them on the street. One day collaborators came into the restaurant at Hotel Atlanta where Pappa was a manager and posted flyers on the windows, stating "JEWS NOT ALLOWED HERE." Pappa got so mad that he tore the poster off the window and brought it home and said, "Look what happened today — this is getting awful!" The next day he was called to the office and, even though his immediate supervisor was not a German sympathizer, Pappa was strongly reprimanded and was told in no uncertain terms that, if it happened again, his supervisor would have to report Pappa to the authorities. That poster had been placed there by the authorities, and it did not matter if Pappa liked it or not, it was going to stay there. Pappa knew that he would otherwise spend considerable time in jail. I still have the poster today to remind me how free this wonderful country is and that we have to be alert to keep it this way.

When was relief to come to Holland? Would there be a sign we could pin our hopes on, to endure the terrible suppression under which we lived every day?

3

Invasion

June 6, 1944, is another one of those days that clearly remains in my mind. It was a rather dreary morning, and it was still raining lightly as I left the house for school. Early that morning, our next door neighbor, *Mevrouw* (Mrs.) Maaskant, told me to tell Mamma that the Allied forces had invaded France.

Allied bombers had dropped leaflets over Rotterdam but, since the curfew was in effect, no one could go out and pick up a leaflet. Picking up a leaflet in itself was very dangerous. If a German soldier saw a person pick up a leaflet during the day, there was a good chance that he would shoot at that person, and it would depend totally on the soldier's marksmanship if someone would get away with an awful scare or, worse, would get shot.

Remember, there was a curfew in effect, and one became a "legal" target. During those curfew hours when no one was allowed on the streets, the Germans would gather all the leaflets. When the curfew was lifted at 7:00 a.m., all the leaflets were already picked up and destroyed.

The Germans tried hard to keep any news favorable to the Allied forces from the Dutch people. There was never any question in the minds of all the Dutch people what the outcome of the war would be; the only question was, how long was the war going to take? So here I was, aware that something big had happened, walking back home for lunch, when I spotted a pamphlet stuck to the wet roof tile of the church. The night before it had been drizzling in Rotterdam. A pamphlet had fallen onto the roof of the church, and the wetness of the rain had acted as a glue and kept the pamphlet from falling to the ground. The Germans obviously could not reach it, and there it was, a beautiful piece of news I would like to get into my hands. It so happened, as I walked by, that the sun was trying to break through the clouds that had been covering the skies all morning. With ever so slight a breeze, the pamphlet broke loose and started fluttering down to the street. The first thing I did was to look all around me to be sure that there was no German soldier in sight. The "coast was clear," and I started to run in the hope that I could get the pamphlet. As I was running, I saw an "old" man (probably 40 years old) running for the same piece of paper. I scooped the pamphlet in midair like an outfielder catches a fly ball and beat the "old" man by two feet. I heard him say: "You got it, kid," and I just ran on because, even at eleven years old, I knew not to exchange any thoughts with a stranger on the street. I knew that I had already done something dangerous by scooping up that pamphlet in clear daylight. I stuffed the pamphlet under my shirt and went home quickly.

On one side of the pamphlet, a message was printed in English, Pappa said, and on the other side the same message was printed in Dutch. It was signed by an American general named Dwight D. Eisenhower. We all read it and thought that the end was now very near. Little did we know that the worst was still to come. Pappa said: "Bob, you know what to do with that pamphlet." I did, and it meant that I should tear it up into small pieces and flush it down the toilet right away so that there was not a chance that it would be found, in the event that Germans were ever to come into the house and search for whatever they wanted to look for. Throughout the war, they had declared many ordinary household items "illegal," so the Germans did not need an excuse to ransack our houses. I told Pappa that I knew the routine, but in fact I was so attached to my find, which had almost escaped my grip, that I hid the pamphlet in one of my books.

✳   ✳   ✳   ✳

In late August of 1944, we went for a week of vacation to Arnhem. We stayed at a bed-and-breakfast and would make little trips, walking in the woods and the heather-covered fields. We noticed that there were an awful lot of German SS troops around the area who looked as if there was no war going on anywhere. We knew that they were SS troops because they were wearing caps with the skull insignia. Later, of course, we found out that those troops were temporarily stationed in the area to rest and would later be redeployed. The vacation was enjoyable, and, after a week, we went home because school was about to start for another year.

On Tuesday, September 5, 1944, a very strange thing happened. We never found out what actually set it off, but the story, which could just as well have been another rumor, went as follows. An Allied soldier got lost behind German lines in Holland, and people saw him. They immediately concluded that he was a scout, that the liberation force was right behind him, and that the liberation of Holland was only hours away. The rumor spread like wildfire, and people were standing along the highways with flowers, ready to welcome the Allied soldiers. People in Rotterdam were told the Allies were in Dordrecht, 20 miles south of Rotterdam, and people north of us said that Rotterdam was liberated. German occupiers packed their belongings, the collaborators were moving out of their houses, and it was bedlam. Dutch flags reappeared, and everyone was happy the war had finally ended for us. The day was called Mad Tuesday. This all happened twelve days before Operation Market Garden began. The German troops were ready to capitulate. Nothing happened, and by evening things were back to the same old routine: the Germans were as nasty as they had been for the past four years, and even the collaborators were returning with all their brassy bravura. Mad Tuesday is depicted in the very beginning of the movie "A Bridge Too Far," but I believe the script writers did not capture the unbelievable electricity that was flowing through the people of occupied Holland, even if it lasted only one day.

Had the Allies realized what was going on in occupied Holland, they could have strolled into the entire nation and liberated it without any loss of life; I am sure of that. Instead, as a reprisal, a large number of political prisoners were summarily executed in Vught by the Germans, who took Mad Tuesday as an unruly uprising.

✳   ✳   ✳   ✳

It was a beautiful sunny day in Rotterdam on Sunday, September 17. Planes were flying over our neighborhood, and we were looking at them. One of our neighbors had a pair of binoculars and said, "They are gliders!"

"Gliders? What are they?" I thought. The neighbor told me where to look, and indeed I saw a cable going from a plane to the one flying right behind him. There were many pairs in that configuration overhead, and once again the Dutch were full of hope that they would be liberated from that awful yoke of occupation.

The irony of the attack at Arnhem was that the English and Polish paratroopers practically jumped right into the quarters of the SSers who were temporarily stationed in Arnhem to rest up before they were assigned to their next deployment.

Monday night, there was a lot of commotion around our neighborhood because the anti-aircraft battery that was deployed at one of our neighborhood soccer fields was on the move. We later found out that they went to Arnhem to join the fight against the British and Polish airborne. The distance to Arnhem was about seventy-five miles, so it did not take too much time for them to be in position to do some real harm to the troops.

As children we were able to find some real "trophy" shrapnel pieces with the anti-aircraft batteries so close to our area. I was the envy of my friends because I found a good-sized piece, about as big as a walnut, embossed with an eagle clasping a swastika in its claws.

Pappa would stand in the darkened kitchen at night and, through the window, watch the German anti-aircraft shoot at the British airplanes on their way to bomb Germany. Large and bright searchlights would light the sky. Once a plane was caught in a searchlight, other lights would join, and as soon as he was illuminated, the pilot would try his best to escape the light because he knew that the guns were going to try to shoot him down.

We heard through the rumor mill that heavy fighting was going on in Arnhem, but we were too far from the fighting to see or experience it first-hand. I remember Thea saying, on September 26 (Mamma's birthday), nine days after Operation Market Garden began, that the attack had failed and the war would last longer and we would have to put up with the Germans even longer.

On October 10, there was a *razzia* (round-up) by the German occupying forces in Rotterdam. All males between 17 and 40 years of age were supposed to be ready to report for work in Germany. They were allowed to bring a minimal amount of clothing and were marched off under armed guards. German soldiers went from house to house to see if there were any "eligible" men hiding in the house. The men who had the nerve to hide somewhere in a closet or attic were dealt with severely if caught.

A soldier, perhaps fifty-five years old, came to our door and rang the bell. Pappa went downstairs and asked what he

BEVEL.

Op bevel der **Duitsche Weermacht** moeten alle mannen in den leeftijd van 17 t/m 40 jaar zich voor den arbeidsinzet aanmelden.

Hiervoor moeten **ALLE** mannen van dezen leeftijd onmiddellijk na ontvangst van dit bevel met de voorgeschreven uitrusting op straat gaan staan.

Alle andere bewoners, ook vrouwen en kinderen, moeten in de huizen blijven totdat de actie ten einde is. De mannen van de genoemde jaargangen, die bij een huiszoeking nog in huis worden aangetroffen, worden gestraft, waarbij hun particulier eigendom zal worden aangesproken.

Bewijzen van vrijstelling van burgerlijke of militaire instanties moeten ter contrôle worden meegebracht. Ook zij, die in het bezit zijn van zulke bewijzen, zijn verplicht zich op straat te begeven.

Er moeten worden medegebracht: warme kleeding, stevige schoenen, dekens, bescherming tegen regen, eetgerei, mes, vork, lepel, drinkbeker en boterhammen voor één dag. Medegebrachte fietsen blijven in het bezit van den eigenaar.

De dagelijksche vergoeding bestaat uit goeden kost, rookartikelen en vijf gulden.

Voor de achterblijvende familieleden zal worden gezorgd.

Het is aan alle bewoners der gemeente verboden hun woonplaats te verlaten.

Op hen, die pogen te ontvluchten of weerstand te bieden, zal worden geschoten.

Translation excerpt: "Men from 17 to 40 have to report for [slave] labor in Germany... Those who flee will be shot"

wanted. The soldier asked if there were any men 17 to 40 in the house. Pappa stood in the downstairs doorway and said no. The hallway was perhaps five feet wide and ten feet long before reaching the steps leading to the second floor where we lived. The German was not interested in climbing yet another staircase. He looked at Pappa, gauged his age, which was 49, and turned around and left. Pappa took great pride standing up to the German, saying, "I did not let that damned Kraut in my home." Ever so small were our victories, but they gave us the satisfaction of having resisted.

The men who were rounded up were sent to Germany to work in the factories. Because the Germans knew that they could not make the Dutch fight the Allies, they had the Dutch take the place of the Germans in the factories, allowing the Germans to head to the front lines to fight for the Third Reich.

One of our neighbors had been in a sanitorium with tuberculosis. He had been completely healed for several years. But, when the round-up happened, he crawled into bed and his wife showed the German soldier a letter from the doctor, which the German could not read but recognized the word "tuberculosis." After reading that word, he could not get out of their house fast enough.

We had a small leak in the third floor bathroom and, regardless of what Pappa tried to do, he could not fix it. So he asked Mamma to call the local plumber. The man said that he would come, but it so happened that he came when Mamma was visiting her sister, my *Tante* Rie. I was home, and the plumber went upstairs, sized up the situation, and started to take up the linoleum that covered the floor. Realizing his next move and remembering what Pappa had hidden under the floor, an act punishable with jail time, I ran to *Tante* Rie and got Mamma to come home immediately. When we arrived back at the house, totally out of breath, the linoleum was back in place, and Mamma said that I had worried about nothing. And so life went on in occupied Holland.

Many people had maps of Europe on their walls to follow the progress of the Allied troops by sticking pins in the map, marking the positions of the Allied lines. Again, it was a dangerous thing to do because if a German came into your home, for which no search warrant was needed, and saw that the map was up-to-date, he would know that you had obtained the troop information from the Dutch broadcast on the BBC. To have a radio and to listen to the BBC was illegal. That would be enough reason to put you in jail.

The heavily-censored news that we heard would tell us that "The headquarters of the Furher has announced the following planned withdrawals." Of course, at no time did they say that the German armed forces were getting beaten, which of course happened day after day. Our legal news was by means of a government-controlled system almost like Musak. The unit, which was rented, was the size of a small speaker with a control box. Four stations were relayed to customers, on which we could receive two Dutch stations and two Belgian stations. During the last six or seven months of the war, electric power was only supplied to the radio distribution center until 8:00 p.m.

One of the biggest figures in the Dutch collaborators' system was Max Blokzijl. He took care of all the German-fed propaganda news, and he would start each night with the opening *Geachte luisteraars* ("Dear listeners"). Sometimes power was cut off just as he said the first syllable of the word *luisteraars*, or *"Geachte luis."* The last two syllables were not transmitted, so the meaning in Dutch was "Dear lice." We would all be in bed by then because there was no heat nor any lights. Besides, we were hungry, so it was better to try to fall asleep and forget all the misery. To hear the collaborator say "Dear lice" would bring a good laugh each time it happened.

✳   ✳   ✳   ✳

School time was getting shorter and shorter; we met two days each week, perhaps for only two-and-a-half hours. City children started to wear wooden shoes, and I asked Mamma if I could get some. My leather shoes were almost gone; I was down to one pair, which had to be saved for Sundays to go to church.

The big game for boys in Holland was soccer, and mothers had an awful time with their sons because they grew up kicking every pebble on the street or any other object lying around outside. Obviously this is not too good for our shoes, and Mamma would constantly admonish me for kicking with the only pair of shoes that I had left. Once I started wearing wooden shoes, kicking pebbles became a little more difficult.

It is hard to believe but, if you put a handful of straw in the bottom, wooden shoes are very warm. Just walking on the straw would "massage" the soles of your feet and blood would circulate more rapidly, so that your feet got very warm, almost uncomfortably warm. Some lucky boys, we thought, had access to hay, and hay, being a finer texture than straw, massaged your feet more gradually. In the winter when it snowed, it became a little difficult to walk on wooden shoes because snow would stick to the bottom and, before you knew it, you were eight inches taller! You had to kick off the caked snow regularly.

Things were getting very scarce, and the Germans would confiscate anything we had if they needed or wanted it. Bicycle tires were scarce. If you were lucky enough to have a pair on your bike, it would not be long before a German soldier would see you and just take the bike.

Pappa rode his bike to work, and he managed to find some wooden tires. They were constructed in such a manner that small strips of wood were fitted to the rim of the wheel, and around that a wooden strip was fastened in a circle. The small pieces of wood would provide the rider a little "give," but it made an awful racket. The Germans were not interested in that kind of tire, so they left people like Pappa alone. Finally, even the wooden tires on Pappa's bicycle gave out, and whatever wood was available had to be used for cooking and heating, so Pappa ended up walking about forty-five minutes to work each day.

During the latter part of the war, in 1944–1945, we did not have many hours of school. In the off hours, the boys in our neighborhood would play. We had to be very careful that we would not be too rough with each other because, if you skinned your knees, the wound would heal slowly because we did not get the proper nourishment. One of my friends was very clever with his excuses, yelling: "Watch out for my scab!" That was the signal for letting go of your playmate.

Since there was nothing for me to do, I often went to the center of Rotterdam to meet Pappa at the end of his workday. Pappa was finished at the hotel at six o'clock, which gave him enough time to walk home before the curfew went into effect. In 1945, there was no more electricity nor gas nor any regularly normal services available. Since there were a number of German soldiers billeted in Hotel Atlanta, extra rations were always available there. Pappa would bring home a few pieces of coke to burn in the stove. Since this was stealing from the German occupiers, he reasoned that it was okay and in a small way even helped the war effort against the Germans.

Well, you know how that goes. Pappa decided that if Mamma would sew some extra big pockets at the very bottom of his overcoat, he could carry more pieces of coke home. However, he had to keep his coat open to avoid having the bags of coke hit his shins while walking home. Any time someone would pass him, he would put his hands in his pockets and would somewhat close his coat and walk more slowly in order not to draw too much attention to his awkward gait. There was one problem, however. The night watchman at the hotel walked home by the same streets Pappa took, and in those days you could not trust anyone. So Pappa took a longer route home to avoid running into the night watchman of the hotel. After the war, Pappa found out that the night watchman had done the same thing — steal the coke and worry about running into Pappa. So all that extra walking was unnecessary, but it was a chance no one could take.

On one of our trips home, we crossed *het Noord Plein*, the North Square in Rotterdam, which was notorious for black market trading. As we walked across the square, a German soldier spotted a black marketeer, but the man took off running. The soldier took his rifle and started to shoot. He ran after the black marketeer and shot several times. I ran after the soldier to see if the guy got away, which he did, but Pappa thought it would have been a whole lot wiser not to be such a good witness in this situation, and called me to stop. I was eleven years old, and excitement had overtaken judgment.

After October or November 1944, we did not have gas nor electric power, and my younger sister Tine and I had to go to the railroad and "sift coals." Holland's soggy soil makes laying a rail bed difficult, so the mode of construction was to lay down approximately four feet of black cinders and rock. On top of that was about six inches of coarse gravel.

This was the bed on which the ties and rails were laid. Since the Germans were short of iron ore, they just pulled up the rails of non-critical rail lines and left the creosoted ties behind. Thus, those rail lines that did not serve them for the war effort were demolished. The same fate befell the copper overhead lines that fed the electric trains; they were torn down for the Germans to use.

Tine and I would shovel the gravel out of a small area and dig up the black cinders and rock mixture. We would put a few small trowels of mixture into a sieve of about 12" x 8" with a 1/4" screen and sift the mixture. It would take us a good part of the morning to get perhaps one or two gallons of coke about the size of popcorn. We would burn it in our small emergency stove in the living room and boil sugar beets for supper. The water was reduced over the fire to make syrup. This was a tricky task because, as the syrup neared its final consistency, it would tend to boil over. You had to watch it constantly, lift the pan off the stove so that the boiling mass would go down again, and return it to the fire, repeating that routine for half an hour or so. At the same time, you had to keep the fire going.

Tulip bulbs were roasted on the back of the stove after someone thought up a way to get more heat from the stove. The contraption was fitted between the stove and the chimney pipe. It was constructed from thin black sheet iron, which was two feet by two feet and about five inches high. Smoke was channeled through the contraption in a zigzag fashion so that the entire surface would be hot. On that hot surface we roasted the tulip bulbs. We would remove the outer shell just as you peel an onion, cut the bulb in half, and take out the small flower bud because it was not supposed to be good to eat. That and cooked sugar beets and syrup were all we had to eat for the last five months of the war.

You might ask: "How does it feel to be hungry?" Just imagine going without a meal for, say, one day. You have that horrible feeling in your stomach. When you are really hungry, that growling in your stomach is with you when you wake up, and it doesn't leave you all day, no matter if you have eaten some sugar beets or tulip bulbs. You can never eat until you have enough, so you go to bed with the same feeling in your stomach with which you began your day. All we could think of was food. Pappa would tell Tine and me these unbelievable stories. Before the war, when there was a party at the hotel, there were dishes placed around the room where the party was held. Each plate held pounds of cheese-blocks for guests to take and eat whenever it pleased them and, best of all, there were enough for the guests to take as many as they would want.

Sixty years later, when communion is served in some Presbyterian churches, a half loaf of bread is passed through the pews, and communicants tear off a small piece of bread symbolizing the body of Christ who was crucified for us. Inadvertently my mind wanders back to the "hunger winter" of '44–'45, and I think that half a loaf would not have made it halfway through the first pew if this had happened in early 1945. Everyone was hungry and, when we were with other people, the subject was always food. But usually when the women were talking together, the subject would move in the direction of, "If we just could have a little soap." "Would life not be a great deal easier if we just had a bucket with some good sudsy and soapy water to do the laundry!"

✳ ✳ ✳ ✳

One day in 1945, one of the boys on the street said that ten more people had been executed in Rotterdam. That was because the resistance movement had liquidated either a German or perhaps a Dutch boy who had joined the Dutch detachment of the German army. Whatever the reason, he had been shot and killed by "the underground," as we used to call the resistance fighters. As a reprisal, ten male citizens previously arrested for political reasons were set against an outside wall of a building and, without a trial, were ex-ecuted. The bodies were left on the ground the entire day. I

34

suppose it's the same as when a driver comes upon an accident. You tell yourself that you are not going to look but, at the last minute, there goes your head turning.

I was going to meet Pappa at the end of the day, and I knew where the execution site was, just 100 feet from the hotel, so I walked by.

Once you set foot on that side of the sidewalk, you had to continue past it. There was a German soldier with a machine gun who said, "Read the notice and move on." Nailed to a post or tree was a bulletin on which the reason was given for having executed the ten men. It was a cold, rainy day, and there, in a vacant lot, were ten men of various ages. It was an awful sight, and it showed to what extent the occupiers were willing to go to make their point.

In the early part of the war, the Germans instituted the *gaarkeuken* (ready kitchen). The ready kitchens were used mainly by Dutch collaborators, and the Dutch who had no use for the occupiers would not have anything to do with them. To partake in such a German-sponsored idea was considered endorsement of their Germanic ways and definitely unpatriotic.

One summer my family went for a week of vacation with my aunt and uncle and their daughter to see friends who had moved to Hilversum. My aunt had arranged the vacation, and she and the hostess, unbeknownst to Mamma, had decided that it was too much trouble to cook a hot meal for eleven people, so we would eat from the ready kitchen.

Mamma decided not to rock the boat and to go along; however, she took Tine and me aside and threatened us with severe punishment if we told anyone that we had eaten from the ready kitchen. Little did we know that in 1945 we would be forced to eat from the ready kitchen, and by then all the ready kitchen was serving was warm water that they called soup. In it was sugar beet pulp, tulip bulbs, and some cabbage greens. Sometimes the ready kitchen served porridge. That was a treat because it seemed to fill one's stomach more. Either soup or porridge was transported in ten-gallon

*The dropping of food by Allied air forces
to starving citizens of Rotterdam.*

milk cans to the distribution places by means of a horse-drawn cart. One time, the old men who worked in the ready kitchen dropped a ten-gallon milk can filled with porridge on the street. In no time people were on their knees ladling the porridge from between the cobblestones and eating it.

✳   ✳   ✳   ✳

In spite of the awful experiences we had, there were, of course, funny moments during the war. Boy Scout groups were outlawed by the Germans because it was an English-based organization. Lord Baden-Powell was the originator; therefore it was illegal to have a troop, be it Cub Scouts or any branch of the organization. Hence, other scout-like groups were formed. Tine and I belonged to a group called Free-Spirited Protestant Youth Organization. Boys and girls had their own branches and were called Free Birds. The groups were divided into bird groups such as Falcons, Eagles, Hawks, etc. I was in the Falcons and we put on a choral cantata for Easter 1945. That time period was during the worst part of the occupation. The German occupiers were attacking the allied troops in Belgium and other places by launching their V1 and V2 rockets. Each launch pad was mobile, and they moved them around after missiles were fired.

This presented a problem for the people in Rotterdam and other parts of occupied Western Holland. Whenever a rocket misfired, it came down right around the place from which it was fired. It is interesting how quickly people adapt to situations. One knew that once the rocket had been fired and the sound of a roar diminished, the deadly beast was away from us and some poor soul down the way had to cope with it, unbeknownst to them. However, if we heard a roar and it did not diminish quickly, we knew that the V1 had misfired and was coming down somewhere close by.

The choral cantata was in the afternoon, and we sang our hearts out. Two big boys were allowed to pump the big organ in the church. Not having any electricity, the air for the pipe organ had to be generated by stepping on — or, more likely, jumping on — the pair of bellows from one to the other. I suppose that was the way it had been done in the old days, and the necessary equipment was still in working condition. So, to keep the reservoir full with an ample supply of compressed air, two of the biggest boys had to pump. At the place in the cantata after Christ had been crucified, we were supposed to make the sound of thunder to illustrate the aftermath: the curtain of the temple was torn, darkness fell, and there was an earthquake. While we were sitting in the choir loft, the boys' choir had to stomp their feet on the wooden floor. When the moment came where we had to "generate the heavenly thunder," we lost half of our congregation because the people thought that a V1 had misfired. We must have done a pretty good job of making thunder!

Near the end of April 1945, the International Red Cross had negotiated with the German command in Holland that something needed to be done for the starving Dutch people. Holland was totally isolated by the Allies, who were in a mad dash towards Berlin. The southern part of Holland had been liberated and parts of the northeast had been as well, but the western part — where Rotterdam, the Hague and Amsterdam are located — was occupied and still under German control.

Realizing that the war was all but over, the Germans allowed the Allied bombers to fly low over Rotterdam and drop tons of food in the fields behind our neighborhood. There was a mad scramble by everyone. I got a can of lard and a small box of powdered eggs and took them home after having tasted some of that good "butter." My friends did not believe me when I told them that I got some eggs because they surely would not have survived a drop out of an airplane. We realized then that it was just a matter of weeks until the total defeat of the Germans. The Swedish Red Cross had been allowed to send tons of wheat to the three major cities, and we ate our first slices of white bread. It looked as if it had been bleached, and it tasted like cake. There was not an overabundance of food coming in by air or from Sweden, but that was a start of something a great deal better.

4

Peace at Last

On May 5, 1945, we were going to bed as usual at about 8 o'clock, when I heard people shouting on the street. This was highly unusual since there was a curfew and no one could be out on the street after 8 o'clock, or else risk the chance of getting shot by a passing German soldier. I looked out the window of my third-story bedroom and heard people shout that the war was over. I ran to Tine's bedroom and told her. Our parents thought that we were fighting and were ready to calm us down. As soon as they heard what we told them, we all got dressed and went out into the street and milled around and were just so excited that we finally were at peace.

The first thought that came to my twelve-year-old mind was, "Well, that will be the end of news bulletins on the radio because there is nothing to report any longer." For five years, the news on the radio had been something about the war, so it seemed logical that there was no longer any need for that kind of information; better yet, we would have no news on the radio any longer.

On the eighth of May, the Canadians rolled into Rotterdam. The first Canadians I saw were two soldiers in a

Jeep. Tine, who was almost 15, had been going to high school and was learning French, German and English. She ran over to the Jeep, and the soldiers stopped the Jeep and talked with her a few minutes. Mamma and I waited on the sidewalk until Tine returned to us, and I asked, "What did they say?" I got the strangest answer from her. She said that she spoke with them in French and not in English. I could not figure out how that could be. I knew that Canada was in the British Empire, and that it was north of the U.S., so therefore they had to speak English.

When I went on to the center of Rotterdam, it was an absolute madhouse. Canadian Army trucks were coming into town, and everyone climbed on the trucks and rode with the liberators. The soldiers did not mind it at all, and we had the ride of our lives. Each truck was a mass of people all over the trucks as if they were a bunch of bees on a tree limb.

* * * *

The only one in the family who was not too excited about what was going on in downtown Rotterdam was Thea. On that day she was celebrating her 24th birthday, and no one outside her immediate family had given it any thought or had come to her and wished her a happy birthday. In Holland, it is a custom to have a birthday party for each member of the family, and all the relatives — aunts, uncles, nephews, nieces, and cousins — come and visit the person whose birthday it is. Thus, throughout the year, family members see each other repeatedly, and family ties are kept strong. Even during the war, this ritual went on under some difficult situations.

Not long after Liberation Day, we received news that Jacob Schotel, Pappa's first cousin, had been executed. We realized that our family had suffered a casualty. Jacob had been a lieutenant in the Dutch army. When the orders of surrender had come on the fourteenth of May 1940, Jacob had decided to bury all the small arms of his company somewhere in a field in the south of the Netherlands and "stick around" because he thought that the war would not last that much longer. While waiting to reclaim his small stash of small arms, Jacob became involved in the Underground Movement. His task was to help the Allied flyers who were shot down over Holland to cross the Belgian border south of Holland and to hand them off to Belgian Resistance fighters. The Belgians, in turn, would pass them on to French Resistance fighters, who would take them through the Pyrenees Mountains to Spain. Once in Spain, the flyers were smuggled to Gibraltar and, from there, they were repatriated to England.

Jacob started with one flyer and became more experienced and braver as time went on. He was later caught with more than a dozen flyers and sent to Vught, a notorious German concentration camp in the south of Holland. Jacob Schotel was executed in early September 1944, after the day the Dutch refer to as Mad Tuesday. Several months after the war ended, a very nice monument was erected in remembrance of Jacob and several other citizens of their small hometown of Driebergen who had lost their lives working for the Resistance.

✳ ✳ ✳ ✳

Soon after Liberation Day, Canadian trucks came around the neighborhood with crackers. It is hard to imagine that that would be such a big deal. Of course, we had been hungry for at least six months and had had meager rations years before that, so anything to eat was a treat. A plain saltine cracker was a terrific treat, and the soldiers had tons of them. Later, we children got hold of some shortening and discovered that covering a cracker with it made for an even better treat. Of course, we believed the shortening to be butter, and when we came home and told Mamma what treat we had received, she warned us that we would tear up our stomachs if we ate too much of that. What a thought, to get sick from eating too many crackers with "butter." Of course, we did not care until we had to pay the piper.

Pappa said that we should retrieve the copper items from under the third floor in the small bathroom. When the planks were removed, to our surprise the copper items were gone. The plumber, who had repaired a leak a few years before, must have stolen the copper because he knew that, if we noticed it was gone, we could not report him to the authorities at that time, out of the fear that we would be arrested.

Things were slowly getting back to normal. Every Sunday, there was a program on the radio that reviewed the progress of repair that the Dutch railroads had made during the past seven days. Besides the ruined railroads that needed to be repaired, the station houses had to be rebuilt. They had been demolished by the desperate Dutch people who were looking for the smallest splinters of wood to fuel their stoves. The way people had scavenged every scrap of wood out of the buildings would have put a termite to shame. So now, an official of the railroad proudly told the Dutch about the progress and which lines were again in service.

Pappa's youngest brother, Jo, was ill with tuberculosis and was dying, due to complications of pneumonia and malnutrition. Before *Oom* Jo died in June, Pappa and Mamma walked to the Hague, about nineteen miles from Rotterdam, to visit him. On the way back to Rotterdam, with about ten miles to go, a Canadian jeep stopped and offered them a ride. They were very pleased that the soldiers had stopped without even having been asked. Some liberators!

Slowly but surely, food items began to be available, a little of this and a little of that: potatoes, bread, cans of corned beef, and pork and beans. All of these were welcome to a population that had been suffering from malnourishment.

5

England, Here I Come

When we heard that there was a program that would send malnourished children to England for four months, Mamma started asking around and found out that one of the leaders of the *Vrije Vogels* (Free Birds), Frans Hengeveld, now a full-fledged medical doctor, knew of the program. He gave me a physical and decided that the equivalent of a ten-pound roast on each side of my chest and the same on my back would be a good start for me. I don't know what my weight was but, being tall for my age and having been on the losing side of a rough "hunger winter," I was certainly qualified as one of the worst cases in Rotterdam, as far as weight was concerned. I have no idea why only boys were chosen from Rotterdam, but that was the way it had been set up, so I was eligible.

After several other tests and after making sure that my parents had not collaborated with the Germans, I was picked as a candidate to be sent to England. On the 26th of July, 1945, I was told to go to the health department and undergo a last check before departure that same afternoon. The only check that was to be performed was to see if any child had head lice. If the nurse found any lice, the only way that a boy could go to England was to have his head shaved and then show up that afternoon ready to go to England. Mamma had done her best to keep us clean, but children will play and come in contact with other children and use their caps, etc. During the war, it was strictly forbidden by Mamma to wear, even for a second, anybody's cap or hat. I knew I did not have any lice; however, just in case, I told Mamma if they found anything I would not have my head shaved.

There was a stigma to being shaven because girls who had dated German soldiers were shaved bald after the liberation. Therefore, being bald did not leave a good impression. I would forgo going to England rather than be bald. Mamma said not to worry because, even if they did shave my head, by the time I came back from England, four months later, my hair would have grown back. I was determined that I would not go that way. When the nurse checked me thoroughly she said, "It's okay; no problem with you," Mamma was proud and gave this look, as if to say "I could have told you." We went home, packed my luggage, just a small suitcase the size of an attaché case, and reported at one of the harbors for getting on the boat to go to England.

The program would send children to England for four months to recover their health. Four months to a country who had fought the Germans for six years and won — that had to be the most exciting thing that any twelve-year-old boy could wish for. Sixty-six Rotterdammers between the ages of eight and twelve embarked on the *Batavier*. The ship seemed small, perhaps because our sleeping quarters were in the front of the ship, a fact that became very noticeable once out at sea. Before we were out at sea, we had about an hour to sail from Rotterdam to the Hook of Holland. We were given life vests and had to wear them constantly. That was not too bad as long as we were up, but when we had to go to sleep wearing those kapok-filled life vests, it was very uncomfortable to lie down. Some of us took them off, but our leader, whom we called *Oom* Tom, insisted that we put them back on again right away.

I remember that a lot of us got seasick the moment the boat was in the North Sea. Later, in England, I heard one of the leaders saying that the most spectacular sight was when two minesweepers met the boat and ran interference for us as we crossed the North Sea to England. Little did we know that it was very dangerous to be on open waters because there were still many mines in the North Sea.

Upon arrival the next day at Gravesend, we were taken to a large building somewhere in London that may have been a hospital or an institution for retired service personnel. Next door was a garrison for French sailors whom we recognized because of their caps. They had the typical dark blue navy sailor caps with a red pompom. A couple of other boys and I crawled out of the window of the room, where we and another fifty or so boys were temporarily housed, and went to the building next to us. Inside the building, soldiers were eating their lunches, and they had what we thought was an overabundance of food. They thought that it was funny that we were (sort of) asking for a slice of bread. Before we knew it, we were eating their leftovers right off their plates, which they thought was funny, and we had a ball. What we did not know was that the medical group accompanying the sixty-six hungry Rotterdam boys had decided that the best way to get us back to normal was to increase our portions slowly so that our systems would not go out of kilter.

We arrived in Doncaster the next day, in the middle of the afternoon, after a three-and-a-half-hour trip on the train from London. I remember that we went through a number of tunnels and found out very quickly that it was a good idea to have the windows closed. The locomotive that pulled the train threw out a lot of soot, and what a mess it made if the windows were open.

As soon as we arrived, we went to an area where there were busses waiting for us. I noticed a photographer and, as he was about to take a picture of the waiting Rotterdammers, I took my suitcase, with just one set of underwear and a couple of handkerchiefs, etc., and proceeded to lift it on

DONCASTER GAZETTE, THURSDAY, AUGUST 2, 1945.

They'll Like Yorkshire

Dutch children arriving at Doncaster Station, to be taken by bus to the Woodlands and Warmsworth Hostels where they will recover their health, undermined under Nazi occupation.

"Dutch children arriving at Doncaster Station, to be taken by bus to the Woodlands and Wadsworth Hostels, where they will recover their health, undermined under Nazi occupation."

my head. That way, if the picture got printed in a newspaper and I was able to get hold of the paper, I would be able to recognize myself. Several days later, I saw a newspaper. The picture was printed with an article, which, of course, I could not read. I asked our leader, Uncle Tom, who had the newspaper, if I could have it, and he gave it to me. I still have it today.

The first place where we stayed was a mine workers' camp. It was newly built, but apparently not used, and so we moved in. It was called Woodlands and was in the Midlands, near Doncaster. After a couple of days, ladies of the Women's Volunteer Service (WVS), came to Woodlands and literally changed the dining hall into what seemed to be a department store with tables full of clothing, shoes, etc. We were supposed to start at one point, pick up a duffel bag, and start stuffing clothes in the bag. After a leader told us to pick out two or three shirts, underwear, handkerchiefs, shoes, and slacks, one of the leaders would check the various items to see if they would fit properly. All of the clothing had labels sewn in it that said that the item was donated by the American Red Cross.

The clothes were beautiful, and a twelve-year-old had the sense that this was an absolute miracle to have someone give us all those woolen things without having anyone asking for ration points or a lot of money! This was all given to us, and we were lucky to get this fantastic gift of much-needed clothing. The slacks were a real treat because Dutch boys of that age would not be wearing slacks. Short pants were the regular dress code for younger boys in Holland, and some lucky boys had what we called plus-fours, the type that golfers used to wear. There was a bonanza of clothing goodies as we went from table to table, and soon my duffel bag was almost filled up. I picked out two beautiful sweaters, one red and one green. After I stuffed in the red sweater, my duffel bag was full.

I was not sure how I could protect my brand new possessions. I was afraid that someone would swipe my newly obtained trophy, so I decided to put on the green sweater, not realizing that all the boys got two sweaters, as well as all the other items. Of course, on a warm July day, that was not the thing to do, so I made a comment that it was hot. A leader suggested that I take off the sweater so that I would be a whole lot more comfortable. "Yes, good luck and I'd lose this sweater," I thought. I would rather be hot than risk the chance that someone was going to steal my proud possession. My mind was still in Holland, and one did not tempt anyone in these scarce times. I said to the leader, "No, I won't take off this beautiful sweater," and that comment was picked up and published by the local press.

I believe we stayed in Doncaster about two weeks and then were transferred to Warmsworth, a similar camp. It too consisted of a number of Quonset huts and a large building in which there was a kitchen and a large dining room. There was a building that housed the infirmary where a nurse took care of all the little things such as cuts, scrapes, and colds. There was a small outbreak of yellow jaundice and a number of children were quarantined. Everybody thought it was really bad luck for those children because they missed all the fun of going swimming and to the movies.

There was one leader, Mr. Buitenhuis, who was a miserably strict disciplinarian. I am convinced that he got pure pleasure out of pestering the children. Besides the sixty-six boys from Rotterdam, there were a number of girls who came from the southern provinces of Holland. The girls and their families had been liberated by the U.S. Army in November 1944. During mealtime, Mr. Buitenhuis would sit on what could be called a serving counter and would not say anything, but look and see if he could spot anyone who talked during the meal. The strict rule was no one could speak during mealtime. If one spoke, he had to finish his or her meal standing. Mr. Buitenhuis would not say anything, but just point. The English people who worked in the camp would show pity for the culprit, but, of course, could not do anything about it.

There were three siblings in the group, two girls and a boy, who were Jewish. We found out later that they had been in Bergen Belsen and were in line to be gassed when the Russians liberated them. One time a strange thing happened in the dining room. We had gotten a big piece of pork for dinner, and the oldest girl got up from her table and forbade her younger brother to eat the pork. He had a naughty smile on his face, which told everyone: "I'll take care of it once you're back at your table." The older sister was very emphatic and let it be known that she was not kidding. I did not know what was going on because we did not see any Jews for many years and, consequently, did not know about their religious beliefs. I do remember that we had one Jewish boy in our class in 1942, named Appie de Vries. The fact that he was Jewish was unknown to us at that time, and one day he did not show up for school any longer. Later, we found out that the poor boy was one of the many millions who were killed.

Life in the camp was good. We had classes in which we learned some English, sang a lot, and played outside. Our favorite song was a canon, sung in three parts, about an owl and a cuckoo, and we sang that almost every day. On Saturday mornings, we would walk to a movie theatre in Doncaster, where there was a regular Saturday morning children's show. All the Dutch children loved it, even though they could not talk with the English children.

We had never seen any cowboy movies, and these were with Roy Rogers and other cowboys. It was terrific! There was a big pipe organ in the theater, and the console would come out of the floor as the organist was playing the "club" song. It is hard to believe that, sixty years later, I can still sing the song in English, of which, at that time, I could not understand the words. However, I heard it so often on Saturday mornings that I could sound out the words. Then, all the popular songs were sung by all the children, as the words were projected on the screen.

We also would be taken to the swimming pool. The leaders separated the boys into two groups, swimmers and non-swimmers. I was petrified because, for all my life, I had been scared of water. Everybody in my family except my parents loved the water. I was scared of water, and it only became worse when they were going to "help" me. I thought that, if any boy in my group found out that I was scared of water, I would be teased as long as I was in Eng-land. I went into the shallow part of the pool and stayed away from everybody. Slowly, but surely, I got more and more at ease in the water, and I healed myself of my fear before I returned to Holland four months later.

When Japan surrendered in August of 1945, we were told that the war was over. Again, it was a strange statement for a twelve-year-old Dutch boy. The war was over for us on May 8, 1945, so what is it that the English are so happy about in August? Obviously, the war came so close to us that it was difficult to comprehend that an awful war was being fought in the Far East, and that we, as children, did not know about the fight against Japan. The night of the end of World War II was celebrated by the people who lived near our camp with a big bonfire. We were invited to be at the bonfire and, when it got dark, a huge fire was started at one of the fields. All of a sudden, the oldest Jewish girl began to scream and was totally out of control. No one could understand what was going through her mind or what the fire had reminded her of that had happened to her so recently. One of the female leaders went to her immediately and took her away to calm her down. It was one more experience that had to be overcome after having gone through the hell of war.

The last Saturday that we were in Warmsworth, before we went to foster parents, we went to the movie theater, which had become a regular routine by now. To our surprise, we were asked to come on the stage with the whole group of sixty-six Rotterdammers and sing our number one canon, the only one we knew. We sang our favorite song, resulting in thunderous applause. As an encore, we sang our national anthem and, this time, we were accompanied by the large theater organ. To my bewilderment, the organist knew the melody. Afterwards, I said to one of the lady leaders that it was rather unusual that the organist knew the Dutch national anthem. The leader said that she had given him the music. Nevertheless, I still thought that it was pretty unusual for someone to play a tune he had never seen before on such a big organ, sheet music or not.

After two months in the two camps, our eating portions were back to normal, even though it seemed at the time that all the boys wanted to make up for all the food they had missed during the five years of war. We went to live with foster parents in Retford, in Nottinghamshire. Retford was a small town, very pretty, with a lot of awfully nice people. This was the first time that I had gotten homesick, even though I did not recognize it as such at the time.

A portion of the sixty-six Rotterdammers were sent to Retford and the other boys and girls went somewhere else. As our bus entered Retford we saw stores with lots of goods in the showcases and, what was most amazing, there was a shoe store that was displaying dozens of pairs of shoes outside in front of the store on a simple rack. Those shoes could have been be picked up by any passer by, and no one in the store would have noticed them being taken. They must have no scarcity of shoes in this country, I thought. I had come from an environment where the bread delivery man had to have an armed police officer accompanying him so he could deliver his bread safely, and I can assure you that the bread was of such a poor quality that not even an animal would eat it today. People were so hungry during the winter of 1944–1945 that decent people would do some awfully crazy things, including stealing shoes from a rack outside a store — if it had been there, of course.

We were welcomed at what turned out to be the town hall. There were about twenty-two boys in our group, all being welcomed by the Lord Mayor of Retford. Lord Mayor Waterfield and other distinguished members of the community gave speeches. There was a tremendous amount of food on the tables and, after the speeches, we were told we could eat what we liked. Well, that was no problem for us, even though we had been in England for two months and were now back to normal rations. We enjoyed all the goodies that the ladies of the community had prepared for us.

I decided to team up with another boy since one family had room for two boys. I asked Jopie Krieg if he wanted to be my roommate, and so we went to Mr. and Mrs. Jessie Bingham. The problem for me was that Mrs. Edith Bingham was not able to pick us up and had sent her friend to pick up Jopie and me. They had gone through a lot of trouble and had succeeded in having someone drive us to the Bingham's home. Jopie and I did not believe our good fortune! A family who wanted us — and they had a car? Then we realized that the car did not belong to our foster family, but they had

The Lord Mayor of Retford, Mr. Waterfield, welcomes Dutch Boys (My eyes and forehead are barely shown in background on right).

arranged with a friend to have him drive us to their home. It would have been too good to be true. By the time I was twelve years old, I had ridden in a car perhaps as much as fifteen minutes, so to think that we might ride in it a few more times was just fantastic.

When we arrived at the Binghams' home, we were let into a very nice, small English home, not any smaller nor bigger than what we were used to in Holland. There were, however, a few differences. The toilet was an outside wooden toilet with a hole in a board, and the toilet paper was yesterday's newspaper. Later, we were sitting in the dining room and looking at a magazine. I was looking at some pictures of ships. Mrs. Bingham, who had not been at the reception, asked us if we liked *chips*. We understood *ships* and nodded our heads and told her that we had come from Holland on a ship, so of course we liked ships.

Mrs. Bingham left the house, went down the street, and bought a big pack of fish and chips wrapped in newspaper.

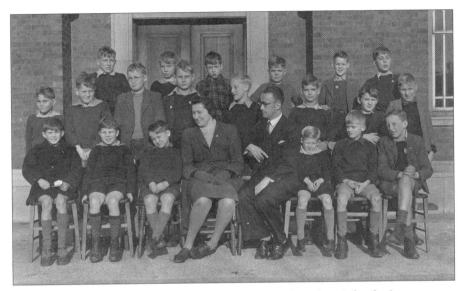

The group of children who went to England, with their leaders, Mr. Buitenhuis and Ms. H. Ada. Bob van Luijn is seated at the right end of the first row; his roommate, Jopie Krieg, is on the right end of the middle row.

Good grief! We had stuffed ourselves at the welcoming party and surely did not have any room for fish and chips. Jopie and I could not understand why in the world Mrs. Bingham would get such a lot of food after we had just stuffed ourselves. After an eventful day we went to bed. For the first week or so, I was not too happy. Although there was enough to do during the day to distract me, I was really homesick during the evenings. Jopie and I were talking about walking back to the camp because we had had such a great time at Warmsworth. We were not too sure how we were going to do it because we did not know the way.

Anyhow, after about a week or so, I got used to the situation, especially when Mr. de Boef came to visit me. He was the superintendent of the Dutch group and gave me a stiff talking to. The afternoon tea was ready, and Mrs. Bingham had prepared her usual big spread. When Mr. de

Boef saw what was ready for tea, he told me that my behavior was shameful and that I should shape up. That was all it took; I was all right from then on. I realized how lucky I was and that I had not shown it to Mr. and Mrs. Bingham.

During the days in Retford, we went to regular English school. The first order of business on a typical school day was gathering in the gym for a short information session attended by the entire student body of the elementary school, concluded by reciting something with a lot of lisping in it. Later, I learned that they were saying the Lord's Prayer; when the student body came to "…and forgive us our trespasses as we forgive our trespassers…" that explained the "lisping" for me. After assembly, we would go to our classes and, first thing after the roll was called, the teacher would collect a half-penny from those boys who wanted a half pint of milk with their lunch. He concluded that ritual with the words "anybody else?" Those were my first English words that I learned in school.

Since I could not understand anything that went on, the teacher would give me arithmetic problems to work on. It was customary to be very strict in school. If a boy had not done his homework, he would be summoned to come to the front of the class and, depending on the severity of the violation, he would get one, two, or even more slaps on his open hand with a bamboo stick. The boy had to hold up his outstretched hand to the side, palm side up, level with his shoulder, and the teacher would hit with all his might across the four fingers. The bamboo stick was from 3/8" to 3/4" in diameter, depending on the personal likes of the teacher. I saw what we at that time thought was a big boy who did everything in his power not to cry when disciplined that way. This was a frightening experience to see that going on, and it was almost a daily routine. It was interesting that the boys would discuss which whipping was worse, the 3/8" stick or the 3/4".

One day, I was caught by a teacher doing something out of order, and he reached for his stick and told me to come up front. I knew the routine by now and was petrified. Immediately, I began to ask him what I was supposed to be doing. Of course my question was asked in Dutch. It had the proper response: the teacher was very embarrassed and asked me if I were one of the refugee children, upon which the entire class answered in unison, "Yes, sir, he is Dutch."

"Sit down and behave" was the teacher's response. My heart was still pounding out of my chest, and I realized that was too close for comfort. I was sure not to do anything that would provoke the teacher again because I did not think my excuse would work twice.

For lunch, we went to a cafeteria that was located somewhere in town. Our group was invited to eat free of charge in the cafeteria, and we were served in the personnel dining room. We were allowed to go back for seconds, thirds, or whatever we wanted. We really ate, and I have a feeling that the owner of the cafeteria was glad that we finally went back to Holland after two months, because we certainly ate more than he could have expected twenty-two boys would eat.

We were in Retford for Guy Fawkes Day, which is celebrated with the setting off of fireworks. Guy Fawkes tried to take revenge against King James I, The Lords and The Commons, assembled in Parliament, because Guy did not agree with the laws against Roman Catholics. It is referred to as the Gun Powder Plot of the year 1605. Guy Fawkes was discovered in time, and the day is commemorated, and all the children there set off fireworks at night.

The English boys were trading and selling lots of small pieces of fireworks during playtime at school, and since the Dutch boys were not acquainted with the custom, they gave us a few pieces so we could share in the festivities on the 5th of November after it got dark. We had a lot of fun with the noisemakers, which did not resemble the sound of guns or bombs.

In the town of Retford the street lights were fed by gas. The street lantern had a pilot light that would stay on constantly, and as it got dark the lamplighter would come through the street on his bicycle carrying a six-foot-long stick with a hook. At dusk, the lamplighter would turn the valve that was near the light source, and the light would illuminate the street.

Sometimes the boys in the street would shinny up the light pole and turn the light off, which was not appreciated by the lamplighter, who somehow knew when to return and warn the group of boys. We, of course, had no idea how he knew. Our fun was innocent enough, and we never hurt anyone or anything.

There were two boys with whom I used to play: Kenneth Stimson and John Cartwright. They were about my age, and we would play cricket and soccer and all the usual things boys do at that age. They would try to teach me how to bowl (pitch) a cricket ball.

At the end of November, it was time for the Dutch boys to go back to Holland. The organization that was in charge of housing us with the various families organized a Christmas party for the whole group and our two leaders. Lord Mayor Waterfield was dressed up as Santa Claus and gave each of us a present. I still have the set of dominoes that Lord Mayor Waterfield gave me.

The next day, Mr. and Mrs. Bingham took Jopie and me to the train station. As the train departed, I saw Mrs. Bingham wipe away a few tears. Again we went to London, and stayed in what may have been the same place we had stayed four months earlier when we arrived from Holland. This time, we all had gained a great deal of weight. I don't know how many pounds I had gained, but I am sure that it was a lot.

6

Back at Home

My suitcase, which I had taken on my journey to England, was now full of presents for Pappa, Mamma, Thea, and Tine. I did not think that things had gotten too much better since I had left, so with all my spending money, a sixpence a week, I had bought candles, soaps, and other such things. When Mrs. Bingham saw what I was buying, she gave me a lot of other similar items. My clothes, courtesy of the American Red Cross, were in a huge duffel bag. My precious sweater was in there, along with two pairs of shoes and all sorts of clothing items that had been given to me. I was wearing my overcoat, an item that I had never had before.

Pappa and Mamma were at the train station when I arrived around the 28th of November 1945. Things were going to be normal again. I was going back to school, but since I had lost almost four months of schooling, I was kept in the fifth grade, which hurt my feelings. However, I could not catch up, so the decision was made, and that was that.

Having overcome my fear of water in England, I took swimming lessons and got my swimming diploma. I was the first in the family who had the nerve to dive off the three-meter diving board. I went to learn lifesaving and became a member of the *ROTTERDAMSE REDDINGS BRIGADE* (Rotterdam Lifesaving Brigade). We even had duty in the winter, on the ice when the lakes froze over; we skated around and were ready to rescue anyone who had fallen through the ice. We had long extension ladders stored at strategic places in the event that they were needed. Luckily, I never had to put my training into practice. I have saved one little girl from drowning, but that happened much later, after I had moved to the U.S.

After the war, there were people who bought surplus war goods. There was a lot of equipment that the Canadian Army did not want to take back, so they left it in Holland. Some enterprising Dutchman had managed to get his hands on a three-ton truck; he placed some wooden benches in it and used it to organize school trips. Since we had not known much about any kind of transportation and had not ridden in too many automobiles, let alone busses, such trips were a real treat for us. The set-up was: a simple canvas cover on the back of the truck, the benches, and an open back with a

1946: Back from England wearing the English green sweater.

tailgate. The children on both outside benches would lean against the canvas, and there was a center bench that children would straddle. We thought that was great! To take the bus on a school trip was a lot of fun.

One day, in the sixth grade, the principal of the elementary school was talking about the beginning of the war. I will never forget one part of his recollection. He was telling us that he had come to school that fateful morning of May 10, 1940, and had closed the school on account of the beginning of the war. He said, "There was a little boy whose older sister read the note on the door, and the boy's comment was: "Oh, good, we don't have school today." Mr. Oosters said that he had to control himself not to do anything to that boy. Even though it was six years later, I did not have the nerve to own up to the fact that I was that boy.

※　※　※　※

If the weather was cold enough, the first order of business was for a schoolboy to be the first to cross the newly frozen lake near the school. The police would keep a sharp eye out for any brave soul who would try to cross before the ice was safe to skate upon. The lake was perhaps 200 yards wide, and it was almost like a badge of honor to be the first one to cross the ice. The weight of the boy would cause the thin ice to move down and the boy would literally glide across the ice, as if it was a frozen wave of water. It was quite dangerous, of course, and the first child had to be fast and not heavy. If the ice was thicker than a predetermined thickness, the ice was considered safe. If this was the case, we would have no school that day, and everybody would get skates and have a great time. At certain places, the police would put a flagpole in the ice and raise the Dutch flag, signaling all was ok. I never tried to be an "early skater" as I was never much of a daredevil.

The thing to do as a boy from Rotterdam was to skate to Gouda. Gouda is perhaps twenty miles from Rotterdam and can be reached by means of a number of small streams, lakes, and other bodies of water, usually by boat, but over the ice in winter. Gouda is a very pretty town and is best known abroad for its cheese. There are, however, two other famous Dutch products originating in the town of Gouda: candles and clay pipes. The pipes are the old-fashioned types one sees in the old Dutch paintings. Some are as long as a yard, while some are made in curls and with faces, or painted in red, white, and blue. The ritual was to skate to Gouda to buy six or seven clay pipes, depending on how much money you had to spend. The vendors would be set up on the ice with a large assortment of clay pipes that one could buy, and they would sew them on the front of your sweater. A long clay pipe, say 20 inches long, was sewn on the back of the sweater. The trick was to skate back to Rotterdam without falling because, if you fell, the first casualty would be the 20-incher.

I was thirteen years old when I made a safe round-trip to Gouda and, after having successfully completed the feat, I took the longest way back to the house, walking slowly back in the hope that the entire neighborhood would see what I had done. Because of the tradition, everyone knew what it meant when a boy or girl would walk through the neighborhood with skates in hand and pipes sewn to his or her sweater.

✳ ✳ ✳ ✳

It was about time to be going to the next school in my life. In Holland, at that time, once a pupil finished the sixth grade of the elementary school, a decision was made as to which school he or she would attend next. There were three paths, all based on the performance of the student during those first six grades. The top of the class would go to a four-year high school, where the student was required to learn five languages (French, German, English, Greek, and Latin), along with Mathematics, Chemistry, and Physics. The middle group of students took French, German, and English, and were prepared for various business careers, such as office managers, clerks, buyers, and sales representatives. The remaining students went to a technical school or to a home-economics-oriented school, as my sister Thea had done. Once being routed into one of these three paths, it was extremely difficult to switch and go into a higher level, although it was not impossible.

Since that decision basically was determined by my performance in the first six grades, it was no surprise to me or my parents that I was destined to go to the technical school. The question became in what trade I was to be

Ambachtsschool, 1947

trained. Mamma and I went to a school in the center of town, where we had a meeting with a counselor. After discussing this, that, and the other with the counselor, he decided that I would be suited for the trade of electrician. Well, that sounded all right with me and the following September I entered the *Ambachtsschool* (Trade School), which stood practically next to the Heineken beer brewery. Every day on the way to school, we could smell the hops, which we did not find unpleasant.

The *Ambachtsschool* taught such trades as electrician, tool and die maker, millwright, auto mechanic, carpenter, cabinet maker, and tailor. The first months were a real struggle for me, since we had three-and-a-half hours of shop practice in the morning and three-and-a-half hours of theory in the afternoon. The theory was drafting, sketching, electrical theory, and math. The shop was a real struggle. We were given a piece of 5" x 3" x 1/2" carbon steel and had specific directions to follow: all six opposing surfaces had to be parallel to each other (three pairs), and all the surfaces had to be perpendicular to all of the adjoining surfaces! However, the most difficult task was to file all of it flat.

When the teacher finally passed my piece of "workmanship," which had taken almost six weeks to complete, it resembled a razor blade more than anything else, but I did learn to file flat. Then we had to file a square piece of 1" x 1" x 5" carbon steel. Once that was completed, we had to file off the corners and make it into an octagon, which we then had to make into a sixteen-sided piece, and this adding of sides continued until the carbon steel resembled a cylinder. Then the trick was to put it on an engine lathe and we found out that all our effort did not yield such a fantastic cylinder. "Now do the same on a lathe," the teacher would say, and in minutes we had a beautiful shiny cylinder. The teacher said: "Remember how much effort it took, and how much quicker a machine can do it for you. Use the tools properly, respect them for their ability, and realize how those tools make work easy for you!"

The next part of shop was low voltage wiring — bells, push buttons, and all sorts of variations. First, one had to draw the wiring diagram of a certain task. Then, one had to complete the actual wiring on a wooden wall, simulating an actual installation. When finished, the buttons could be pushed and it would work. All this was done on a ladder.

The wooden wall, which had been used by hundreds of students over the years, looked as if the wall had been used as a shotgun target. In the next class, we would do 220 volts wiring in conduit. We had to bend thin wall conduit, at which we became pretty good after a number of months. Then we had to splice high-voltage cables, that is, wire-armored lead-shielded cables, and it was a very tricky task to do correctly. Every time a layer of shielding was removed, the remainder had to be tied back to a predetermined number of millimeters, etc. In short, when we graduated, we had a good basis on which we could start our apprenticeship.

❋   ❋   ❋   ❋

At eighteen years of age, Tine graduated with very good grades from the school that prepared her for a career in the business world. She was the type of student who excelled in languages, as well as in math. She was fluent in three languages (French, German, and English) and decided to apply for a job at the telegraph branch of the Dutch postal service. Tine had pen pals in England and Switzerland, and she was able to write to them in their native tongues. She was somewhat worried because she did not pick up the skill of transmitting messages in Morse code as quickly as she thought that she should.

Tine joined an amateur theater group that put on plays once or twice a year, and she was making her stage début on the evening of November 3, 1948. A band had been hired to play after the performance, and the actors and audience would dance until one or two o'clock in the morning. Needless to say, at fifteen years old, I was not about to stay for the dance where they turned down the overhead lights and shuffled around the dance floor. I decided to go home and said goodbye to the family (which was a lot of people, as this was Tine's first try at an important part in the play). Before I left, I found Tine and, while touching her coifed hair, said, "See you, sis. Good job."

The last picture with all three of us:
Thea, Tine, and me. 1948

The next morning, I went to the technical school and just saw Tine getting ready to go to her job at the Main Post Office in downtown Rotterdam. Since we had an hour-and-a-half for lunch, I went home for the usual lunch that Mamma had ready for me.

However, *Oom* Jan met me before I could get in the house. He told me that Tine had died ten minutes after she had left the house that morning. She was on her bicycle, riding with hundreds of others to the center of town. The "ribbon" of the bicyclers was usually ten people wide and Tine, being too impatient to poke around at a leisurely speed, decided to pass the crowd. She looked around and saw a truck passing the bicyclers on her left. As soon as the truck had passed, she pulled out only to discover, to her horror, that the truck had a trailer with five tons of sugar beets on it. Witnesses said that Tine panicked, threw up her hands, and fell. The right rear tire of the trailer ran over the back of her head, killing her instantly.

The police came to the house and told Mamma what had happened, and the truck driver came to the house offering his condolences. The man was terribly upset. He had no idea what had happened until he had been stopped several hundred yards down the street, because he had not felt anything when Tine fell under the trailer.

Because of the kind of person Tine had been, and the friends she had made, her funeral was an enormous one with an unbelievable number of flowers. All our neighbors showed their sorrow by taking down the curtains from their front windows and substituting white bed sheets in their place, making the entire street a very eerie and sad sight.

Pappa had been brought up very religiously, but Mamma's family did not go to church. After the service was completed at the cemetery, we quietly walked back to the horse-drawn carriage, and Pappa said, "Bob, we've taken her home." Because of his upbringing, Pappa was able to find a ray of solace in the middle of tragedy, even though his grief was unbearable.

7

Working for a Living

In the fall of 1949, I entered the work force. The standard electrician's clothing was a blue coverall. He would change out of the coverall into street clothes as soon as the day's work had stopped, and most often he would go home in a coat and tie. The Dutch are very proud people and one's clothing should not tell a stranger whether one is an office clerk, a car mechanic, or, in my case, an electrician.

Once I had my diploma, I went to work for a small company in Vlaardingen. The company repaired motors and motor-starters. To get to work, I had to ride my bicycle to the train station, park my bike (for which I had to pay a weekly parking fee), and ride the train for twenty minutes. The train tickets were provided by the employer, so the train did not cost me anything. The work week was forty-eight-hours long, with a half-day on Saturday. My hourly rate was 25 cents per hour, which at that time was roughly the equivalent of seven-and-a-half cents per hour in American money! After four months, I was fired.

Although they fired me without providing a good reason, they did give me a recommendation letter, which stated that I had worked there for four months and had left on my own accord. The following week, I started with another small company, which was closer to home, and got to do all sorts of things with electrical motors. However, when work slowed down, the last person hired had to go. Being that lucky someone, I was again fired without a real reason and received a nice letter stating that I had left on my own accord. I could not help but start to think that there was something that I was not doing right. I waited a couple of weeks and, this time, I took a job with a "big company" called A de Hoop NV. It was a local company that had about 350 employees, including two graduate engineers, and was considered big in the electrical field. There were basically two divisions, the inside and the outside services. I thought the outside service was the interesting part. They had a crew consisting of perhaps 100 electricians, whose task was to go onto the ships that came into the harbor for repairs. That kind of work sounded very interesting and exciting.

Before we could do that, though, we had to work first in the factory, and I started off in the warehouse. Our job was to gather orders for the outside crew and cut certain types of cable to the required lengths. It sounds kind of simple, but by doing that for a few weeks, one learned very quickly the various kinds of cable that were available. All these cables were lead-shielded and protected by a woven covering of steel threads, which were the thickness of a thread used by a shoemaker. The steel webbing was hard to cut and was supposed to resist salt-spray out on the ocean.

When the company received a special order to supply the electrical panels for a large number of Navy destroyers, I was given the opportunity to work in the special group that was being formed to do that kind of work. The specifications were very exact as to how to tie the bundles of insulated wires. In addition, the terminations of the wires were soldered, and the inspectors were very critical as to how much solder would be permitted on each of the terminals. I was offered the opportunity to work on those panels and, after some time, I became proficient at it and was made the lead electrician in a group of about eight people. We had several girls in the group, who were also very good at the task.

One day we were kind of joking as to who could do it the best — a woman or a man. Well, I opened my mouth and said, "A man, of course!" Before I could say another word, the girls decided that there should be a contest and that I, with my big mouth, should be the man. Not being sure how to get out of that situation I said, seemingly without hesitation, "OK, I'll show you." The whole group and a few others made up the rules and were going to witness the contest. The task took about six minutes. Both of us started at the same time and "raced" to the completion, knowing that if there was one wrong termination the match would be won by the opponent. I finished the task faster than the girl by less than two seconds. After proper inspections, both contestants were found to have made acceptable terminations, which made me the winner. After working in that department for about a year, I was given the opportunity to work in the outside service, which, while using the skills I had learned in school and on the various jobs as an electrician, offered a broader experience.

When I started working on the outside service, I was about nineteen years old and ready for a new adventure. One of my first assignments was in a small town called Puttershoek, the home of a large sugar beet factory. (Needless to say, I thought that those damned things had been outlawed after the war!). Puttershoek is a town about eighteen miles to the south of Rotterdam and, six days a week, I rode there on my bicycle. The company gave us an extra sixteen guilders, about $4.00, to ride a train that was pulled by a steam locomotive. Instead, I rode my bike and kept the money. It was fall and I rode my bicycle through rain, sleet, and snow. The factory was expanding, and it was my job to do the basic electrical wiring and the splicing of many cables for the expansion.

After most of the work was done, I was transferred to another job, which was rewiring a Victory Ship. One of the tasks was to wire the lights in the masts. There were about twenty-five electricians assigned to the job, and all but one had a fear of heights. Except for me, all of the other electricians had been on ships before and knew that the coming winter meant cold times working with the steel masts. I started the task and progressed fairly well until it got very cold. Mamma knitted me a pair of gloves with the fingers left unfinished. Having the fingertips of the gloves open, I would be able to feel the work while still having some protection from the elements. I would climb up the mast, mount one or two cable straps, and then climb down. Upon reaching the deck, I would slap my hands on my shoulders so that the blood would flow a little faster, warming my hands. I finished the job, and when the ship sailed later that spring, I saw it depart Rotterdam in the late afternoon, heading for the Hook of Holland, towards the sea. As I watched it sailing away, I saw the mast lights lit and felt a tremendous sense of pride knowing that I had single-handedly done that.

From then on, a number of different jobs were assigned to me, and I became good enough to go out to ships without a helper. If a ship was anchored in the middle of the river, I would have to take a water taxi. That was a regular service for workers who had to do business on a particular ship. One Greek ship sticks in my mind. I was told to go to a particular ship and see what they needed. The water taxi took me to this Greek ship, and the boatswain spoke with me in broken English. As he was talking, I was thinking, "I've learned a little English in England, so no sweat." The problem was that the top light, on the forward mast, was not working. The boatswain gave me a spare bulb, of which the bulbous part was as large as a grapefruit. There was a rope all the way to the top and he had rounded up a boatswain's-chair. The boatswain's-chair is nothing more than a six-inch-wide board about two feet long, with a rope secured through the end of each side. The rope ends were knotted together, terminating

69

with a cleat about forty inches from the board. So, basically, a boatswain's chair was a triangle whose base was the board and whose equal sides were ropes.

The boatswain secured the chair to the rope that ran all the way to the top of the mast, where the light was mounted. I selected the tools I thought I would need and let the boatswain hoist me up the mast. Everything going up went well, and I sort of enjoyed the ride. However, the ride came to a sudden stop when the cleat that carried the boatswain's-chair hit the block over which the rope was running. Because of the distance between the cleat on my seat, plus the six inches of block and the height of the light fixture, I was stopped roughly five feet below where I needed to be. My only choice was to stand up on the seat while holding onto the mast for dear life. Due to its basic configuration, the boatswain's chair was obviously not stable, and standing in it high above a steel deck was like attempting to balance on a board placed loosely on top of a basketball. I had never anticipated a situation like this, and I certainly had not taken that job for excitement of that kind.

However, like it or not, that was the job. So, with all the nerve I could muster, I managed to stand up, hold on, and start to open the light fixture. As if being in such a precarious position weren't enough, I was also fully aware that I could not drop any screws, bolts, or other parts of the light fixture, because then I would have to make the journey all the way down and up again. I succeeded in taking the burned-out light bulb out of the fixture and screwing in the new light bulb. As I was closing the light fixture, I made the stupid mistake of looking down at what was to be seen on deck. I saw nothing but a steel deck and a Greek boatswain holding my rope with his left hand as tight as he could, while vigorously and repeatedly crossing himself with his right hand! An unbelievable emotion of horrendous fear overcame me. My thought was that if a seasoned seaman was that concerned or unsure about my safety, what was I doing up here? I was shaking all over, and waited a little while before

I slowly went down into the sitting position on the boatswain's-chair. When sitting securely in the seat, I signaled to be lowered, and descended safely back to the deck. I was sure that there would be no next time if that kind of work had to be done again. If the situation ever presented itself again, I decided that I would lie and say that I, like the other men, had a fear of heights.

Later that year, I was transferred back into the factory and was building panels with heavy copper conductors. I knew that that would not last too long because there was a military draft in Holland, and I was sure to be drafted to do my part in the eventual defense of my country.

8

In the Royal Dutch Army

At that time, Holland had the so-called "filler system." Every two months, a certain number of draftees were called up for an eighteen-month stint in the Army, Navy, or Air Force. At the same time, the group that had just completed their eighteen-month stint, now fully trained, were discharged. My notice came and told me to report on November 26, 1953, in Ossendrecht, which is in the south of Holland. I was to be trained in Anti-Aircraft Artillery. It sounded exciting, and with a feeling of looking forward to a new adventure, I told my boss that I was drafted and had to report for duty. He told me to be back at work as soon as I was discharged, which was a good prospect. The train that took me to Bergen op Zoom was full of men my age who were all going to Ossendrecht. There was a festive mood on the train, and everybody was friends with everybody, and it promised to be a great eighteen months. As we arrived at Bergen op Zoom, busses were waiting for us and took us to a post with about four thousand soldiers. We were told in which of the barracks we were to sleep. After fatigues were issued, the first thing that we were told to do was to fill a large bag with wheat straw. We later found out that we had just made our mattresses, the same mattresses on which we were going to sleep for the next four months.

That was just about the end of the festivities. I was still in my civilian clothes, and stood in one of the halls with about thirty other men who were all assigned to the same sleeping quarters. What turned out to be a Sergeant First Class walked up to me and screamed at me to take my hands out of my own civilian pants pockets. I thought, "Yes, this is going to be a different world altogether." I had arrived at boot camp! From sunup to sundown, we were in classes, out on the drill field, in the gym, or in the field. I never in my life had seen Dutch heather up so close as I did in those months. (Years later, I wanted to have some in my garden to remind me that life had not always been easy.) At the time, I thought things could not be any worse. We had to overcome obstacles that could not be overcome by a normal city boy. The tough thing to get used to was all the running we had to do. Before I went in the army, the only time that I ran was if I wanted to catch a streetcar or a bus. The dreaded signal to run from one class to the next class became old very quickly. I believe it was surprising to all of us when the running routine became second nature because, after a month or two, we did not even think about it when we had to run.

There was one problem with the Dutch army in 1953: with all the clothing that was issued to us the first two days, there were no khaki fatigues for a guy six-feet four-and-a-half-inches tall. Besides me, there was only one other inductee with white fatigues instead of khaki fatigues. Well, every time a drill sergeant wanted someone to demonstrate what needed to be done, whom do you think he would pick out of the "battery" of about a hundred and eighty soldiers? Sure enough, the one with the white fatigues. I never knew that I could climb a twenty-foot rope, scale a nine-foot brick wall, or run up crazy wooden inclines. It was not that I wanted to do it; it was because the drill sergeants were able to scare the hell out of me and make me do things I did not know could be done by a human being. In retrospect, it was good for me because I learned what discipline was, and it has served me the rest of my life.

After about two or three weeks, we were issued regular uniforms that we wore when we were on leave. The first thing we had to do was sew our regiment name on our sleeves. I was in the Waalhaven regiment. In the Anti-Aircraft Artillery, the regiments were named after Dutch military airports established before WWII. Waalhaven was in the south of Rotterdam, so it made sense to have the anti-aircraft troops who came predominantly from Rotterdam in the Waalhaven regiment. On the left sleeve was the Dutch Lion patch. The lion was depicted with seven arrows in his claw representing the seven original Dutch provinces. The Dutch motto was embroidered under the lion: *"Je maintiendrai"* ("I will maintain"). If anyone wore the jacket with the lion patch over civilian clothes, the military police could arrest him for being out of uniform. The patch with the lion and the national motto made you a soldier.

After about four weeks, we were given our first leave, and we all went home on the train. We were not allowed to wear civilian clothes while on leave. However, Dutch men who were drafted wanted to show that they did not like the duty, so everybody put on their civilian clothes to go to town. Neighbors saw me in my civvies, so I was considered a normal Dutch boy.

Later that week, our neighbor Mrs. Berggren said to Mamma: "Bob has been in the service for more than four weeks and does not seem to have gained any weight!"

Highly insulted, Mamma answered, "My boy does not need to go into the Army to gain weight; he gets fed well at home!"

❄ ❄ ❄ ❄

The first time I had to be on guard duty was the coldest night of the entire year; the temperature was minus 13 degrees Fahrenheit. Therefore, the military followed the unusual procedure of having on-duty soldiers stand guard for only one hour, followed by two hours of break. During normal conditions, a guard would be on-duty for two hours, followed by four hours off-duty. We were supplied with two cartridges for our rifles, and I had to guard an ammunition bunker. The place was spooky and surrounded by pine trees. The frost was so hard that branches of the pine trees were snapping off and falling down, making spooky noises that broke the snow-deadened silence. I was sure that the lieutenant of the guard was sneaking up on me to see if I was alert, or could it have been a Russian trying to get the best of me? Needless to say, I was scared to death and was always glad to have no unusual things to report when I was relieved.

One day, I was told to report to an office on the base. I had no idea what was going to happen or why. A captain was sitting at a table in the office; I saluted and told him who I was, and he told me to sit down. He was a nice guy and chatted with me. He asked me how I liked the army, and I told him that it was all right. He asked me if I had any complaints, and I told him I did not. He asked again, and I thought I had better give him some kind of answer, so I said something like, "Since you press me for it, I think it's ridiculous that they are doing all this hollering and shouting. If they tell me something I'll do it; they don't have to yell at me." He "whole-heartedly agreed," and I found out later that I had blown a chance to go to NCO school. The one thing good about that was that enlisted men had to serve eighteen months, and NCOs had to serve three additional months. If I had gone to NCO school, I might have missed meeting my Uncle Albert, who had lived in America for more than thirty-eight years, and who was on his first trip back to Holland after his retirement from the Newport News shipyard.

Two things that happened during boot camp stand out in my mind. One very cold day we were going on "maneuvers." In the Dutch army, at that time, they never told you what you were going to do on a particular day. When we went out, we had no idea if we would be out just for the morning, all day, or what. We were going through the fields, and we had a

75

short second lieutenant of the infantry training us. At a given point, we came to a small stream that was about seven feet wide. Of course, by now it was an accepted practice to take the tallest guy in the battery and let him be the first one to do the next routine. The lieutenant picked me out and went through the motions as to how to jump across a stream. The basic maneuver was this: hold your rifle with both out-stretched arms in front of your chest, jump, and, as soon as you are off the ground, bring the rifle quickly to your chest. The weight of the single-bolt-action Lee Enfield, about eleven pounds, was to help you get that extra little inch out of your jump.

"OK, soldier, go and jump" was the order. I knew I would not be able to get across keeping my feet dry, but I knew that there was no chance of saying "let's do this another way." Lo and behold, I jumped and cleared the stream with room to spare. Being on the other side, I decided that I was going to observe how well the other soldiers in the battery did. Some landed in the stream and some got their heels wet. It was lots of fun for those that cleared the stream. The last person to attempt the jump was the short, five-foot-four lieutenant. Sure enough, he landed in the water. I stood six feet from him and laughed out loud. That happened to be a huge mistake on my part, as I would find out after we had lunch. It was customary to have the tallest soldiers marching in the front and the shortest in the back. The short soldiers would always gripe about my stride because they had a hard time keeping up. We found out that we were going to be out all day in this horrible, cold weather, with only our fatigues to keep us warm. A truck came and brought us our lunch — soup and some sandwiches. We ate the soup as quickly as we could because our mess tins were below freezing point, and the soup did not stay warm at all.

As soon as we were finished with our lunch, we started again. We approached a stream that was about two feet deep. The lieutenant ordered me to get in and start walking with the rest of the battery behind me. The only problem was that there was a thin layer of ice on it. The ice was probably not thicker than 1/16 of an inch. I could not break the ice with my shins so, with each step I took, I had to get my foot above the ice, break it, and take the next step. If that was not bad enough, the lieutenant, who was walking on the side of the stream right behind me, yelled "airplane." We were trained to take cover instantly once that warning was given. I took one step to the closest shoulder and lunged to the side of the stream.

Royal Dutch Army

That little lieutenant almost had a heart attack. He let me know in no uncertain terms that, once "airplane" was yelled, we were supposed to drop, wherever we were. Well, a minute later, the order came again, and I let my Lee Enfield do the ice breaking for me and went completely under. I don't know how the others made out, but I knew this was pay-back time and I had better ignore everybody. I learned that it is in your best interest to try not to show your feelings when it relates to a higher-ranked individual. About thirty soldiers ended up in sickbay with pneumonia, and it turned out to be a big stink because the chief of staff, a four-star general, came to our battery and asked how things were going. Fat chance that anybody was going to say anything to a four-star general. I learned my lesson and found out that, white fatigues or not, I would do a lot better just sitting there and watching what would happen next.

Near the end of our boot camp, we went to Roozendaal for a shooting exercise. We were issued five or six cartridges and that was all. We were told to keep track of the empty shells because we had to turn them in afterwards. Our first lieutenant was a fantastic guy; everybody liked him, and when he praised you, that was the biggest compliment that you could get. He was big and strong, had a red moustache, and was a Green Beret. The lieutenant decided to try a little test on the entire group of about 350 recruits and NCO's. He decided to run back to the post, interspersed with some short pieces of speed walking. We were wearing fatigues, boots, and our back packs, all while carrying a Lee Enfield. I was, as usual, up front, and every time he looked back and gave the signal to run, I could not resist trying. I had no time to look around me; all I saw was that big, red-mustached, grinning face, and I could not refuse to follow. We managed to run most of the nearly eight miles in fifty-six minutes, and when we arrived at the post, we found out that most of the guys had quit and less than fifty of us had arrived! If I had seen anyone quit in front of me, I would probably have quit myself. It was an accomplishment of which I was proud and showed me that people can do a great deal more than we think we are capable of.

The last day in boot camp was on a Saturday, around March 21, 1954. We were to pack everything according to the handbook and have everything ready to go on leave for ten days. I caught quite a break with the scheduling, as my birthday is on the thirtieth and I would be able to spend it at home! In Holland, birthdays are a big thing. Your friends and family members come for a party that lasts until the last train leaves the local station.

As the morning progressed, the last thing that needed to be done was to empty our "mattresses" of wheat straw. We emptied them all into a pile, which must have ended up being 20 feet high. I decided to work on top of the straw pile with a pitchfork. The straw was to be burned later that morning. After working for about half an hour with a pitchfork, I decided to give another soldier a chance to work on top. Rather than sliding down, I decided to jump in what appeared to be a big thick pile of straw, ten feet lower. One foot landed, indeed, in a thick pile; however, the other hit a hole, and I sprained my ankle pretty badly. I had my boots and anklets on, and got on the train still feeling that sore ankle. When I came home, I had a hard time putting any weight on it. By Monday morning, my ankle was so swollen that I could not see my toes any longer. Mamma got worried and sent me to the local Army sickbay; I did not want to do it, but she insisted. Of course, they put me in a bed and discharged me the day after my birthday, just in time to report for duty in Crailo. I was told that they did not call off the birthday party at the house and had a great time without me!

※　※　※　※

Crailo is a small town near Hilversum. It's in a beautiful part of the country, and it was considered a choice assignment. There were five groups, called batteries, and one maintenance group. We had five 90-millimeter anti-aircraft guns. They were old World War II guns, but so were our bolt-action Lee Enfield rifles. The big guns were radar-controlled, and we spent days cleaning and setting them up. Since I had spent ten days in the sickbay, I wasn't about to start work right away. I had a letter from the military doctor saying that I was not ready for full duty. I made sure I kept that status as long as I could. Finally, when the doctor at the Crailo post gave me a release to start full duty, my battery First Lieutenant thought that I had been on light duty for too long and he put me in charge of the warehouse, from which I issued supplies to maintain the guns. The timing was perfect and, not too long after that, I was able to get some help from one of my friends in the battery who became my assistant.

My hobby was photography, and I decided to start taking pictures, which I developed at home while I was on leave.

Twice a month, we would get one weekend leave. I would print the photographs I had taken and sell them to the guys. (The business went so well that I recouped the expense of all my darkroom equipment and had enough money left over to go on a vacation in Northern Italy after I had completed my military service.)

Our regiment went twice to Den Helder, a coastal town in the northern part of Holland. We shot our 90-millimeter guns there with the North Sea as our safe backdrop. Our target was a windbag that was pulled through the sky on a long rope by a small aircraft. The officers purposely cranked the timing of the fuse a little late so that we would not hit the windbag too often. One time, someone decided that we were going to let the radar do part of the tracking. As the plane turned around at the end of the run, the plane and the bag appeared to be at the same spot, so the radar locked on the plane and not the bag. We got one shot off, fortunately missing the plane before we realized what was wrong. Meanwhile, the pilot of the plane, who was not too happy, dropped the windbag and said he was going home!

The general consensus of the guys was that you were a sissy if you put cotton in your ears, so most of us were around the guns without ear protection while they were shooting. At night, my ears were ringing, and I must have damaged some of my hearing at that time. The last fourteen months did not go as fast as all of us draftees wanted, but, finally, in May 1955, I was honorably discharged and returned to civilian life.

9

Back in Civilian Life

I went back to de Hoop and resumed my career as a journeyman electrician. To help me in my chances for promotion, I went to night school. Since I had gone the direction of the *Ambachtsschool,* or trade school, I had to do a great deal of work to catch up with a track that would possibly get me into the MTS. The MTS was a technical school which, upon completion, would put someone on an equal footing with students who had completed two years of an engineering curriculum at a fully accredited engineering college or university in the U.S. About a month after I was discharged from the Army, Pappa's brother Albert and his wife came from America to Holland. He had retired from the Newport News Shipyard in Virginia and brought his brand new DeSoto automobile with him. Pappa's five other brothers were all living in the Hague.

I should explain that *Opa* (Grandfather) van Luijn had been a head conductor on the Dutch railroad. His assignment was the run between Amsterdam and Cologne, Germany. For whatever reason, *Opa* and *Oma* decided to live in Germany while that assignment lasted. Two sons, one of them Albert, were born in Emmerich, Germany, a town close to the Netherlands, just over the German border. When Opa was reassigned, the family moved back to Holland and re-established themselves in the Hague. Albert, their third living child, grew up and became a millwright/machinist and met a girl who lived in Uithoorn, a small town outside of Amsterdam. Grietje de Wit's father was a cooper, and her oldest brother had taken over the business of making barrels and cheese forms for the farmers in the area. Albert had served his country as a sailor in the Royal Dutch Navy, liked the sailing, and therefore decided, after he was discharged, that a career as an engineer in the merchant marine would be enjoyable, not to mention well-paying. He married his sweetheart, Grietje, and sailed two weeks later, leaving his new bride in Holland.

The destination of the freighter was the United States. It was 1917, and World War I was going on. By this time, America had joined the fight. Holland, however, stayed out of the war by declaring neutrality. Neutral or not, as Uncle Albert's ship neared the American continent, his ship was torpedoed by a German submarine. Albert and his crewmates floated in the Atlantic Ocean for thirty-six hours and were picked up by an American destroyer. Due to Holland's neutrality, Albert and his fellow shipmates had no way of getting back to Holland. The destroyer dropped them in Norfolk, Virginia. Albert found his way to Newport News and applied for a millwright's job at the Newport News Shipyard. He was happy working and contemplated staying in the States, provided his wife Grietje was willing to come and join him. Realizing that Uithoorn was a small Dutch town in which the de Wit family was well established, Albert wrote her a letter at the end of the war, expecting an answer he did not want to hear. To his surprise Grietje's answer was, "I'll meet you in Newport News and will be on the next boat to the USA."

In 1928, while working in America, Pappa had visited his brother and sister-in-law for Christmas. Pappa was homesick because he had been in the States for more than two years and had been unable to get Mamma and my sister Thea to come and join him. He had been classified as a deserter, and not one shipping company would let Mamma and Thea on a ship to America.

Uncle Albert had always been talked about at home because he lived in America. Pappa would say repeatedly: "Everything is possible in America." When Albert retired from the Newport News shipyard in 1954, he had spent thirty-seven years with the shipyard and had finished his career as an inspector. In 1955, just about the time I was discharged from the Royal Dutch Army, Uncle Albert and Aunt Gre (Grietje had been shortened to Gre) had decided to come to Holland for three months. Of course, the sight of a big American car was absolutely unbelievable. In those days, many American tourists would come to Europe by boat with their cars. Uncle Albert would take us around the neighborhood and we were the envy of all.

One afternoon, Uncle Albert was sitting in our living room and asked me: "Why are you not coming to the States?"

My answer was, "I need a sponsor and that is something I don't have."

Uncle Albert said, "We will sponsor you" and looked at his wife Gre. I looked at Tante Gre and asked if it was OK with her.

She said, "Sure, you are welcome, and we would love to have you." Boy, what a chance, what an opportunity!

At that very moment, I got up, excused myself, and rode my bicycle to the American Consulate in Rotterdam. In my "fluent" English, I told the lady at the counter that I would like to have a visa to go to the USA. The lady smiled and informed me that there was a quota system, meaning that only a limited number of immigrants were allowed to enter the U.S. each year, and that it was going to take a while before my application would come to the top for consideration. Taking some papers that I had to fill out, I went home terribly disappointed because I was ready to go and was not looking forward to a time in the future. I went back to work at de Hoop NV, thinking it would not be long before I would immigrate to the USA., the land of opportunity.

In the meantime, I went to night school and continued to study in case I couldn't emigrate. Even though I did not tell anybody about my plans, it became known at work what I was doing at night, and that effort yielded an unexpected result — an opportunity for promotion. I became eligible for a job in Testing. The company did all sorts of electrical repairs on ships that came into Rotterdam's harbor. This way, the components that could not be repaired on-site could be sent to the plant for more extensive work. As soon as a motor arrived, the four electrical mechanics in Testing had to evaluate what was wrong with the component and recommend how it should be repaired. When the work was completed, we, in Testing, would get the electrical item back and test it to make sure that it would perform as well as it did when it was newly built, or, in other words, perform according to its ratings on the nameplate. It was very interesting work, and it would give someone a tremendous challenge because not all motors simply needed new bearings. As time went on, I became more and more proficient at analyzing what was wrong with the various generators and motors.

✳ ✳ ✳ ✳

Hourly employees wore blue coveralls in Holland. If you were salaried and paid by the month, you would wear khaki coveralls, which, in itself, was a real status symbol. Mamma would wash my coveralls every week and hang them on the dry line at home. Living on the second and third floor in town, the only way she could do this was to hang the clothes on a set of drying lines that were fixed in front of the back balcony. Only six feet of width was available, so the normal way of coping with that situation was to have four parallel lines, each six feet long, in front of each other. The separation between lines was about six inches. The underwear and other such items were hung on the "inside" lines, and shirts and sheets were hung on the outside line. The moment I was promoted to monthly salaried status, my khaki coveralls hung on the outside line. In no time flat, the neighborhood knew that I was wearing khaki coveralls instead of blue ones and concluded that Bob must be doing well in his job!

Time went on, and I went on a two-week vacation to Austria and was hoping that my name would soon come to the top at the American Consulate in downtown Rotterdam. Night school was four evenings a week, and I was back on the drafting board at the school for some hours each week. Everything was going okay. One evening, we had an exceptionally hard test in math. All the guys in the class were griping, and at the end of the period, the teacher collected the twenty-odd papers and turned around to do something else. I did not see it, but somehow the test papers disappeared from the teacher's table.

There were a number of older boys in the class who had been in Indonesia as soldiers for two years. In 1945, when Indonesia was still known as the Dutch East Indies, a movement by the natives that started at the end of the Japanese occupation led to a strong effort for the Dutch East Indies to become an independent country. The Dutch government, not too keen on giving up its colony, sent Dutch troops over for a two-year stint to keep order. These Dutch troops had gone through some very rough times in the Dutch East Indies. Before that, the same age group had gone through the war as slave laborers in Germany, or had hidden from the Germans to avoid having to go to Germany, or had served in the resistance. These guys had gone through hell and were determined that they were not going to put up with something unreasonable in night school; as a matter of fact, they decided it was going much too far. One of them swiped the test papers, and the teacher could not find them. After looking in vain for the test papers, the teacher turned around once more and realized what had happened. He asked if anyone had seen the test papers. No one answered, so he looked one more time and said, "I get the message: this test was too hard, so we'll do it over tomorrow night." There was no honor system in the school and the general consensus was, if you could get away with it, more power to you. In Holland, cheating on your taxes is fine as long as you don't get caught, and the same attitude worked in school.

I enjoyed the job in Testing and thought that I had done relatively well. There was a particular part that came into the shop rather regularly. It was a motor-generator set that was used on small freighters. It consisted of a small electric motor that had a number of generators all built into one machine on a common shaft. Various voltages were its output; for instance, one output was a high-frequency power source that was used in the radio room, while other outputs were for lights, etc. After I had worked on a few of them, I became "the expert," and whenever one came into the shop, I would get it and evaluate it. Since I was hoping to be admitted to the USA one day, I wrote down the name of the manufacturer. It was the General Electric Company in Schenectady, New York. That was a strange-sounding name for a town, but I would hope to go there one day and find out if I could get a plant tour and see the M-G set being manufactured.

10

A Letter from the U.S. Consulate

January 1957 came and nothing exceptional happened until about the twentieth of the month. There was an official letter in the mail from the American Consulate. My heart was pounding out of my chest as I opened the letter. I was told to be at the consulate in the morning and to report for a physical examination the following week. I took the day off and rode my Moped to the American Consulate. (Since I was a monthly salaried employee, I could afford a second-hand Moped, which was a dream compared to my bicycle.)

The consulate was an office on the second and third floors of a large office building in the center of Rotterdam. When I reported, I was told to go to the third floor and undress down to my skivvies. On the third floor, there was a large room with no furniture except for a table and a chair. Since there was no one regularly occupying any of the third floor, the space was not heated. The temperature of the room must have been only 45 degrees Fahrenheit. The floor was covered with the ubiquitous brown vinyl tiles of similar places and, since it was so cold, I kept on my socks. A few minutes later, the doctor came in and checked me out. He listened to my lungs, checked all sorts of things, and finally told me to take off my socks. He very thoroughly checked my right foot and proceeded to separate each of my toes and look between them. I thought, "What in the world is he looking for? Is this something they do in America?"

After he repeated his thorough inspection of my left foot, he looked again under my foot and then he finally asked me, with a puzzled look on his face, "Why the socks?"

I answered, "Doctor, the floor is cold!"

He erupted in a thunderous laugh and said, "OK, get dressed." I was given a piece of paper to take to the government-owned medical department in Rotterdam, where I was going to be given a smallpox vaccination and have a few x-rays taken. The Dutch medical department sent the information to the American Consulate in Rotterdam, and after it was decided that everything was received in good condition, a decision would be made as to whether or not I would get a visa. Three days after I was vaccinated, I became slightly ill, but that was nothing to worry about. The scab on my arm fell off and everything was all right. I was ready for the final phase of getting a visa.

I received another letter from the consulate, announcing that my request for a visa had been approved! I had until the end of April 1957 to be on my way to the States, starting a new life in the land of opportunity! I was on a constant high and decided to tell my employer at the end of February. My last day of work was the twenty-ninth of March, and I had my twenty-fourth birthday party on March thirtieth, which turned out to be a farewell party. My uncles, aunts, cousins, and friends came to the house, gave me presents, and wished me good luck. I had two weeks off before I left Rotterdam on the S.S. Rijndam on April 13, 1957.

The way the cost was calculated for the trip across the Atlantic Ocean was a typical response by the Dutch government to people wanting to emigrate. When the war ended, a large number of young men wanted to leave Holland. Many of them had fought in the Dutch Underground against the German occupiers, knowing well and good that if they were caught, execution was the penalty. Many of them probably missed that excitement and were looking for other adventures. In addition, many families wanted to take advantage of opportunities in other countries that were not then available in Holland. Whatever their reasons, there were a number of countries to which thousands of Dutch people emigrated, the most popular being: New Zealand, Australia, South Africa, Canada, and the USA. The United States was the only country that had any restrictions for the people wanting to immigrate. One had to have a visa, and that could be gotten if someone in the U.S. would be responsible for

The four of us before I immigrated to the U.S. (1957)

that person or family. The Dutch government had promulgated a new law that would financially assist those who wanted to emigrate. A person or his entire family could emigrate to any country he wished, with the only stipulation being that he would pay at least three times the amount of money the person or family had paid in federal income tax in Holland for the preceding full calendar year. The shortfall in cost of the passage would be paid by the Dutch government. A family of six would have paid very little in taxes, so the

Dutch government was in essence paying their way to wherever they wanted to go. It almost seemed as if they were
trying to run the good workers out of Holland. Everybody
knew that they were taking a chance, starting all over in a
strange country, so it took a lot of outright guts to pick up
and start all over in a new land. In my case, it was a little
easier because I was going to live with my aunt and uncle.
When I tripled the taxes that I had paid in 1956, the difference was about ten dollars. I decided to take the govern-
ment-paid ticket to the U.S., which included a train ticket
that would take me from New York City to Newport News,
Virginia. Even though I knew that Uncle Albert would pick
me up in Hoboken, where the S.S. Rijndam would dock, I
figured it was best to have the ticket to Virginia, in case
Uncle Albert was delayed.

After having visited a number of friends and relatives
before departure, the day of my voyage soon arrived. Early
on Saturday, April 13, 1957, I woke up for the last time in the
small room that had been my own place for the past twenty-
one years. I was very excited and ordered a taxi to take the
four of us (Pappa, Mamma, Thea, and me) to the dock from
which the boat would depart. After the passengers had
checked in, family and friends were allowed to come aboard
to spend an hour or so on the ship. The signal for the guests
to leave the ship was the first loud blast on the boat's horn.
As much as I wanted to go to America, I had that uncomfortable feeling in the pit of my stomach, and was hoping that
the ship would burst into flames, forcing me to get off and
stop my great adventure. Of course, nothing happened, and I
said farewell to my family. Mamma's last words to me, before
she left the ship, were: "See, I promised you that I would not
cry." I could not handle crying women, and I still have a hard
time with it. A final blast on the ship's horn, and the greatest
adventure of my life had begun.

✳   ✳   ✳   ✳

April 13, 1957
Leaving Malvastraat 6C for good

On the ship, the first order of business was a lifeboat drill, for which we were instructed to go to our lifeboat station on the deck. As we passed A de Hoop, NV, my employer for six years, I smiled and thought, "This is going to be some chance I am getting." My luggage consisted of four suitcases and a trunk that Pappa had brought back from America when he returned in 1929. The suitcases contained clothing, books, photo albums, and tools. I brought files, pliers, and the rest of the hand tools with which I had been making a good living. After all my expenses had been paid, I exchanged my last Dutch *guilders* for thirty-five American dollars and faced the future with a great deal of optimism and excitement.

The trip across took ten days. First we went to Southampton, England, then to Le Havre, France, followed by Cobb, Ireland, and then across to Halifax, Nova Scotia. The crossing was fantastic. We had two days that were a little rough, and at one point I did not feel 100% but, as a whole, things went fine. The food was very good and I ate some new, unfamiliar vegetables. The washroom, where there were showers and basins to wash and shave, had hot running water. During the first few days, I would rinse my

91

mouth with warm water because I had a tooth that was sensitive to cold water. After doing this for a few days, I decided to stop because I did not want to get used to it. After the war, we had gotten a *geyser* or "point of use" water heater for the bathtub, but that was the only running hot water in our house, so I figured that hot running water was a luxury, afforded only on luxury ships and not in homes.

We docked just long enough to board additional passengers at each stop, but when we stopped in Halifax on Sunday, April 21, it was announced that passengers who were going to New York were allowed to debark at 3:00 p.m. as long as they were back within three hours. I had never been to North America so I jumped at a chance to visit Halifax, even if for a short time, to look around the town. I soon noticed that all the houses had their electric power strung overhead instead of neatly buried underground as it was done in Holland. Also, I noticed things that looked like garbage cans (the transformers) hanging on power poles and thought, "Boy, this looks messy! I am glad that I am going to the States because I know it will be neater there." Little did I know! On Monday night, several boys with whom I shared a cabin asked the cabin steward to wake us the next morning so that we could see the Statue of Liberty as we sailed past it. The steward did wake us; however, it was so foggy that we could not see a thing.

Later, when it was light, I saw the ship being moored as a deckhand threw ashore a weighted light line, which was caught by a man at the dock. He proceeded to pull in the main line, which would securely tie the ship down. A thought, of which I am still rather ashamed, went through my mind: "Buddy, you are ahead of me now — you can speak English — but I am going to pass you." As soon as we had been served our breakfast, we had to pack and get ready for Customs and Immigration Service. The immigration officer asked me a lot of questions about the regulations that I had previously promised to obey. The three things that I had to do as soon as I settled were to report to the Selective Service

S.S. Rijndam

Board, get a Social Security card, and be sure to register each January at a U.S. post office in order to keep my green card valid.

When I came ashore I could only find three suitcases. The luggage was arranged in alphabetical order and, being a Dutch boy, I went to the "L's". There are so many "vans" that in Holland the "van" is listed in the telephone book after the name. I would be listed as Luijn, Robert van. My uncle had spotted me and said, "Are you ready?" I told him that I had lost two pieces of luggage; he said to look with the "V's" and, sure enough, there were the two missing pieces. The breakfast steward had noticed that there were a couple of nice apples left on the table and told me to take the apples. I took them and put them on top of my bag. When the customs officer saw the apples, he confiscated them. I could not understand why, as I just had eaten one, but I did not care and gave them to him.

After a few more minutes, we took my stuff to the car and were on the way to Virginia. My uncle said, "I'm not sure if I know exactly how to get to the New Jersey Turnpike, so when I pull over, pick someone and ask: 'Excuse me sir, can you tell me where the New Jersey Turnpike is?'" I rehearsed the phrase over and over again, and after a few dry runs, I told my uncle that I was ready to ask someone. My uncle pulled over to a man on the sidewalk, and I rolled down the window and asked: "Excuse me, sir, can you tell me where the New Jersey Turnpike is?" The man looked at me with an amazed look on his face and answered: "I no have no car; I know not New Jersey Turnpike". My uncle laughed and said, "Welcome to America, just another foreigner."

At lunch time, we stopped at a restaurant on the Turnpike, and I told my uncle that I had to go to the bathroom. He said that it was probably around the corner. Having been in England five times, I knew how to find a toilet; however, the place had nothing so I went back to the table where we were sitting and told my uncle that there was no bathroom. He said again that it must be around the corner, and I replied that the only thing I saw was a "restroom." Well, I had just learned my first essential American word! We got back in the car and proceeded on our journey south.

In Quantico, Virginia, we had to stop because there was such a horrendous downpour that we could not see the road. The next morning, we approached Richmond, Virginia, and picked up Route 60. "This is the route on which we live," Uncle Albert said. Route, road, it all was the same to my Dutch ears, so I started to anticipate where the house was because I had no idea how far Newport News was from Richmond. After half an hour, I gave up craning my neck and decided that I would see the house once we were nearly there. Of course, it was a long while, and I could not figure out why he had said that he lived on that "route."

While driving down to Newport News, I kept thinking about how lucky I was. There were three things that I would have that I had never had before. My "new" family had a car, a telephone, and a television set. The only way that I had seen television in Holland was through the window of a radio and television shop, and that was really something.

94

We finally arrived at the van Luyn house. It was a small house that turned out to have three rooms: a living room, an eat-in kitchen, and a bedroom for my aunt and uncle. There was also a full bathroom, which completed the house, the only problem being that there was no shower, meaning only baths could be taken.

While my uncle's full-time job was as an inspector at the Newport News Shipyard, a sideline he and my aunt had was a chicken hatchery. There was an incubator, which could hold 6,000 eggs at a time, and they had about 250 Rhode Island Red chickens. Each week 1,000 eggs went into the incubator, and nearly a thousand baby chicks were ready to be mailed out. The eggs that did not go into the incubator were sold to people who would come to the house. The property was on a piece of land measuring about ten acres. The hen house had a second story to it, where there was a sleep-sofa for me to sleep on.

Virginia must have gone through a heat wave right after I arrived because it was either near or over 100 degrees every day. After a few miserable nights on the second floor in the chicken house, I asked if I could sleep in the garden house. It was a small shack, measuring about ten by ten feet, with both a wooden and a screen door. The beauty was that it was not as hot as the area above the hen house. I could decorate my place and feel more comfortable. There was neither water nor heat in the place, but I wired it for electricity and was very proud of my small heaven in America.

11

Work in the States

On April 30, I began my career as an electrician in Warwick, a small town adjacent to Newport News. I had tried to start working at the Newport News Shipyards but, since I was not an American citizen, I could not get hired. The electrical company that hired me was Butterworth & Moss, which did all sorts of electrical wiring in the area. My salary was $1.25 per hour, and I worked from 7:30 in the morning until dark. Ironically, as a foreigner I was not allowed to work at the shipyards, but the very first job I was assigned was rewiring a number of barracks at Fort Monroe. I believe it was the headquarters of the U.S. Continental Army Command.

From there, I went on to wiring houses and had to learn the American system. The wire sizes were very confusing for me. The European system is based on the metric system; for instance, one-and-a-half square millimeters of copper conductor could carry 15 amperes, two-and-a-half square millimeters could carry 20 amperes. The larger the cross section, the larger the current-carrying capacity. The American system goes: #12 wire carries 20 amperes, #14 carries 15 amperes, and so on. The larger the current, the smaller the number would become. Now, if the need arises to carry more current and the number gets to #2, the wire size becomes 0, 00, and 000. No one could say that there was any logic to it, but that was the way it was. I was determined to learn it because I was going to be successful. That was for sure.

＊　＊　＊　＊

On the Fourth of July, the neighbor's daughter, who was engaged to a boy who had a speedboat, asked me if I would like to go for a ride with them. She said that they were going water skiing. I told her that I would love to, and that afternoon I got to try water skiing. Even more exciting, after my second attempt, I was actually skiing! It was the thrill of my life, and I had a great time. Later that day, Uncle Albert and I went to a parade, where Albert pointed out several men who had rather large rings on their fingers. He reverently told me that they were shipyard engineers and that they had graduated from Virginia's best engineering college, Virginia Polytechnic Institute.

During the week, I worked all over the Peninsula, and I remember one large house that we were roughing-in for Mr. and Mrs. Benson; Mr. Benson was the owner of a concrete mixing company. The job involved mounting receptacle boxes for switches, duplex receptacles, and ceiling octagonal boxes at various places. A man saw me putting in a box that was supposed to put a spotlight over the fireplace. He looked scruffy and asked me what I was doing. I told him, and he said, "Move that to the back a little." I nodded and continued what I was doing. Kyle Ford, the electrician with whom I was working, came by, while I was still in the same area of the house, and I told him that the guy with holes in his blue jeans said something about moving the spotlight location. My partner replied, "You'd better do it; he is the owner." I could not believe it — a man wearing scruffy clothes being the owner of a very expensive house! Boy, this country *is* different!

One job was an expansion of the office of a consulting engineering firm. I wired the whole place, and then, at night, I drew a diagram as to how I had wired the office and gave it to the owner of the company, Dutch drafting symbols and all. There was a young girl working there as a receptionist, doing typing work. I thought that she was a very pretty girl and that I would not mind dating her. I knew that my English was not that good and was sure that, if I asked her, she would laugh and I would blush. I did not want to face that situation. Luckily, there was a telephone number written on the telephone that sat on her desk (normal in the States, but not in Holland). I knew that there was a pay phone right outside the office, in the parking lot, and I mustered up all my courage and decided to go outside and call her. I said something to the effect that I was the electrician who was fixing the fluorescent fixture over her desk and would like a date with her. She giggled (my anticipation of a girl laughing at me had been correct) and she told me to call back tomorrow after she had discussed it with her parents. I walked back into the office, and she gave me a friendly smile, so I waited until the next day and went through the same ritual.

In those days, in Holland, when two people had a first date, the couple met somewhere well known in town. They would probably meet in front of City Hall or under the clock at the Central Train Station, and the boy might not yet know where the girl lived.

When I called again the next day, she told me that we would have a date and that I was supposed to come to her house. I asked her for her name, and she said it was Joanne Beecroft. I told her that I did not have a car, but that I would be there at eight o'clock. She said, "It does not matter if you have no car, just come to the house." When I arrived at the house — my uncle had taken me and I told him that I would somehow find my way home — I rang the bell and found Joanne home alone.

That made me very uncomfortable and I did not know what to think of it. In Holland, one is invited into the girl's home only when the parents want to take a look at you, and you'd better be prepared to tell them that you have a steady job and a good income, etc. Here, I was told that her parents had gone out to play canasta with some friends. Joanne and I looked at a college yearbook and just talked. Later that evening, her parents came home, and I was introduced to Doctor and Mrs. Beecroft. When it was time for me to go home, I was about to leave when they asked me how was I going to get home. I said I would walk, that it was no problem because it was only about three or four miles. "Absolutely not!" Mrs. Beecroft said. She offered to drive me to the chicken farm, and that was that.

Joanne and I had a few more dates and one evening we all watched television. In those days, *The $64,000 Question* was a very popular TV program. Each week on the show the contestant was asked a question. If the correct answer was given, he or she won $2,000. If they answered correctly, a week later, they won $4,000, and $8,000 the week after that. That particular night, there was a twelve-year-old boy named Robert Storm answering electrical questions: "For $16,000 give me the formula of the following diagram." It was an arrangement of some capacitors connected parallel and in series. As all people do, I looked at the question and beat Robert Storm by a fraction of a second with the correct answer. All three, Joanne and her parents, said that I just had won $16,000! Joanne had just finished her freshman year at Mary Baldwin College, in Staunton, Virginia, and she and her parents said in unison that I should go to college. What? Me, 24 years old, going to college and quitting my good job? No sir, that was ridiculous. Plus, I was about ready to learn to drive and was close to buying my own car. Right now the world was at my feet. I had done my share of studying, and it was time to make, and save, some real money!

On our next date, the subject of college came up again and I quickly brushed it off. However, the following date would cause a reaction that I could not have imagined in my wildest dreams, and it was definitely going to change my life.

As had become the routine, I made my way down to her house somehow, and this time we went to see a movie in Hampton. It was *Guys and Dolls*. It was a fun movie, and I wondered why there had been so much talk in Holland about banning it before I left for the States. The Dutch censors had decided that the movie was not respectful of the Salvation Army. Joanne, as usual, was driving a 1956 Chevy; I still had no car and did not know how to drive one. As we were driving somewhere in Hampton, not quite in Newport News, Joanne started the college thing again and I responded with: "I am a journeyman electrician. I have trained for it, and I am making good money ($1.25 per hour), and I have no intention of throwing it all away by quitting and going to college." Joanne looked at me and said:

"Why don't you admit it?"

"Admit what?" I asked.

"The fact that you are too stupid to go to college!"

"Hold the phone," I thought, and said, "Please pull over and stop the car."

When she did, I shook hands and said to her:

"I don't think that you should spend any more time with someone who is too stupid to go to college."

I got out of the car and walked the fifteen miles back to my aunt and uncle's house, paving the road with some choice Dutch curse words. Who in the world did she think she was to tell me that?

The next day, in the truck on our way to the next job, I asked Kyle Ford if he knew where the local high school was and whether he knew if they had any night classes. He showed me where it was and told me that the classes started again in September.

12

My First Car

In July or early August, I was able to buy a second-hand car. It was a two-door 1949 Ford. It cost me $200, and I thought I had arrived. The car was in good condition and had 70,000 miles on it. I started to drive it to work before I even had my license! I learned how to drive it and, at night, I would go to the licensing bureau and parallel park between two wood slats about four inches by one inch and six feet long, which were lying on the ground. I would line up various points of the building relative to the side windows in the car and, after a while, I could park backwards as if my eyes were next to the wheels. I passed the test and got my license.

Now, I could start to do something about that insult Joanne had served me earlier. I would go to the high school and register for night classes. School met three nights a week and I enrolled in math. I was not interested in what kind of math it was; I wanted to learn the terms in English. I did not know what "parentheses," "brackets," or any of those terms were, so I took level-1 algebra.

The teacher, Mr. Huller, instructed three levels in the same classroom. He would work with group 1, give them exercises, proceed with group 2, and then group 3. I did the work quickly and watched him work on the blackboard. One evening as he was working with group 3, he made a mistake. I put my hand up, and Mr. Huller responded saying, "No, I'm working with group 3; wait until I come back to group 1." I shook my head and pointed.

He said, "What's the matter?"

I said: "I can't say."

"What is it?" he asked again.

All I could say was: "You're wrong".

Boy, that got the whole class's attention, and everyone started to laugh, so he told me to come to the board and gave me the chalk. I made a few changes and sat down. He looked and said:

"You are correct; stay after class."

When the class was over and everyone was gone, he asked me what the idea was — being in group 1 and understanding group 3 work. I told him that I wanted to learn the English terms and thought going to night school was a good way to do it. He asked, "But why?"

Well, now I had to "'fess up," and I was too shy to tell him that here, in America, a twenty-four-year-old electrician had something to prove that was bigger than algebra 1, 2, or 3. I told him, somewhat timidly, "I want to go to college" — something that I had not told a single solitary person.

He responded with: "Great, let's see what we can do to accomplish that. Go in group 3 as a starter." I asked him if I could do group 2 and group 3 at the same time.

He looked doubtful and said, "OK, but I am not giving you any extra time for the exam at the end of the quarter."

I could not have cared less. All I wanted was to learn the math terms so that, if I got admitted into a college, at least I would understand the various terms that were used in mathematics. At the end of the quarter, I passed both tests in the time allotted for one, so I thought that I was on the right track. In the meantime, I had decided to leave Butterworth & Moss and start working for Colonial Williamsburg as a maintenance electrician. It was a lot of fun to work in all the restored houses and buildings, and work was done in such a manner that we would have to hide the electrical outlets as much as possible to maintain the atmosphere of the early years of the 1700s in Colonial America. While working there, I was learning a good bit about American history.

In December, I reached a milestone in my life in America. I owned a car and had $1,000 in a savings account. I treated Aunt Gre and Uncle Albert by taking them out to eat at a famous seafood place in Yorktown, Nick's Seafood.

My First Car: 1949 Ford

✳ ✳ ✳ ✳

Around that time, I was given a helper. He was about two years older than I and had graduated from the College of William & Mary. Widdy Fennell was a nice boy, but he had one problem — he had ten thumbs on two left hands! I could not figure out how he would be helpful to me, except to hand me a hammer and not too big a screwdriver. What I found out later was that Widdy's father was the manager of the Williamsburg Inn, and Widdy had to kill some time and make some spending money while awaiting the start of law school at the University of Virginia, in Charlottesville.

Widdy had served three years in the U.S. Navy as an officer, after graduating from the College of William and Mary. Again, I had no idea what a fantastic stroke of luck had come my way. We worked well together and had a lot of laughs. Fortunately, Colonial Williamsburg was not interested in speed; rather, neatness and high quality work were of the first order. Therefore, having a helper who did not speed up our tasks was of very little importance to the company.

In February 1958, Widdy asked me if I was interested in going to Washington, D.C. Well, of course, I would love to go to the city of which I had heard a great deal, and I would be able to see all those famous buildings and sights. Widdy said that he knew four girls who were living in an apartment in Georgetown, a part of D.C., and that two of the girls were going home for the weekend, leaving two bedrooms available for us to sleep in. I was not used to the idea of sleeping in an apartment where two girls were sleeping. Widdy assured me that the boys would be upstairs in separate bedrooms and the girls downstairs. So we went and had a fantastic time. The two girls were both from Yorktown — Lettie Shields was the daughter of Judge and Mrs. Shields and Elaine Abbott was the daughter of Mr. and Mrs. Stanley W. Abbott. Stanley Abbott was the U.S. Park Service Superintendent of the Yorktown-Williamsburg-Jamestown Colonial Parkway. Friday night, Elaine had a date, so Widdy and I took Lettie to a jazz club in Georgetown. Then, on Sunday night, Lettie had a date with someone, and we took Elaine to the Officers Club at Bolling Air Force Base. Widdy had his Navy identification, and we had a great time there.

When we weren't taking the girls out, Widdy and I saw as many of the sights as we could. We walked all the way up the Washington Monument, went to the Lincoln Memorial (where I tried to read aloud the Gettysburg Address), and saw all sorts of other great things. What a weekend! It was just marvelous.

On Sunday morning, everybody was reading the funnies. "What a crazy habit for college graduates to do," I thought, so I went to the kitchen and proceeded to give the stove a good cleaning. I cleaned the pots and the pans until they looked as if they were new. Everybody else was reading those colored strips, which I thought were intended for children.

The following weeks, we were talking about what we had done. As we drove to Washington for that fabulous weekend, I had confided in Widdy the plan that I would try to go to college. I had selected Virginia Polytechnic Institute because my uncle had spoken highly about the school and it was a state institution. Its tuition, room, and board were costs which I could probably handle. Obviously, I had to apply in order to have a chance to be admitted, so I had decided that I was not about to say that I was going to college; rather, I would say, "If I get to go." Widdy had cut right through it, and before we had arrived in Washington, he said, "You are going to tell the girls that you are going to VPI." The thought of assuming that I would be admitted before I even had applied made me somewhat uncomfortable, but I had not argued when he said, "Robert is going to VPI next fall."

Finally, April came along and I took a couple of days off to go to VPI and try to find out what I needed to do to get admitted. My uncle's neighbor's son, Robert Mangum, was a football player at VPI, and he had told me that he would find me a bed somewhere in his dormitory, so I slept in the dorm where all the football players were housed. That should have impressed me, but since I did not know a thing about football, it just passed me by.

Next morning, I went to Burruss Hall, the building where the admissions office was. They told me that I had to take some tests. All morning and afternoon, I took test after test. One English test stands out in my mind. The examiner gave us a starting time and let us read for perhaps five minutes. It was a story about a crow that stole silver and was put in jail. Crow? "That must not be a bird; that must be the way you spell *crook*." I reread the sentence, which still did not make any sense. "Stop," was the instruction, "Mark your test paper as to where you were reading — the number of the line can be found in the left margin." I wrote down the number of the line. Then, the next part was a comprehension test of what I had read. Well, it does not take a nuclear physicist to figure out that I did not do too well on the English part of my test! After all the various tests were taken, I had to report to a person who had graded all the tests that I had taken that day. When I sat down in an office in Burruss Hall, the man looked at my test scores and looked up at me:

"You've done very well on your tests, but your English is atrocious."

Upon which I responded, "Sir, I never took any English in my life."

In disgust he threw the papers on his desk, looked at me sternly and said, "Son, I see a lot of boys in this job, but I never heard a poorer excuse."

"It is the truth, sir; I've never taken English."

Looking back at my papers, he asked, "Where were you born?"

"In Rotterdam, Holland," I said.

"How long have you been in this country?"

"Today, the twenty-third of April, it is one year, sir."

"Is there some reason why you picked today?" he asked

"Yes sir, today I will have lived in Virginia one year, and therefore, I will be considered a Virginia resident, and I understand that, in this state, tuition costs less for an in-state student. That is, if you admit me."

He smiled and said:

"You did fine on your English."

The next thing he did was to send me to the Dean of the Engineering School, Dr. John Whittemore. Dean Whittemore looked at my Dutch papers that showed all the schooling I had taken in Holland, my night classes, etc. He picked up the phone and asked the person he called if he had a minute to look at some Dutch papers. He put down the phone and sent me across the campus to the School of Agriculture, where I met Dr. Wybe Kroontje. "Could that be a former Dutchman?"

I thought. As it turned out, Wybe Kroontje was also from Rotterdam, and he was now a professor of agronomy at VPI. He looked over all my papers, said that everything looked fine, and told me to go back to Dean Wittemoore. Wybe Kroontje obviously had called Dean Whittemore while I was walking back to the Dean's office, and when I returned to his office, the Dean suggested that I should enroll in summer school and should take freshman English, as well as anything else I wanted to take.

He said, "This will give you a feel for college life, and if you can handle the English language at this time. If you decide you want to wait another year before you get started, then you haven't spent too much money because the first summer term lasts six weeks and costs half the amount of a regular quarter." If I remember correctly, it cost $167.00 for six weeks for room, board, laundry, and tuition.

I was so happy that I went right to the bookstore and bought a Virginia Polytechnic Institute decal to go on the rear window of my '49 Ford. About a week later, I received a letter from VPI officially admitting me. I was happy and could not wait to give Joanne Beecroft a call. Joanne, unbeknownst to her, had challenged me almost a year earlier, and I could not wait to tell her that I had been admitted to VPI. My aunt and uncle took the news with less enthusiasm, but that did not register with me. I had a date with the girl who was the reason for my becoming, at age 25, a college student.

I had talked with my boss, Harry Sutton, at Colonial Williamsburg, and told him what my plans were. He was delighted and told me that his son was a rising senior at VPI. Harry said, "Robert, you always have a job here. Whenever you have vacation, we want you to come back and work — even if it is for a week during Easter vacation." That was a terrific deal because, even though I had enough saved for perhaps a couple of years, I was sure that I would need to replenish my bank account to be able to afford all four years.

After calling Joanne with the big news, I drove my '49 Ford, with its Virginia Polytechnic Institute decal on the back window, to Joanne's and showed her the letter from the Admissions Office. The whole family was happy for me and congratulated me. I did not say anything at that time, but I knew, and Joanne knew, that she was the reason for my having succeeded in being admitted to VPI.

13

College

VPI's first summer session started around the fifteenth of June. Three weeks before I was to start college, my uncle asked me at the breakfast table how long I had been in the States.

I answered him, "Twelve, no, thirteen, months, sir."

"Well, I think it's time for you to move out."

Good morning! I did not know that the difference from going from a high to a low would be so awful. I was twenty-five and did not know what to say. I tried to gather my composure, hoping to avoid showing the shock that my uncle had thrust upon me. Quickly, I said, "I am sorry that I cannot respond any faster, but it so happens that I have to change the power at a flower shop on the Duke of Gloucester Street in Williamsburg." The store was rented by Colonial Williamsburg to a local florist, and they needed their electrical service changed. Well, with all the self-control I could muster, I said to my uncle, "I can't move out tonight because I have to change the power and will be working all through the night, so that when I cut off the power for a few hours, the flowers in the cooler won't wilt." I tried to act calm, but the only thought I had was, "What am I going to do?"

I went to work and told my helper Widdy that I was in real trouble and needed to find a place to live. Widdy said, "Don't worry; things will be all right." That is easily said, I thought, but I have to find something, and I can't look while I'm working.

My mind switched to the work at hand, and I started to work. That night, everything went fine; the service was changed and my intentional power outage did not cause any of the flowers to die. I worked the rest of the following day and went to bed early that second day.

The next day was a Friday, and we had a normal day at work.

During work, Widdy asked me, "Do you remember Elaine Abbott?"

I said, "Yes, of course, we met Elaine and Lettie Shields in Washington, in February."

Widdy continued, "The Abbotts are having an open house in Yorktown, and Elaine asked me if we could give them a hand tonight, tidying things up a little. Elaine needs some help fixing up the basement and hanging a few pictures, etc." Well, I thought, I'm not in the mood to go out and have some fun but, at the same time, it was better for me to start looking for a place to live on Saturday, when I would have all day, so I agreed to help.

Widdy and I mopped, swept, cleaned the basement, and hung some pictures on the wall. The basement was very nice, with a great deal of space. It took us about three hours, during which I was introduced to Mr. and Mrs. Abbott. When it was time to leave, Elaine walked with me to the car, and in the yard she said, "You have seen the basement, and we would be honored if you would stay with us; that is, if the basement bedroom, shower, and separate entrance would fit your requirements." Goodness! How in the world did that happen to me? Just as the world seemed to close in on me, I got an offer like this? I asked her if she was serious, and she said, "Yes, of course."

The following morning, Saturday, I loaded my car with all my belongings and moved to Yorktown. Uncle Albert asked me where I was going, and I told him that I was invited to live with the Superintendent of the Colonial Parkway's family, in the house that belonged to the National Park Service. My uncle looked very surprised and could not figure out how I had managed that so quickly. I did not elaborate as to how I had managed to meet such an outstanding, well-respected family.

I was convinced that there were two reasons why I was told to leave my uncle and aunt's place. The first was an incident that happened early in my stay with my aunt and uncle. During the beginning of my stay in America, I would get letters from friends and family in Holland. One day, I received a letter from a niece of Aunt Gre. I barely knew the girl, so I had a suspicion that there was more to it than what it appeared at the time. Rumors had gone around in the family, when Uncle Albert came to Holland, that he was sweet on the girl, who was in the latter part of her forties. Two or three letters later, I received a letter from her with an enclosed letter in it. She asked me to give it to Uncle Albert, without the knowledge of Aunt Gre. I thought, "Wait a minute, Aunt Gre is fixing my meals and washing my clothes!" I could not think of treating her in this manner. I waited until I had a moment alone with Uncle Albert and told him what I had received. I also told him that it was none of my business what he wanted to do, but that he should not expect me to be a part of his deceit and that I was going to return the letter to the girl.

I believe that the other reason for my eviction was monetary. I am sure that Uncle Albert thought that I was expecting him to help pay for my expenses at VPI. Of course, that was not my intention at all.

✳   ✳   ✳   ✳

I became a part of the Abbott family, as if I had lived there all my life. There were three children in the family. Elaine was a few years younger than I, Carlton was about six years younger, and Gale was the youngest, a vivacious teenager of about seventeen. Every night during dinner, I was learning the American ways: the way Americans use their utensils at the dinner table, which is rather different from the Dutch; what and how we say certain things; and other important items of which I should be aware.

As I came home in the evening after working at Colonial Williamsburg, I would take a swim in the York River, the shore of which came to the back of the house. Then I would go sit in the gazebo, have a couple of highballs — bourbon and soda — and listen to Stanley Abbott, who was a terrific individual with an unending stream of philosophical thoughts and was, in addition, an artist of the highest order. Stan was educated at Cornell University in landscape architecture. A fresh breeze blew from the York River, and Stanley Abbott was telling me all sorts of thoughts that came to his mind. What an education! What a terrific blessing to be exposed to those thoughts. Stanley Abbott, to whom I would refer as "Pappa Abbott," was the sole designer of the Blue Ridge Parkway, and, in the late twenties, had negotiated for and bought every square foot of the property from the various farmers who owned the property, before the federal government could claim it to develop and build a national park. Pappa Abbott had also designed the Mississippi Parkway and had also, as a matter of fact, worked on Connecticut's Merritt Parkway, during the Depression (on the board of which was Gerard Swope, the third president of the General Electric Company, the significance of which I learned later in my life). We would talk every night, and I got an appreciation for things I had never thought about.

✳   ✳   ✳   ✳

Three weeks later, after Colonial Williamsburg had given me a leave of absence, I got up early and pulled out of the Abbotts' driveway around 4 a.m. At that very moment, I had that same strange feeling of uncertainty in the pit of my stomach that I had had before leaving Holland. This time, instead of hoping for a fire, I thought, "Please, let me have a dead battery in the car." Of course, it started right up and my next adventure had begun. In the early morning, I arrived at VPI and went to the War Memorial Gym, where students were supposed to register for the classes they were taking during the first summer session. I signed up for English and math. English was from 8:00 A.M. until 8:50 A.M., and math was from10:00 A.M. until 11:50 A.M. Both of the classes met five days a week. The rest of the day we had for reading and homework. I was excited; my college career was to begin the following day, and I was as ready as anyone could be. At least, that is what I thought.

The next morning at eight o'clock sharp, Mr. Dayton Kohler walked into the English class and proceeded to call the roll. My name was still spelled "van Luijn," so I don't remember how he pronounced it, but I was waiting for it and said, like everybody else, "Here." Mr. Kohler proceeded to

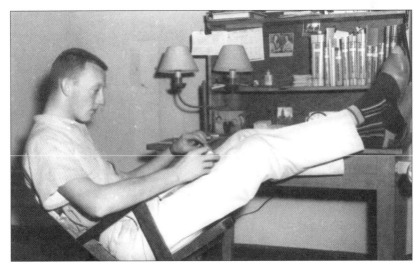

Freshman at VPI, Fall of 1958

tell us what text we were to use, what two parallels we had to read, and what kind of dictionary we were to have. Boy, I had it all under control! I had it all because the Abbotts had given me a beautiful dictionary. Then he said, "The assignment for tomorrow is to review pages one through fifteen." I did not know what the word "assignment" meant; I wrote down what I heard and made sure once back in my dorm room that I would ask my roommate, Don Shorter (a boy of about twenty years old, who had already worked for a few years in the engineering department at the Salem General Electric plant). The next words out of the professor's mouth were: "Class dismissed." Everybody got up and left the room. Cold sweat broke out! I thought, "Holy smoke, I have just gone through an American college lecture, and I haven't got the faintest idea what happened." I walked up to the front of the class and asked Professor Kohler if we had any homework. He was still muddling with the papers on his desk, and he said, without looking up,

"Your assignment is to review pages one through fifteen."

My answer was, "Yes sir, I heard that, but I want to know about homework."

At this, he looked up with an expression that clearly said, "Oh, my Lord, I've got a real case here." Sternly he said, "Your homework is to review pages one through fifteen." Well, that was one word I did not have to ask Don Shorter what the meaning was!

Embarrassed, I left the room, went back to my dorm room, and waited for my math class to start. Math was no problem, since I had been to night school in Newport News and now knew what brackets and parentheses were in English, and the rest fell in place. Back in the room, I started to do my homework (sorry, my "assignment"). I could not figure out what was going on. Somehow, on the pages I was reading, they assigned a title to a word, referring to it as a verb or a noun. I was trying to figure out what that meant, but I was totally lost. I must have read those fifteen pages at least ten times, but I could not figure out what was happening.

Two days of classes did not seem to help too much, until, all of a sudden, it dawned on me that they were doing basic grammar. In Holland, I was in the third or fourth grade when we had discussed and learned about verbs, nouns, and adjectives! I had not anticipated that they would go over such basic grammar rules in a college class but, of course, as it turned out, it was to my benefit to learn from the ground up, so to say. Once I realized what was going on, I could at least follow what they were talking about.

At the end of the week, we were told to turn in an autobiography. Okay, I had a dictionary and I knew how to write about myself, so I should do all right with this. I sat down and started my life story with an opening sentence that started as follows. "I am born in Rotterdam, the Netherlands." In Dutch, it is *I am born* because if I said *I was born*, then I am obviously dead. I checked every word I wrote down, except the "ands" and the "ifs," with my dictionary. I ended it with the following mandatory sentence: "On my honor I have neither given nor received any help on this autobiography." I was so proud of it that I gave it to my roommate Don Shorter so he could read it. He read it, and his response gave me an inkling that things might not be as good as I thought that they were. He said, "You really will learn a lot when the professor returns the paper to you." I thought it was a strange comment because I had checked every word in the dictionary and was sure that I did not have any spelling mistakes.

Two days later, I received my autobiography, corrected. There was more red ink on my masterpiece than the original blue of my pen. On top there was a big "F " At the bottom of my paper, written in bold letters, were the words: "SEE ME." The way that the professors of English corrected papers was to refer one to the handbook. For instance, 25A was a "superfluous comma" (I read it as *super-fluwus)*. I did not know the word "superfluous," therefore put the accent on the

115

wrong syllable and could not make heads or tails out of it. One of my friends, Lester Rowe, who had nicknamed me "Dutch", told me that Mr. Kohler taught the same class again from 9:00 A.M. until 9:50 A.M., so I went to see Mr. Kohler again and asked him if I could sit through the second class, as long as I promised not to say anything during the second session. He kind of smiled and jokingly said that there was nobody in school who wanted to listen to him again for an hour. I was glad that I could, and I thought that I learned a lot. At the end of the six-week session, I received an A in math and a D in English. I passed, but I thought, "I have to live here the rest of my life, so I must do better." I decided to take the same course again in September, this time with another professor. To my disappointment, I got another D. To make matters worse for myself, I was unaware of the Quality Credit Average and, being on a three-point system, I had put myself in a hole, which I would be faced with at a later day.

After the first summer session, I worked at Colonial Williamsburg until the start of school in September. My major was electrical engineering. I took all sorts of courses and, for me, one was particularly interesting. It was Western Civilization. In Holland, we had learned that the Dutch had defeated the Spanish Armada. During my two months in Retford, England, I had heard that this same Spanish Armada was destroyed by the English. Here, at VPI, I was taught that a heavy storm blew the Spanish Armada apart, the end result being that the Dutch and the English destroyed the pieces that were left. The only trouble I had with Western Civilization was that the papers had to be written in English. My first year, the only thing that kept me from flunking out of VPI was my math.

* * * *

In the summer of 1959, Pappa Abbott arranged for me to be hired in the Glass House in Jamestown. In 1957, because of the 350th anniversary of the first colony in Virginia, the glass industry of West Virginia, in cooperation with the National Park Service, had decided to build a replica of the building in which the first industry in the new colony was housed. It was a large post and beam structure that was left open on all four sides and had a thatched roof. In it was a glassmaking facility. We had two glass blowers and I was the salesman. We sold the vases for $2.50 and showed the tourists how glass was made. The glass was green in color due to the chemicals in the local sand, which is what we used. I had been in the country for two years and had started to speak better English, so I thought that I would be able to handle almost any situation.

It so happened that, one day, a female tourist who visited the Glass House did something that embarrassed her, but it was funny. She caught me laughing and looked at me with a very disapproving expression. I thought that this was the right time and place to use my newly-learned English idiom. I said: "I am not laughing at you ma'am, I am laughing because of you." This attempt by me to use the idiom made it worse.

One day, Pappa Abbott was guiding a VIP through the Jamestown park; he was Mr. Arthur I. Ginsburg, president of Fort Worth Pipe and Supply Company of Fort Worth, Texas. Mr. Ginsburg had flown into Newport News airport in his own converted DC-3. He was accompanied by his wife, their two daughters, his pilot, and his co-pilot. They were on their way to make a large donation to Virginia Military Institute. I explained the process at the Glass House, upon which Mr. Ginsburg asked me if we had to train to have an English accent to work in this job. It tickled me to have Mr. Ginsburg think that I had an English accent, and I told him, "No sir, I immigrated two years ago from Holland."

After that little exchange, Mr. Ginsburg asked me, "Would you like to join us for dinner tonight at the King's Arms Restaurant?"

I glanced quickly at Pappa Abbott, who faintly nodded, and I said, "I would love to do that, sir; thank you for asking me."

That evening, we were in a special room for what turned out to be a party of eleven. I was standing in the back of the room and let everybody select a place until there was one seat open. The seat that was empty was to the left of Mr. Ginsburg. He again asked me about the Glass House and wondered if I worked there year 'round. I told him: "No, sir, I am a student, and this is my summer job."

"Are you an exchange student?" was the next question.

"No, sir, I am a permanent resident in the USA, and I am working my way through VPI."

"Why did you pick such a lousy school?" (At that time, VPI and VMI were the two big rivals in the state of Virginia).

I smiled and said: "It is the one I could afford, sir."

Working at the Glass House the entire summer, I met a lot of people who were on vacation. There were two situations that come readily to my mind. The first one was the day that a family visited the Glass House and asked the usual questions. As I remember it, there were four in the party: the parents, a boy, and a girl. As happened so often, the boy wanted a souvenir from the Glass House, and he selected a paperweight. The cost was fifty cents; it was a small glob of glass in which we pressed a die leaving the Jamestown date. The mother decided, for one reason or another, that her son had more than his share and was not about to buy yet another souvenir. The boy persisted, which finally drew a reaction from his mother. She said that, if he wanted it that much, he had to pay for it with his own money. The boy agreed and whipped out a silver dollar to pay for the paperweight. I could not believe my eyes, and my excitement at seeing a silver dollar gave away the fact that I had never seen one. As a matter of fact, I thought it was something that had been gone for many years. I called it to the lady's attention that her boy was about to spend his silver dollar. The response was that I should not worry because he had a few left over from a trip they had made the year before. "Out west they still have plenty of silver dollars," she said. The family being my witness, I showed that I exchanged the silver dollar with a paper one I had in my pocket. They got a kick out of my reaction, and I have been carrying the silver dollar ever since.

The second situation had to do with two girls. After I had explained the glassblowing process, I asked one girl where her home was. She said, "Originally, I'm from Long Island but, after I graduated from college, I moved and am working and living in Schenectady, New York." I asked her how to spell Schenectady, and, yes, it was the same place where my MG sets, which we had repaired at A de Hoop, NV, were fabricated. To be sure, I asked if there was a General Electric plant. She laughed and said, "That's why I chose Schenectady. That's where all the single young engineers work!" We had a couple of dates while she was in the area, and I asked her for her address. I wrote her and asked if she could find me a rooming house where I could spend a few days inexpensively, so that I could see her and go to the GE plant while she was teaching.

After I finished my summer job at the Glass House, I decided to visit Schenectady, New York. I drove my '49 Ford all the way there, and found the GE plant and my rooming house. The first full day in Schenectady, I went to the employment office early in the morning. There were two entrances. One was labeled "Hourly" and the other "Salaried." I decided to go to the salaried door, and I showed my Dutch letter from A. de Hoop, NV, in which it was written that de Hoop was a certified repair facility for GE equipment. The lady at the desk asked me to sit down and picked up the phone. In about five minutes, a gentleman drove up in a station wagon and asked if I had eaten. I said, yes, I had, and that I was very much interested in seeing their facility. I believe that, in 1959, there were more than 25,000 people working there, so this was a big place. The gentleman proceeded to show me all over the place. We walked over the entire manufacturing floor and saw Vertical Turret Lathes that were so big that the operator was sitting on a small step ladder in the machine observing the cutting tool as the ma-

Class portrait taken in 1958

chine was turning. This was fantastic. We went into the afternoon, at which time he took me over to the Research and Development Department. He pointed out what I later realized was Knolls Laboratory, the nuclear facility. He said he was sorry that he could not show that for security reasons. "Boy! The way they treat a rising sophomore in this company is fantastic," I thought. "When, and if, I graduate from VPI, there is no question where I would like to work. Imagine how they must treat their employees! Even though I never saw where they were building the MG set, nor found out if they were still in production, I was still duly impressed.

The summer went its normal way, and upon my arrival in Blacksburg, after driving from Schenectady, I walked over to the Student Activity Building (SAB), where the mailboxes were. There was one letter in the box from the Dean of Engineering, Dean Whittemore. "Please come to see me," it said. I could not figure out what in the world the Dean wanted from me, and I worried a little about something I may not have done properly. When I came in his office, Dean Whittemore said, "In my position as Dean, I receive mail from people during the summer months telling me about my Engineering students and, often, it is news I would rather not hear." Wow, was "laughing because of you" catching up with me? I did not know, but was expecting a sound tongue lashing at the least.

He said, "I've received a letter that makes me very proud; do you remember meeting Mr. Ginsburg from Fort Worth?"

I said, "Yes, sir, I do".

"He sent me a check for $750.00 for your tuition"

I almost passed out.

"What do you think I ought to do with it?" continued the Dean.

I said that, if he agreed, it would be nice if he would credit my account with $250.00 each quarter during the coming year. He said that was an excellent idea and said again how pleased he was.

Near the end of that sophomore year, I realized that I might not make it in electrical engineering and decided to switch to industrial engineering. Things were not necessarily easier, but it seemed that a big pressure was lifted from me, and I was making better grades.

✳   ✳   ✳   ✳

The following summer, Pappa Abbott thought that it would be a nice idea if I were to go to the Grand Teton National Park. With some sufficient string-pulling on Pappa Abbott's part, I landed a three-month position as the head groundsman at the Jackson Lake Lodge in the Grand Teton National Park, Wyoming. However, there was one stipulation

— I had to report for work two days after I had finished my last exam for that quarter. The only way that I could make that was for me to fly to Wyoming and report for work. Mamma Abbott purchased a ticket for me, and I started the summer in a financial hole. The Grand Tetons were beautiful, and the work was lots of fun. I had five college-age boys working for me, whose job it was to cut wood and keep the grounds spic and span.

The reason Pappa Abbott was able to get me the job was that the Jackson Lake Lodge was one of the very few concessions in the Grand Teton National Park, and he knew the park superintendent. Also, the Jackson Lake Lodge is a part of the Rockefeller Foundation. Years back, Mr. John D. Rockefeller, Jr. would go to the Grand Tetons and enjoy the unbelievable beauty of the surroundings. Mr. Rockefeller decided to purchase as much land as he thought necessary to protect this lovely piece of nature in America. He had a lawyer friend, Mr. Fabian, whom he commissioned to purchase thousands of acres, pretending that it was for Mr. Fabian's use. When the required acreage was gathered, Mr. Fabian deeded the land to Mr. Rockefeller, who in turn gave it to the United States so that it could be designated as a national park. Mr. Rockefeller was allowed to build the Jackson Lake Lodge on the property, and Mr. Fabian was allowed to have his home built on a small piece of property. Since Colonial Williamsburg in Virginia was also funded by the Rockefeller Foundation, it was not difficult for them to find out if I had done a good job as one of their maintenance electricians.

The personnel at the Jackson Lake Lodge consisted of about a half-dozen professionals from a hotel in Phoenix, Arizona, and the rest were college students hired for the summer. The students lived in two dormitories, one each for the boys and the girls. I arrived at Jackson Lake Lodge two days after I had been sweating over one of my final exams in Blacksburg and, that afternoon, I decided to go to the personnel dining room to enjoy my first dinner there. The food was the same food that was sold to the guests, so it was good and there was plenty of it. As I walked to the dining room, a girl came out of the girls' dormitory and we walked to the dining room together.

"Where do you come from?" I asked.

"The Virgin Islands"

"Oh, that's interesting," I said. I did not have the faintest idea where that was.

"So, where are you from?"

"Yorktown, Virginia."

"Where did you work last year?"

"In Jamestown, in the national park where there is a Glass House, the first industry in the colonies."

"You received a silver dollar there last year!"

I was stunned. "How in the world do you know that?"

She proceeded to tell me that her father was the park superintendent of the Virgin Islands National Park and that she had wanted to work at the Grand Teton National Park. Her dad had decided that it was too far, unless she could find a way to get to Wyoming. She found out that a ranger, who was at the Everglades National Park in Florida, was on his way to a conference at Glacier National Park and was taking his family with him for a vacation, so she got a ride with them. While they had been driving the past four days, they had talked and the wife had recalled that Dutch boy who had been so excited to see his first silver dollar. I showed the girl the silver dollar, and she offered to take me to the head ranger's house to see the family again. The moment I walked into the house, the lady said, "You're the silver dollar guy from Jamestown." Indeed, we live in a small, small world.

✳ ✳ ✳ ✳

When September came along, I went back to VPI and started my junior year. However, even with having had a very busy summer, I was not financially able to make it through to the following summer. In December, I decided to quit school for one quarter. I was not going to borrow any money because I knew that the pressure of trying to finish school was high enough, and that I could not handle any additional worry. Unfortunately, I realized only later that there were a few required courses that were taught only once a year, so I actually added a year to my college career. I went back to my toolbox and worked again for Colonial Williamsburg. By the following summer, I realized that my bank account was still a bit small and decided to work a few more hours a week. I decided that if I could put a little variety in my tasks it would be easier, and it wouldn't feel like I was working all the time. I worked full time for Colonial Williamsburg as a maintenance electrician. At night, I was an usher at the *The Common Glory*, an outdoor show that told the story of the War of Independence. My tasks included: seating people as they arrived at the open-air theater, selling soft drinks during intermission, and, during the second act, acting as an English soldier who was killed in the decisive battle of Yorktown. We had sixty performances and, by the end of the season, I could recite Patrick Henry's call to arms — "The battle, sir, is not for the strong alone...." This was fun! On Sunday and Monday nights, when there was no *Common Glory* performance, I was a lifeguard at the Williamsburg Inn pool. That left Saturday, which gave me a chance to take on a job as a helper to a carpenter who worked at Colonial Williamsburg and was making some extra money on weekends.

The easiest of these jobs was as a lifeguard because it typically involved sitting high above the deep end of the pool, watching the tourists have a good time. However, on the last evening of the summer, the day before I was going back to school, I had to pull out a little girl whose big sister had teased her into the deep end of the pool, and she was going under. I still remember the fear in the little girl's eyes and the bubbles coming out of her mouth as she went slowly under the surface of the water. Her parents, who were sitting nearby, had not seen the incident and were slightly perturbed with me when they saw me mildly reprimanding the older sister.

* * * *

During the school year, I worked at the dishwashing machine in the dining hall at VPI. For the Thanksgiving holiday of my junior year, I stayed at school and had a blind date at Hollins College. Linda Rogers (my date) and I went to the annual Thanksgiving game between VPI and VMI, which took place in Victory Stadium in Roanoke, Virginia. When Christmas came, I went back to work at Colonial Williamsburg, and I made enough money to pay for my tuition and my books, plus $15 to spare!

Returning to VPI the following January, I had another date at Hollins College on the first Sunday night, and it had snowed. When we returned, it was about 10:45 P.M. The girls had to be in at 11:00 P.M., otherwise they would be "campused." There were two girls walking back to the dorm on the narrow driveway, and there was snow about 12" deep on each side of the road. I decided to drive off the cleared path and get in the snow so that the girls would not have to walk through the snow to let me by. Of course, I got stuck, and there was no way that I could get out of it. Finally, I asked my date to call a wrecker as soon as she walked back in the dorm. The wrecker came, and I was free in a minute.

"How much do I owe you?"

"$15.00," he replied

"That's all I have!" was my desperate plea.

"That's all I need," he answered.

Now, I was completely broke and had no chance to make any money until Easter vacation. Luckily, I had enough gas in the tank so I drove back to Blacksburg rather downhearted.

The next day, the feeling had not left me, but I had to go to class and could not do anything about my financial situation. As I walked from my morning classes to the mailbox at the SAB to see if I had any mail, I saw that there was a blood drive by the American Red Cross. "Well, that's the least I can do for my fellow man," I thought, and walked in. I filled out the paperwork and ended up on the stretcher that was outfitted so that one could donate blood. The nurse was a very nice lady and asked all the regular questions and, as she was about to put the needle in my arm, I said:

"Be careful, this blood was made in Holland!"

She looked at me and asked: "Are you an exchange student?"

"No, ma'am, I am not; I am a student who was born in Rotterdam, Holland."

"So you are on a scholarship here at VPI." Boy, would that be lovely!

"No m'am, I am working my way through college."

"Where are you working?" was her next question.

"Well, that's a bit of a problem; I don't have a job right now, but, during the various breaks in the year, I work for Colonial Williamsburg as a maintenance electrician." She took a paper towel and wrote down something and proceeded to take a pint of Dutch blood. I did not think about the nurse and the discussion any longer.

A few days later, there was a letter in my mailbox. The return address stated that it was from Electrotech, a small manufacturing company in town that was making slip ring assemblies for missiles. The letter said something to the effect that the undersigned would like to talk with me. I did not recognize the name of the person who wrote the letter, but I thought that the next day would be a good time to go and see what it was all about.

I went to Electrotech and met the general manager, who asked me if I was interested in a part-time job! Good grief, what an offer and what timing! I quickly said, "Yes, sir, I surely would be very much interested in having a part-time job." As I was talking, I kept thinking who in the world is this kind gentleman and how is it that he picked me? I could not come up with a good answer, until my eyes wandered past his face and focused on a photograph on the credenza behind him. I saw a very nice-looking lady and there was the answer — she was the nurse who had taken my blood a few days ago! He asked me if I wanted to work in engineering or in production. Afraid of asking what would be involved in either choice, I took production. I don't remember exactly how much I was paid but, whatever it was, it was a fortune in my book. I had a timecard and was able to come in whenever I could and stay as long as I wanted, receiving a check according to the hours I had worked. My toothpaste and soap money was taken care of, and I still had a good bit extra. Had it not been for the "cutesy" comment about blood made in Holland and preventing two girls from walking into a snowdrift, this all would not have happened. I worked there the rest of the school year and was asked to work for the summer months. I could not take them up on the offer because I could earn more at Colonial Williamsburg and had promised them that I would come back in the summer.

14

No More Dutchman

The highlight of my senior year came on the nineteenth of November, 1962. In the spring of 1962, I had started an application to become an American citizen. I filled out papers and went to the campus police department, where my fingerprints were taken. When all formalities were completed, I thought it was just a matter of time before I would become an American citizen. I received a booklet containing information that was going to be part of my examination. I studied it and was waiting for the call that would direct me to an office where the examination would take place. In late spring, I was summoned to the Federal Courthouse in Roanoke, where I was to be examined.

Full of excitement, I went with two of my friends — Don Shorter, who had been my freshman roommate, and Ernie Evans — because I was told to bring two witnesses with me. Ernie Evans, a friend and a Civil Engineering student, was a big man, about 6'4" tall and probably 245 pounds, without an ounce of fat on his frame. We walked into the Federal Courthouse, and I was told to go into an office, in which a woman sat waiting for me.

She was with the Immigration and Naturalization Service. She told me to sit down, looked at my papers, and said, "Oh, we've got a college student here, a smart one."

"No ma'am, not exactly," I answered.

She followed up with the comment: "Let's start with changing your name. It'll be very easy to do as you get naturalized, and it will save you a lot of trouble throughout your life in the USA. You can pick anything you like — Jones or whatever you choose."

"No, thank you, ma'am, I like my name the way it is."

"*van Luijn* will be very difficult in the U.S. At least put it together and start it with a capital V."

"No, ma'am, that is not the way I want to do it." I sensed that things were not going too well and that this was not going to be just a formality. "OK, I will drop the dots," I finally said

"You will drop the whats?" she asked.

"The dots over the Y."

She could not figure out what I was willing to do, so I explained to her that if she were to write an *i* and a *j* longhand, she would write the same figure as a *y*, the only difference being that the *ij* would be written with dots above the *y*. After my explanation, she agreed that my name would be changed to *van Luyn*. She said, very casually, "Since you are a college student, you should not have any trouble in telling me what the three branches of government are." First of all, I had never heard of the term "branches," and I thought I was still waiting to be tested. I looked blankly at her, and she responded with:

"I flunk you!"

I just about died. I had flunked the exam before I knew that it had even begun! I looked at her in bewilderment, and she repeated her statement:

"You flunked!"

I went out of the office to where Don and Ernie were waiting. Upon seeing me, Ernie asked, "Done already?"

"She flunked me," I said.

"You're kidding," Ernie responded.

"No, she flunked me," I repeated.

Ernie got up, walked into the woman's office without knocking, slammed his fist on the desk, and said, "Lady, there is no guy in this country who deserves to be a citizen of this country more than Robert van Luijn, and you had better pass him, or I will raise some hell with my congressman."

I ran in after Ernie, pleading, "Ernie, get the hell out of here; she will have me deported."

Ernie was getting mad, and the woman did not want a scene in her office. She told me, "OK, I will see you again at 4:30 p.m., right here, and I will examine you thoroughly."

Ernie and Don went back to Blacksburg, and I went to the public library to bury myself in anything I could find that would help me prepare for my looming exam. I read and re-read anything that I thought would help me. I studied without stopping for lunch; this was too important. I could not lose this opportunity a second time.

With a heavy heart, I went back to the Federal Courthouse. Inside, a Hungarian immigrant was being quizzed. He was asked something about the Senate, and so help me, his answer was *the Washington Senators,* the former Washington D.C. baseball team. The same woman who had quizzed me smiled, corrected his answer, and proceeded to the next question. After she had passed him, I began to think that I had just caught her at the wrong time of the day (or rather *she had caught me* at the wrong time). Anyhow, my second chance began.

The questions were fired at me in a rapid sequence:
"Who designed the Great Seal of the United States of America?"
"What is on the reverse side of the Great Seal of the United States of America?"
"Are you going to be President of the USA?"
To this last question, I answered, "No."
"Why not, aren't you good enough?" she asked.

I replied, "I was not born a U.S. citizen and am not eligible."

She continued:

"Describe the Great Seal of America and, yes, name the three branches of the government."

"What does it take to become a U.S. Representative or U.S. Senator?"

Due to the fact that I had correctly answered all of her questions, she finally relaxed a little. The exam lasted about twenty minutes, but it seemed to have lasted an hour. At last she relented and said, "You have passed."

Boy, I couldn't wait to go back to Blacksburg and tell my buddies that it was just a matter of time until I would become a full-fledged American citizen! Two years earlier, when the presidential elections had been going on, I had voiced my opinion that I thought that Senator Kennedy would make a good President. I had no idea about Republicans and Democrats, I just liked the man and thought that he would do well as President. The vast majority of the students at VPI were for Nixon, and my friends started to stuff pro-Nixon flyers in my pockets, jackets, books, and anything else they could get their hands on. During the election, they pasted a large poster on the door of my dorm room that read, "I am for John Kennedy." Under those words was written: "We sure are happy he is still a damned foreigner and can't vote!" I thought I'd fix that, so, after passing my naturalization test, I wrote a letter to President Kennedy, asking him for an autographed photograph of the president under whom I would become a U.S. citizen.

A few weeks later, I received a letter from Evelyn Lincoln, the President's secretary, with a nice note and a photograph of the President, under which he had written: "To Robert van Luyn with very best wishes, John Kennedy." I would keep the letter, without telling anyone, until the day I became a citizen.

In early November, I received a letter, saying that I had to report to the Federal Courthouse in Harrisonburg, Virginia. I was asked to surrender my green card and to proceed into the courtroom with roughly thirty or forty other people. Oom Albert had come to Harrisonburg from Newport News to see me become a citizen of the United States of America. While the judge was listening to us declare our *Oath of Allegiance* to the United States, I noticed the woman from the Immigration and Naturalization Service frantically scanning the crowd of participants to see if all repeated the oath. The judge congratulated us all, and we were invited to enjoy a fantastic feast prepared by the local chapter of the Daughters of the American Revolution. The ladies gave all of us a small, silk American flag, and it was a very nice gathering.

While I was munching away at my snacks, the woman from the Immigration and Naturalization Service came up to me and said, "Mr. van Luyn, you must have wondered why I gave you such a hard time during the examination."

I lied and said, "No, ma'am, I did not."

"Well," she said, "I am sure that you are going to be a Congressman one day, and I wanted to make sure that you would start based on a good foundation."

I smiled and held on tightly to my naturalization certificate. I could not have cared less about that day in Roanoke, earlier that year. Looking at that wonderful document that made me an American citizen, I saw the Great Seal of America and realized I had come from the Dutch lion to the American eagle. I also noticed that the American eagle had thirteen arrows in his claw, six more than the Dutch lion!

I went back to Blacksburg and was welcomed by my friends, who gave me a congratulatory card with many signatures, including those of a number of faculty members. With the card came a gift, a fifth of Virginia Gentleman. I was so happy! It was something I had been looking forward to since the day I had arrived in the U.S., five-and-a-half years earlier. I wrote my parents, and they congratulated me. They sent me a celebratory card every year, as if it was another birthday, until my mother passed away.

15

The End Is in Sight

As a soon-to-be graduate engineer, December 1962 was the time to start interviewing for a job. My experience with small companies in Holland had told me that the future would be brighter with a large company. The companies would announce when they would come to the campus, and one could sign up for an interview. If the interview went well, the student would get a follow-up letter, inviting him to a plant location for a further interview. I decided to try with big companies only, so I interviewed with Alcoa, DuPont, Westinghouse, Hamilton Standard, Newport News Shipyard, and IBM. I had not seen that the General Electric Company was interviewing, so I went ahead with other large companies, hoping to see an announcement soon. I still had my Schenectady experience fresh in my mind and was waiting for GE to come for the interviews because they were the company I was most interested in.

When I interviewed with DuPont, the interviewer told me that, since I was born and raised in Holland, he would make sure that I would go to Dordrecht, Holland, where they had just started a new plant. I told him, "Thank you very much, but I did not immigrate to the U.S. so that I could get an education and go back to Holland." The interviews continued, and one could sign up as many times as he wished.

After being interviewed by Alcoa, I received a letter to visit their plant in Tennessee, which I did. By the end of the visit, I had an offer for employment as an engineer. A confirmation letter followed less than a week later. That was a relief; now I knew that, when I graduated, I would have a job, so the pressure was off. I received invitations for interview trips from almost all of the companies that interviewed me. Since I had an offer in my pocket, I could start to be choosy. The Westinghouse Company did not invite me for a plant tour, but gave me an offer. The DuPont Company asked me to come to their Parlin, New Jersey, plant, where DuPont was manufacturing X-ray films for medical use. After arriving at the plant at 8:00 a.m., I was taken by a gentleman to a production meeting, at which they discussed what had happened during the preceding night-shift, i.e. the number of films produced, what type, etc.

As we came out of the meeting my escort said, "Did you notice the man with the red hair?"

"Yes, sir, I did."

"You are going to take his job."

"That is very interesting; what is his job?" I asked.

He told me that the redhead was the night supervisor in a particular part of the plant. I knew I had an offer from Alcoa, and I was not about to take a job on the night shift. I told him that I had not half-killed myself for the last five years so that I could work on a night shift.

"But the plant manager started his career on the night shift!" was his response.

I told him that the interview was over and that I was ready to go back to Blacksburg. He seemed very surprised and said, "Forget it; I will see if I can get you something better."

My confidence in DuPont was gone, and I was no longer interested in working there. What was most interesting was the fact that DuPont was not about to give up on me. They wrote me several letters from Wilmington, Delaware, and basically told me that I could tell them what I would like to do, and they would find such a position in their organization, if at all possible. First to Holland, and then on the night shift! I did not like the idea of going to work for a company that would suggest that I should work in situations that did not interest me in the slightest.

At last, General Electric came for campus interviews. I immediately signed up, and I noticed that a description of the company said that they would only interview the top ten percent of the graduating class. I decided to ignore that item and signed up anyhow.

When the day came for the interview, I entered the room and, after the introductions, handed the interviewer my resumé. He looked at the first few lines and said, "We at the General Electric Company hire only the top ten percent of the class."

I was in a ten-percent group — it was just the bottom portion of the class!

"Sir, I had a rather difficult time the first two years I came here. I had to learn English, as well as my engineering courses."

"Sorry, I can't do a thing for you,." he said, closing the folder into which he had earlier placed my resumé.

He looked at his watch and realized we had most of the allotted twenty minutes left, so he decided to shoot the breeze with me.

"Where in Holland were you born?"
"What did you do in Holland? "
"Are you here with your family?"
"What do you think of this country?"

I answered the questions, and then it happened. The next question was going to seal the deal, and I did not know it was coming, and certainly had not planned how to answer it.

"Have you ever had a disappointment since you've been in the U.S.?"

"No, sir, but you are about to give me my first," I said.

The expression on his face not only changed, it almost looked apologetic, and he said "Don't you do that to me!"

"Sir, you asked me a fair question, and I gave you an honest answer."

We shook hands and, in less than a week, I had an interview trip with GE, closely followed by an offer to start work in Philadelphia, Pennsylvania, as soon as I graduated. I ended up with seven offers and, of course, remembering the way I had been treated in Schenectady at the GE plant three years earlier, there was no doubt for whom I would choose to work.

* * * *

That Christmas was going to be a great one. I was ready to go back to Colonial Williamsburg. When I got there, not only was my job waiting for me, but Harry Sutton had a new task for me, in addition to my regular forty hours. I was asked to turn off all the Christmas lights in seven major buildings in the restored area. Regardless of how long it took me, I would be paid for two hours of overtime. Once I got the routine down, I could complete the job in twenty minutes.

Again, this was the time I had to make enough money to pay for my tuition, books, and incidentals for the rest of the college year. I still had not borrowed any money, but I was running low. A day before my last at Colonial Williamsburg, I figured that I had enough for tuition, but not enough for books, soap and toothpaste. "What am I going to do?" I thought. I finally decided to swallow my pride and go to Uncle Albert to ask if I could borrow $75.00. I went to the house and, after the regular pleasantries, asked if Uncle Albert would help me. The answer was a short "No." I made my manners and went back to Williamsburg, fussing at myself. I should have known better than to ask him.

The next morning, still mad at myself for having asked my uncle for help, I was not in a very good mood. While driving me to a task at one of the properties of Colonial Williamsburg, my boss, Harry Sutton, knowing me very well, noticed that something was bothering me.

"What's the matter, Robert?"

"Nothing, sir."

Harry stopped the truck and looked at me. "I know you better than that. Out with it. Let's hear it. What's the trouble?"

He knew I had an uncle in Newport News, and he sensed there was some trouble relative to my uncle.

"Were you in Newport News last night?" he asked.

Out it came. I told him how lousy I felt after I had been refused a loan of $75.00.

Harry said, "Don't worry and do your work; we will all get together late this afternoon and have a little party for New Year's."

At about 3:00 p.m., we all gathered at the warehouse and had some cookies, fruit cake, and eggnog (which definitely had a more robust body than when it was bought earlier in the day at the local grocery store!). Mr. Otis O'Dell came to make a little speech. He was the vice-president of Buildings and Grounds at Colonial Williamsburg. He said that he was very pleased that, in spite of the budget crunch, everyone had performed very well, and he told us how proud he was of the teamwork of the whole organization.

He went on further, saying, "Today something happened that hit me right between the eyes." He turned to me and said, "Van, you've got a lot of friends here!" I looked at him with what must have been a puzzled look on my face. He walked over to me, and handed me an envelope that felt as if it were full of money.

"Van, you better get the hell out of VPI because you're going to have a lot of Daddies here looking for you if you don't." I did not know what to do or say, but managed to stammer a few words telling them how much I appreciated their concern. Later, I looked in the envelope and counted more than $76.00. Harry Sutton must have spoken with the guys, and they all pitched in for me. Knowing that there were only five months left until graduation, I headed back to Blacksburg with enough money to cover my tuition, books, soap, and toothpaste.

* * * *

In the meantime, I had gotten a part-time job at a local florist. I learned how to make floral wreaths and sprays for funerals, and was getting the hang of it. Jimmy Childress, my boss, let me work as much as my classes and homework would allow. At the time, I was still dating Linda Rogers at Hollins College, and I had met a nice young woman who was "signing out" the girls when they went on dates off-campus. Suzanne Manges, who was working as assistant to the Social Dean at Hollins, was about twenty-four years old, and I thought I could get her a date with a student who was a little older. We might enjoy a double date. So I checked with some of my GI Bill friends; these were the students who had been in the service and were going through college on the GI Bill. Like me, they were older than the usual college students. One of them was willing to go on a double date, and we took Suzanne and Linda Rogers to a VPI basketball game. It so happened that Suzanne was from Blacksburg, a fact that was unknown to me.

"After the game, we could go to my mother's house and look at her brand new color TV," Suzanne suggested.

Well, we saw the TV. The Mitch Miller Show was on. The picture was in color but was so terribly misaligned that it looked like a badly printed issue of the Sunday morning funnies. Afterwards, we took the girls back to Hollins, and I forgot about the evening.

A few months later, while I was working in the back of the florist shop, Mrs. Manges came into the flower shop and, unbeknownst to me, saw me and spoke with the florist about me. As soon as she was gone, Jimmy called me up front and told me to quit working for him.

"Your troubles are over," he stated.

"What are you talking about?" I asked.

He explained that Mrs. Manges was a well-known person in town, and that all I had to do was date her daughter and my troubles would be over. I told him that I knew Suzanne, but I was not interested in dating her, even though I was not dating at Hollins College any longer.

About a couple of weeks later, during the Easter holidays, I got a call in the dorm. There was a pay telephone in the hall and, when it rang, someone would pick it up and yell for whoever was wanted on the phone.

"Dutch!" was the yell, and I went to the phone.

To my surprise, Mrs. Manges was on the line. I'll never forget what she said,

> "Dutch, my Suzanne has her former college roommate visiting over at Hollins College. She is a beautiful, beautiful girl with a gorgeous, gorgeous voice. I think that it would be nice if you and a nice young man would take the girls out for a cup of coffee."

Aware of the earlier conversation I had had with Jimmy about dating Suzanne, I had a suspicion of what Mrs. Manges might have in mind. I thought, "Americans have a tendency to exaggerate a bit, so if I reduce the beauty and vocal ability by fifty percent, I would still end up with a beautiful girl with a gorgeous voice; plus, she's twenty-four years old." I had better figure this out and see how I could meet her.

The best thing to do was to get one of my buddies to go with me, as long as he wasn't too aggressive. I asked Jim Patterson, a German Club member, and he was glad to go with me, even though he did not know what I had in the back of my mind. Jim and I drove over to Hollins College. It so happened that Suzanne was still at work and would come to her campus apartment at around eight o'clock. Jim and I went to the dormitory where Suzanne was the house-mother, and rang the bell. Yes, the girl who opened the door was classy and beautiful, indeed. The three of us talked a little, and soon, Suzanne was back from work. She suggested that we go somewhere to have a cup of coffee.

We decided to go to the Brown Derby, a nice small restaurant in Roanoke, and Jim drove Suzanne's car, a new Plymouth Fury "hardtop." He loved cars, so he offered to drive the car, and I got to sit in the back with this beautiful girl, Gertrude Florrid, who, I found out later, was a third grade teacher from Atlanta, Georgia. All was working out fine thus far, and I was thinking that this is a really classy and beautiful girl whom I will never see again. I decided that the best thing for me to do was to be a perfect gentleman so that when she went back to Atlanta, she'd remember me as "that nice guy from VPI." We talked about this and that and, somewhere during the conversation, she told me that she was a "teetotaler." That went straight over my head, and I did not have the slightest idea what she meant by that expression.

We took the girls back to Hollins College, and on the way back to VPI, Jim and I were talking about the beautiful car and how nice it rode. Later that week, I thought back on the evening and what a classy girl I had met. I thought that I could write her and invite her for Senior Weekend. There is a Dutch saying that goes, "No, you have. Yes, you may get," which is similar to "nothing ventured, nothing gained." So I called Suzanne at Hollins and asked her for Gertude's name and address. Lo and behold, Gertrude wrote back and said that she would come for Senior Weekend.

As was the custom, when girls were coming to Blacksburg for the formal dances or for concerts that were sponsored by the dance clubs, the boy would find a room with a local family for a nominal amount. Since Trudy (her nickname) had met Mrs. Manges several times while at Agnes Scott College, she felt free to ask if she could stay with her for that particular weekend.

I had a slight problem when contemplating the weekend arrangements. I had wrecked my Ford in a single car wreck on an icy road in Christiansburg that past January. After that, I was planning to get a car before I graduated, so that I had something to take with me to GE, in June. Well, I bit the bullet, and went to a local car dealer on the day I was supposed to be picking up Trudy from the airport in Roanoke, which was thirty-five miles away. I bought a second-hand Pontiac and, just as I was about to leave in my "new" car, it would not start.

Sweat broke out on my brow; I did not know what to do. I went to Mrs. Manges and told her of my troubles. She said, "You could use my car, but I don't have insurance for you."

Desperate to be on time, and with no other means to get there, I said, "Do not worry, ma'am, give me your keys; I have insurance myself." My determination must have overwhelmed her because, minutes later, I was cruising down Route 460 in her big Lincoln Continental.

The airplane arrived on time at Roanoke's airport, and I started to worry if I would recognize Trudy. For the life of me, I could not recall her face. Of course, I recognized her the moment I saw her. As soon as she got into the car, I told her that it wasn't mine and that her hostess had been kind enough to let me borrow the car to pick her up.

The weekend was full of activities. The Kingston Trio gave a concert on campus because the two dance clubs — German Club and Cotillion Club — had joined forces to sponsor it together. I had to "work" as an usher, and the club members had promised not to take the best seats in the house. Our promise did not count for our dates, so Trudy was able to have a good seat in Burruss Hall.

In addition to the Kingston Trio, the German Club members had their "privates" at Dixie Caverns. The "privates" was a dance get-together, with all the German Club members celebrating the successful Spring Formals on which we all had worked so hard. Also, Casey Jones and several other German Club members were living in downtown Blacksburg in what we called the Penthouse, and on many occasions we had a good time filling the apartment to its capacity.

On Saturday morning, I went back to the car dealer and told him that he had sold me a lemon, and we negotiated amicably. I left the dealership as the proud owner of a 1960 Ford Falcon. It was a nice little car that would serve me well for the next three years.

In spite of my car troubles at the start of the weekend, everything else went smoothly. Mrs. Manges was a gracious hostess, Trudy enjoyed meeting my friends, and the concert and dance were terrific. When I took Trudy to the Roanoke airport on Sunday afternoon, there was an air show going on but, regardless of the additonal traffic, I got her to the plane on time. The future was looking great, and I was glad to be heading towards graduation.

16

Graduation

Pappa had retired from the Hotel-Restaurant Atlanta in 1962, and Mamma and Pappa decided that they were going to come to the U.S. for my graduation and stay until October. I was excited because I had not seen them for six years and had only spoken with them once over the telephone; the Abbotts had treated me with a call to Holland. In those days, my parents and I wrote air-mail letters back and forth every month. Their plans to come to graduation were the best thing that could happen. Talk about a graduation present — that was terrific!

On the sixth of June 1963, I drove my 1960 Falcon to New York and arrived there around noon. While looking for the pier where the boat was to dock, I drove through Bloomfield Street in Hoboken. Bloomfield Street was where Pappa's rooming house had been when he was in the U.S. during the late twenties; he had talked about it hundreds of times, so much so that, in my mind, it was almost an address that had been my own. As soon as I had my parents and their luggage in the car, I took them to Bloomfield Street and asked Pappa if he recognized anything. He got all excited and said,

"Mamma, can you imagine? You are driving through Bloomfield Street in your son's automobile, and we are in America together at last!"

I started my drive to Blacksburg but, since I had driven from VPI to New York that morning, I was not able to go all the way back that same day. I stopped around the Quantico, Virginia, area and got a motel room. I did not have enough money for two rooms, but I did not tell my parents this, and I slept in the car. The next morning, I went to my parents' room and told them that my shower did not work, asking if they would mind letting me shower in their room. Soon, we were on the road again and on our way to Blacksburg.

Lester Rowe, with whom I had been friends throughout my years at VPI, had married a Radford College student who had lived with her uncle and aunt, Leamon and Helen Simmons of Christiansburg, Virginia. I had gotten to know the Simmons family during the five years that I had been at VPI, so, when they found out that my parents were coming for my graduation, they insisted that my parents stay with them. What a lovely offer, one that I appreciated very much.

That Friday evening, we all were invited for supper at the Simmons'. While Mr. Simmons was grilling the steaks outside, my parents and I were talking up a storm, catching up on all the things that had happened on both sides of the Atlantic Ocean during the six years that we had been apart. Thea, forty-two-years old, had gotten married just a few days before Mamma and Pappa had sailed, and all sorts of other things were discussed to get me up to date.

Mamma had decided that, if Thea was going to get married, she should do it before Pappa and Mamma left for the States to see me graduate. They were not about to leave the country with an engaged daughter alone in their house with the possibility that her fiancé would come over. The Dutch were still very proper in those days, and Mamma was not going to take any chances. While the three of us were sitting at the Simmons' dining room table, I heard the details of the wonderful party after the wedding.

144

My parents told me that the wedding night of Thea was another happening. Thea had decided that, regardless of where they were going to spend their honeymoon, they would spend the first night in a Rotterdam hotel. At about midnight, there was a hard knock on their room's door, and Thea's husband, Gerard Kleijn, went to see what was going on. Thea was peeking from under the blankets and saw, to her surprise, that two officers of the vice squad were checking on what was going on. It turned out that Thea had signed the registry using her maiden name. She had to get up and tell the officers that she and Gerard were on their honeymoon, and that she was not yet used to her married name because she had signed her name the other way for many years. After having shown the officers the wedding certificate, the situation was cleared up.

While we were sitting at the table in Christiansburg, reacquainting ourselves and laughing about what all had happened, one of the Simmons' three sons came in with a steak. I must admit that it was a big one, probably 3/4" thick. He placed the plate of steak in front of Pappa and, while I continued talking, Pappa said, "My goodness, they want me to carve." It tickled me because I had acclimated enough, while living in America for six years, to know what was about to happen. Less than a minute later, Mamma received an equally large steak, which caused Mamma to say, "I have to carve, too!" When the next steak appeared, my Pappa figured out what was about to happen, and all he could utter was, "God Almighty, look at the meat we are going to eat tonight!" The size of the steaks did not surprise me, and I realized again how much America had spoiled me in the last six years.

The next day, I took my parents to the campus of VPI and showed them the War Memorial Chapel and the organ with the Dutch organ pipes that I had seen being assembled. During their installation, I had recognized the name of the Dutch town where the pipes were made, had talked with the installer, and had even been allowed to tune a rank of pipes.

Graduation: Sunday June 9, 1963

When the organ was dedicated, the installer announced that he would play a Dutch hymn in honor of a Dutch friend he had made at VPI. The hymn was *"Wilt heden nu treden,"* sung in America at Thanksgiving with the words "We gather together...."

At the time of my graduation, VPI had a student body of about 6200 students. On graduation night, there was a reception for the students who would go through baccalaureate exercises. The reception line included several members of the faculty, in particular Dr. T. Marshall Hahn, president of the college. Since I knew Dr. Hahn personally, I thought I would have a little fun. I introduced my parents to Dr. Hahn the Dutch way, saying, "Pappa, I would like you to meet the president of the college, Professor Doctor Engineer T. Marshall Hahn." Dr. Hahn had a twinkle in his eye when he looked at me, then said to my dad, "Pappa Dutch, you think that you are proud of your son; let me assure you that we are much prouder of him than you could be." Pappa did not believe his ears and walked away muttering, "What a democracy — a Professor Doctor Engineer calling me Pappa Dutch — what a democracy!" I loved it, and Pappa enjoyed that introduction the rest of the evening.

On Sunday we graduated — the first class to hold Commencement exercises in the newly built Cassell Coliseum. Uncle Albert, who came to VPI to see me graduate, had insisted that Pappa and Mamma stay with them for a spell while I was getting situated in Philadelphia. Later that day, I drove Pappa and Mamma to Uncle Albert and Aunt Gre's house in Newport News.

✳ ✳ ✳ ✳

I had told the manager of employment of General Electric that I would report for work on Wednesday, June 12. I stayed with friends in Williamsburg until I had to leave. On Tuesday, the eleventh, I drove my 1960 Ford Falcon to Philadelphia. I had the address of the plant, so I figured that I would first find the GE plant and then find a place to stay for the night. On Wednesday, after work, I would look for a semi-permanent place, since my first assignment was going to be for one year. I drove into Philadelphia and asked where 69th Street and Elmwood was.

After a few attempts, I arrived on a street called Lynwood Avenue. I saw a large plant across the railroad with a big GE logo on the roof. Lynwood Avenue was a one-way street, so I got out of the car, looked around, and tried to get my bearings so I would be able to find the plant the following day. As I looked, a man walked up to me and started to talk to me.

"They call me Duke; I live around here. What are you looking for?"

"Well, I was looking for General Electric, but I've found it. Tomorrow, I will start to work there as an engineer."

Duke asked, "Do you know where you're going to stay tonight?"

"No, not yet, but I'm going to find a nearby motel somewhere."

"No need, buddy, I'll find you something."

I said that it was kind of him, but really not necessary.

"No bother, buddy."

He started ringing the bells of the houses where he knew that widows were living on Lynwood Avenue. The second bell he rang was at Lena Pride's house. She appeared to be in her seventies.

"Lena, don't you want to rent a room to this real nice young engineer who is going to work for General Electric tomorrow?"

"No, I think not right now, Duke."

"Oh, come on Lena, you can spare one of your bedrooms for this nice young man."

All along, I tried to tell Duke that it was kind of him, but it was really not necessary for him to try to find me a place to stay. Duke would not listen.

"Come on Lena, it will be OK."

"All right" Lena said, "I guess it would be OK."

I knew that I could always find a more permanent place later in the week, and Lena's price of $7.00 a day was something I certainly could live with.

I took a few items out of my car while Duke went to the hardware store to have a key made for me, which he purchased with a dollar he had borrowed from Lena. I could not believe it! This guy, whom I had never met before in my life, just took over and found me a place to live.

The next morning, Lena had the coffee made. Lena sat me down at the kitchen table and, with a cup of coffee and danish, my breakfast was complete. I told Lena that I would eat lunch at the plant and would walk to a small restaurant for supper. When Lena heard this, she said that she could fix me a bowl of soup for supper and increase my rent to ten dollars a day. I didn't realize then that I would be living at Lena's for a year until I was transferred.

17

General Electric

On Wednesday morning, at General Electric's Philadelphia Switchgear plant, I filled out a number of forms at the employment office. The manager of personnel welcomed me and said that he had one question.

He asked, "Why were you so determined to start to work on a Wednesday? Why not wait until Monday, next week?"

It flashed through my mind that I had a $3200 debt for clothes and the car. "Sir, I need the money. I'm broke, and I need to get to work."

"Well, that is as good a reason as anything," he responded.

The training program that I was going to be completing, the *Manufacturing Training Program*, was structured in such a way that engineers would work in six different phases of manufacturing at three geographical locations. There were three plants in the Philadelphia area; hence, the assignments were considered as one assignment location. My first assignment was in Materials at the Switchgear plant. Large electric breakers were built there, the ones that can be seen in the field at large sub-stations. My task was to schedule the arrival from contractors of all of the hardware that was needed at a sub-station site for the completion of the installation of the switches, making certain that those parts arrived at the specific location on time. It was not terribly interesting. However, I knew the assignment would last only six months. I got a good idea of what was needed for the job and knew that this wasn't what I wanted to do once I completed the training program.

✳   ✳   ✳   ✳

With the Fourth of July coming up soon, I felt that my first Independence Day as an American citizen should be celebrated! I asked Bob Jeckel, a materials specialist in the unit in which I was working, what would be happening on the Fourth.

"We will have a day off," he told me.

"Yes, I know that, but is anything happening in this historic city, say at Independence Hall?"

"I'm not sure, but check. I seem to remember that the Vice-President is coming to Independence Hall."

I checked and found out that Lyndon Johnson was going to be at Independence Hall on the Fourth, around ten o'clock. Needless to say, that was where I was going to be.

I left Lena Pride's home early that morning because I wanted to make sure that I would get a good place at the event. On arriving at Independence Hall, I noticed a podium with chairs, and, in front of those, about six hundred chairs. This was the place, and I decided not to be too obvious. I sat down in the back row and watched as people would come, continuously moving closer to the front. It was a little after eight o'clock, so I was the first one there. A little while later, a Philadelphia policeman, who had nothing better to do, strolled over to me and said,

"Do you have a ticket?"

Rather than saying no, I asked him, "How do I get a ticket?"

"Go to that trailer," he said, pointing to a temporary trailer off to the side of Independence Hall, "and ask for one."

I walked to the trailer and went in. A young lady was sitting behind a desk and asked me what she could do for me.

"I would like to have a ticket, please."

"What color would you like, red or blue?"

Not having any idea what the coding was, and not wanting to tell her that I did not know the difference (because that would tell her that I had no idea of the rules that could apply), I said, "Blue, please."

She handed me a blue ticket and I went back to my seat in the back. The police officer had noticed me coming back and decided to check with me. The same routine again:

"Do you have a ticket?"

Triumphantly I produced my newly obtained blue ticket.

"Oh, you should be sitting on the front row with that color," he responded.

Hey, things are looking up! I went to the front row and had the best seat in all of Philadelphia. On the podium were the VIPs, among whom were Lady Bird Johnson and Johnny Carson, the well-known host of the *Tonight Show*. I was a little perturbed that the public, who filled the entire place, seemed more interested in seeing Lady Bird than the Vice-President of the United States! "That's America," I thought. I had a wonderful time and thought that my first Fourth of July as an American citizen had been celebrated in the best way possible. The next day, I thanked Bob Jeckel for telling me about the event, which caused Bob to say,

"It's in the paper; did you see it?"

"No, I did not," I responded.

Bob looked in his briefcase and showed me the *Philadelphia Inquirer*. There, on the front page, was a photograph taken from the back of the podium, showing the Vice-President, several other people, and the crowd. Right there, in the front row, was a brand new U.S. citizen wearing sunglasses and listening intently to the Vice-President of the United States! I wrote to the *Inquirer*, ordering and receiving a glossy print of the event.

* * * *

Trudy and I were corresponding regularly, and the courtship had now developed into a letter-a-day type of relationship. In one of her letters, she told me that, in the middle of July, she was going to go to Silver Spring, Maryland, and spend some time with her Aunt Lois (her mother's sister). Lois Myers was the vivacious widow of Arthur Myers, Sr., a Georgia Tech engineer who had worked as a consulting engineer for a large construction company in the Washington, D.C., area. Since Silver Spring, Maryland, was not far from Philadelphia, I was invited to stay at Aunt Lois' while Trudy was there. We had a wonderful weekend, and I took Trudy to Newport News to meet my parents, who were still staying with Uncle Albert and Aunt Gre until I could find a temporary place for them in Philadelphia. The four of us (Pappa, Mamma, Trudy, and I) went over to Yorktown, where we met the entire Abbott family.

That was the second date Trudy and I had, and the next one was on the weekend of Labor Day, 1963. I went to Atlanta and was introduced to the Florrid family. Richard Florrid was a man of about five feet six inches tall, and I could tell that he was a strong athletic type of person. I later found out that he had been a professional baseball player, following his very successful college career completed by being the pitcher for Georgia Tech's 1928 Southern Conference championship team. Trudy's Mama was a serious, smart lady who took her time in sizing up this tall engineer who seemed to be making an impression on her one and only child. It was another wonderful weekend.

During this visit, I stayed at a local motel and saw Atlanta for the first time in my life, becoming duly educated in the happenings of the War Between the States. We went to

Grant Park, where the famous Cyclorama is. It is a circular painting, about seventy feet in diameter, and the visitor stands inside the circle after having entered through a tunnel. Depicted was the Battle of Atlanta, in which Sherman had burned the city. The display is arranged in such a manner that one sees actual sand and figures in the foreground; however, at some point, reality changes into painting; it is quite an interesting display. When Trudy showed me the pictures of Sherman having a five-day beard, I could almost see flames shooting out of her eyes with a disdain that I hoped I would never see again in my life. In contrast, Robert E. Lee's picture was the gentleman-like portrait of what one would think of when picturing a "Southern Gentleman."

✳ ✳ ✳ ✳

Back in Philadelphia, I asked Lena if she knew of anyone who would rent out part of a house, so that I could move my parents to Philadelphia. They had been at Uncle Albert and Aunt Gre's for six weeks, and I wanted to bring them closer to me. Of course, Lena knew an elderly spinster, Elsie, who was willing to rent me two bedrooms and a bathroom, plus the use of the kitchen. Elsie charged me twenty dollars a week, and it was as if I was home again. I gave my mother forty dollars a week to buy groceries, and we had a wonderful time. While I went to work, they walked around the neighborhood and visited the various sights in Philadelphia. On the summer evenings, Pappa and I would sit on the front porch, drinking our Dutch gin that they had brought with them from Holland. Elsie was a strict churchgoer, and Lena had warned me not to have alcoholic beverages in Elsie's home. To make sure that we would not upset Elsie, Pappa and I would have our Dutch gin from a cup and saucer, making it appear as if we were having a cup of tea. Those devious Dutch people!

One day, Mamma showed me that she had discovered, at a discount, a nice brand of canned roast beef stew. I was

Thursday, October 31, 1963

MR. AND MRS. C. G. VAN LUIJN

Visitors From Holland

Mr. and Mrs. C. G. van Luijn
of Rotterdam, Holland, and
their son, Robert, of Philadelphia, Pa., were guests this
weekend of Mr. and Mrs. L.
E. Simmons and their family,
of Christiansburg.
    Mr. and Mrs. van Luijn were
guests of the Simmons family last spring when they were
here for their son's graduation from VPI. They have
spent the summer with him in
Philadelphia where he is employed by General Electric.
    While here this weekend
Robert attended the home-
coming activities at VPI.
    Mr. and Mrs. van Luijn will
leave from Philadelphia on
Friday to return to their home
in Holland.

Visitors From Holland

"Mr. and Mrs. C. G. van Luijn of Rotterdam, Holland, and their son, Robert, of Philadelphia, Pa. were guests this weekend of Mr. and Mrs. L. E. Simmons and their family, of Christiansburg.

Mr. and Mrs. van Luijn were guests of the Simmons family last spring when they were here for their son's graduation from VPI. They have spent the summer with him in Philadelphia where he is employed by General Electric.

While here this weekend Robert attended the homecoming activities of VPI.

Mr. and Mrs. van Luijn will leave from Philadelphia on Friday to return to their home in Holland."

quite happy that she showed me her lucky find before she served us the "beef stew." She could not read the label and was unaware that it was really a can of dog food!

✳   ✳   ✳   ✳

In October, my parents returned to Rotterdam on the *S.S. Rotterdam*, a beautiful ship. I had asked my boss if I could take a day off to take my parents to the ship in New York, but he said that since I did not have a year with the company, he could not allow me to be absent. Well, I went to work, left at lunchtime, picked up Pappa and Mamma, and drove to New York. When I approached the pier where the ship was moored, there was a great deal of commotion.

*Waiting for the ship
to depart.*

There were helicopters in the air circling the ship, Coast
Guard boats in the water around the ship, and a number of
cameramen constantly filming the people waving at the
passengers. I thought that it was strange and started to
worry because I wanted to get back to GE to finish the work
that I had left at noon, but the departure time seemed to be
slipping away.

Finally, the ship departed, and I jumped in the car to get
back to Philadelphia. While driving on the New Jersey Turnpike, I heard that Marshall Tito had just left on the *S.S.
Rotterdam* and that there had been a delay in departure
because of a bomb scare. I thought, "Holy smoke, they left
over a thousand passengers on the ship, but Tito, the President of Yugoslavia, could not enter the ship until all was
safe!" I was back at my desk a little after four o'clock, and
my boss, Marsden Lawley, came into the area.

"Bob, I thought that you were taking your parents to the
boat!"

"Yes, sir. I did and came back to work."

"Oh, that was not necessary."

"That's OK, sir. I made it, and they are on the Atlantic by
now."

Thanksgiving was approaching, and Trudy was making plans to visit friends in Philadelphia. "Oh, boy, we are going to have a ball!" I thought. I was looking into getting tickets for the Army-Navy game and an off-Broadway show. To top it all off, we would take Trudy's friends, with whom she would stay, to Bookbinder's, a famous seafood restaurant in Philadelphia.

On the twenty-first of November, President Kennedy was assassinated, and the Army-Navy game was postponed. Trudy still came for the Thanksgiving holidays, and we saw the Thanksgiving Parade in downtown Philly, which featured some "Mummers" with all their elaborate costumes, playing their banjos. We had Thanksgiving dinner with Louise and Ben Mills, a sister and brother who were friends of the Florrid family. That evening, we went to the Shubert Theater and saw "The Girl Who Came to Dinner," with Jose Ferrer and Florence Henderson. I was feeling terrific because I had arranged enough of a mixture of events so that Trudy would be properly entertained after having flown in from Atlanta the previous day. The next evening, it was off to Bookbinder's for dinner. After we had ordered, Trudy and I were busy talking with Trudy's hosts when the waitress came back to ask if Trudy would mind if French fries were substituted for the baked potato that she had just ordered. The waitress explained, "We just ran out of baked potatoes."

"Why, sure, that's all right," said Trudy.

The meal was served, and about ten minutes after the four of us started to eat, the waitress came back again to inform Trudy that they had some more baked potatoes.

"Would you still like the baked potato?" Trudy replied that if it was not too much of a problem, she would appreciate having the baked potato.

As the waitress walked away to fetch the potato, I said, "She wants to show you that she is looking after you; she is working for a good tip."

Minutes later, the girl reappeared with the potato on a small plate and proceeded to move it onto Trudy's plate.

Then she grabbed a cloth napkin from the table and proceeded to scrape the French fries from Trudy's plate. Needless to say, we were dumbfounded. Trudy looked at me and, with a poker-face expression, commented, "Working for a good tip, heh?"

* * * *

The routine at work was getting old, and I was itching to get to my second assignment. Meanwhile, in order to make sure that all the orders for a specific substation had been processed, I had to go into the dispatcher's office and go through file cabinets that had thousands of orders. I repeated this routine many times a day and realized, as I was going through the files, that the orders were mixed up and hard to find. As I was looking for a specific one, I would put the orders in the correct order, so that I would not have to go through that mess again, reducing my search time. That turned out to be a bad move, and I received my first contact notice from the union. I did not realize that the office people were in a union and that, by putting the papers in the correct order, I was taking work away from the office workers who were not doing it in the first place! Of course, I stopped doing it and had to put up with the aggravation.

I celebrated Christmas in Atlanta with Trudy and her parents, staying with Mr. Florrid's sister and brother-in-law, the McClures. We had a wonderful time, and I started to feel that I was being accepted by the family.

Trudy was still teaching in Atlanta. In 1959, she had graduated from Agnes Scott College with high honors and had been elected to the Phi Beta Kappa Society. She had successfully completed her major in voice and, at the same time, had taken the courses necessary for certification in education. Trudy has a gorgeous voice and was a paid soloist at College Park Methodist Church. I could not figure out what she saw in me, but I was not about to argue about it.

18

Spacecraft

In December, I was sent to my second assignment, which was at Valley Forge, twenty miles from Philadelphia. General Electric had a facility there named "Spacecraft." They were building spacecrafts there, and this was absolutely the most far-out, advanced science that was being done in the world at the time. What a break! Can you imagine? Here I am, six months out of VPI, and working on spacecrafts? Unbelievable! About a week or so after I started as a quality control engineer, the first weather satellite, Nimbus I, was launched, and it sent back photographs from space showing the continents and cloud covers. This was spectacular in 1963; it sounded like something out of a science fiction magazine.

I received letters from my parents, with newspaper clippings of photographs taken over Holland by Nimbus I. I was in charge of four components that were going to be installed on Nimbus II, III, and IV. I had to test if the components were good, and I also had to "life" test them. Once the test was started, there was only a very short period of time within which the test could be stopped and restarted. It had been statistically determined as to how many days of testing were sufficient, without degrading the parts to the point that they would have too much wear on them. If, for whatever reason, the test was stopped after the first two days, the parts were considered scrap because starting the needed cycle over again would test them too long. One of my components was the Shutter Position Indicator.

During the lengthy countdown of a spacecraft launch, all sorts of systems are tested as to whether or not they are still in working condition. My particular test was on the components for Nimbus II and would last twenty-one days, nonstop. I went to the men in the laboratory who would monitor the test twenty-four hours a day, and I said, "Please, guys, watch my Shutter Position Indicators and, if anything goes wrong, do not shut down the test. I don't care what time of the day or night it is, I want to know it. Please call me right away." I told the technicians on all four shifts and gave them my desk and home phone numbers.

"We've heard that before!" they said, smiling.

All went well for about the first sixteen days, but then one night, at about two o'clock in the morning, the telephone rang. I had the feeling that it was Valley Forge and that something had happened that needed my attention. The man on the other end of the line informed me that the test had failed.

"Don't break the vacuum on my test set-up; I'll be right there," I said. I heard something that could be interpreted as a chuckle. I quickly got dressed and, in less than half an hour, I was in the laboratory.

The test was conducted in a glass-enclosed dome about 18" wide and about 24" tall. A vacuum was pulled on the inside, where the parts were being tested. There were about eight or ten connectors feeding terminals inside, onto which electrical wires would be connected, if needed, for a particular test. Each airtight connector, containing thirty-six thin wires, was hooked up to the test rig. Each screwed tightly to the testing device. The lab technicians were sitting at a table and looked over their shoulders as I walked in.

"You want us to shut down the test since you're here now?" they asked.

"No, let's wait just a minute," I answered, realizing that the moment they threw the switch, I would have a bunch of scrap on my hands, even if it turned out later that the switches were in perfect order. Too much time testing would have gone by, and I would not be able to start the test again.

Indeed, one of my switches was not responding any longer, but I did not know why. The switch contacts could have failed, the outside wire to the switch could have a break in it, or the wire inside the glass dome could have loosened. I checked everything that I could see without disturbing the set-up.

"Does anybody here know where I can find a wiring diagram of the feed-through connectors?" I asked.

One technician got up and brought me a large drawing with hundreds of wires shown on it.

"Now, let's see. Which switch is not responding?'

They gave me the number. I looked at the feed-through diagram and said,

"That's connector D, let's take that puppy loose." I started to unscrew the bottom of the connector, which contained a spider web of wires crammed into a very small space.

"Connector D, wire 23," I said. Now the guys were getting out of their chairs and were looking over my shoulder. It was a wild guess, but I thought it was worth a try, so I pulled on the wire that was connected to pin #23 and, sure enough, the solder joint had broken loose.

"Anybody have a soldering iron around here?" I asked.

Two technicians went to their toolboxes, and one gave me his soldering iron. It had been a while since I had had that little contest with that girl at de Hoop NV, but I knew I had not forgotten how to solder. I completed the connection and screwed the connector tight again.

"Let's try to see if the switch responds correctly, now," I said.

And, luckily, the test continued without a hitch.

"Good, that came out OK," I said.

As if nothing happened, I looked on my watch, saying, "I think I can still get a few hours of sleep if I hurry."

I left, drove back to Philadelphia, and showed up for work the next morning at the regular time.

I never told anybody anything about what had happened that night. I felt that the guys were probably expecting me to say something to my boss or at least to my co-workers. I did not, the result being that whenever I had to run a test, the lab technicians would pick my work first, and my fellow engineers would be left wondering why I could get the lab people to react quicker for me than for them.

Later in May, we were testing the assembled Nimbus II vehicle in a large vacuum chamber. The diameter was thirty-nine feet, and it would take days of pumping before we reached a vacuum equal to that of outer space. The chamber could be cooled as well as heated, all to simulate conditions that exist in outer space. There was a lot of work to be done, and I was asked to do it on the graveyard shift. What made the graveyard shift attractive was that they paid extra, and often my relief shift would not come in and I would work a double shift, receiving overtime and other such incentives. It reminded me of the job offer in Parlin, New Jersey, with DuPont. Well, this is different, I reasoned, because it's only for a few months. Besides, I was now engaged to be married to that Georgia Peach and needed all the money I could get my hands on for the wedding; plus I still had a debt to pay that I had incurred during my last year at VPI. Sounded like old times again but, this time, I saw the light at the end of the proverbial tunnel before it really got dark to start with.

Nimbus II was placed in the thirty-nine-foot Thermal Vacuum Chamber and was undergoing tests as a completed vehicle. We would monitor all the output signals and, early in the morning, would report the progress we had made during the night. To allow all interested parties access to the report, we would record the report on a tape recorder on the

161

telephone. I thought that it was fun, so I proceeded to record the message every morning as I was about to finish the graveyard shift. One of my colleagues, Al Merkle, jokingly said that they were making some comments about the guy with a foreign accent on the recorder. We had some laughs about it and I did not think anything of it. Later Al said something again, at which time I said, "Al, do you think someone minds my accent?" Al very carefully mentioned that the "B" level manager had made a remark (my boss was a "C" level, a lower reporting level). Of course, it did not bother me, but I stopped doing it; however, it was funny that they were very careful in telling me, as if they thought that I would cause a ruckus over such an insignificant thing. I knew that I had an accent and it certainly did not bother me, and I was trying to minimize it as much as I possibly could.

I had requested that my next location would be in a manufacturing plant somewhere in the South. There was no plant in Atlanta, so I was hoping that my second year in the training program would be somewhere where Trudy would be happy. She had been teaching in the Atlanta school system for five years, as an elementary school and music teacher. Since she had never lived outside the metropolitan area of Atlanta and was an only child, I thought we would have a better start if the first time outside of Atlanta would be somewhere in the South. Soon, I found out that my second location in the training program would be in Hickory, North Carolina.

On my last day at Valley Forge, I decided that I would go and see the "B" level manager. I was not going to say anything about having to stop recording the test report, but I wanted to meet the man and thank him for the assignment. I went to his office and asked his secretary if I could see him for just a couple of minutes. She asked me for my name and went into his adjoining office. She came back and said that he was very busy and had no time at the moment. I said that I was sorry that I could not come back, as I was leaving for Hickory, North Carolina. I asked her if she would please convey to him that I thought that my assignment had been very interesting, and that I hoped that it would be continued so that other young engineers, as well as the General Electric Company, would benefit in the future from the experience.

"Just wait a minute" said the secretary.

She went back into the office, and this time she said he could see me for just a minute. I went in and conveyed to him my thoughts, and was about to leave when he said,

"Aren't you the person who recorded the test reports about the status of Nimbus II while it was in the thirty-nine-foot Thermal Vacuum Chamber?"

"Yes, I am, sir"

"Well, I enjoyed listening to you each morning," he said. I thanked him and told him that I enjoyed doing it!

* * * *

Well, Hickory, North Carolina, is definitely in the South, but I believe the word "North" preceding the state name gave my future in-laws cold chills. In Hickory, the GE Company was manufacturing distribution transformers. Those were the "garbage cans" that I first had observed hanging on power poles in Nova Scotia, seven years earlier. I was assigned to the maintenance department as a facilities engineer. This was right down my alley; I knew how to do the electrical work, and had no problems writing instructions as to how the mechanics should do certain tasks in the plant.

After becoming engaged on Palm Sunday, almost a year after we had met, Trudy and I set the wedding date for August 1, 1964, in Atlanta, Georgia, at Calvary Methodist Church. Since my parents had come over for my graduation the year before, they were unable to come back for our wedding. Miriam and Bill Mitchell, longtime friends of Trudy's parents, offered to sit on the groom's side in the church, and graciously offered to have the rehearsal dinner at their home in Atlanta's historic Ansley Park. My best man was Pappa Abbott with Don Shorter, my college roommate, and Widdy Fennell being two of the groomsmen. Bill Mitchell, Jr., Trudy's childhood friend, and George Gray, Trudy's cousin-in-law, filled out the party of four. Trudy's college classmate, Susannah Masten, was the maid of honor, and two first cousins, Jeanne McClure Gray and Margaret Collings Frady, were the bridesmatrons. It was a very nice affair; however, I did not enjoy the fact that, after I had greeted hundreds of people in the receiving line (most of whom I did not know), I had no time left to spend with my buddies, whom I had not seen in a few years. My new bride whispered into my ear that it was expected that I should at least act as if I was eager to get away from everybody, and we left to change into our travel clothes.

I was still driving my 1960 Ford Falcon; I had noticed that it did not shift too smoothly, and I was wondering what was wrong. We stayed at the Holiday Inn in Atlanta and, on Sunday morning, we were on our way to the Smoky Mountains of Tennessee and North Carolina. Trudy had the top layer of our wedding cake in a hatbox on her lap. About fifteen miles out of town, my car died. The shifter was not working, and here I was in Marietta, unable to move. I got out of the car and lifted the hood, in the hope that whatever was wrong could be easily spotted. Of course, I could not tell what the problem was.

Just as I was wondering what to do, three young boys stopped their car behind us. They were in an old car, and judging by the awful noise it made, it seemed that their car did not have a muffler. They asked me what my problem was, and I told them that my transmission was probably shot. One boy said, "You're in luck; there is a garage about 200 feet from here. Let us take you to the motel right next to it, and tomorrow morning you can have them fix your transmission."

Boy, that was something; I did not have much money in my pocket nor in my checking account and now, at the start of our honeymoon — an unexpected expense. How do we solve this? Well, the boys took us to the Georgian Oaks Motel in their car that sounded as if it was about to explode. An elderly lady at the registration desk looked rather doubtful over her glasses as Trudy and I entered the lobby.

"Ma'am, my car broke down, and these young men have been so nice to us and brought us here. Have you got a room for us?" The lady had me sign in as Trudy thanked the boys, who left the grounds of the motel with a tremendous roar from the muffler-less car.

The next morning, I went to the garage and the manager said that he would fix the car, and that it would be ready around 11:30 a.m. When I came back to the garage, I asked with a heavy heart what the expense was.

The bill was $42.00. I said, "Please, sir, we are on our honeymoon, and I would appreciate it very much if you could wait until next Friday to cash this check because I have only enough to cover our trip."

"No, problem, I'll take care of that." was his answer.

The '60 Falcon ran like a top, and we all but forgot about the rough start of our honeymoon. We had a wonderful four days in the Smoky Mountains. We swung by Atlanta on our way back to Hickory, where I had to be back at work the following Monday morning.

❋ ❋ ❋ ❋

Trudy had looked for a teaching position in both the Hickory and the Newton-Conover school systems. Needless to say, I was not surprised that she was successful and was offered a position in both systems. After she thought about the differences, she decided to work in the Hickory City Schools, since the school where she would be working was just a block from where we had rented an apartment. It all worked out very well. The Viewmont Apartments had been built as emergency housing during World War II. It was a small development of several single-story duplexes, spread over several acres on a quiet street in a north Hickory neighborhood. Our apartment had a living room, a dining area, a

165

kitchen, two bedrooms, and a bathroom. The apartment was located on a corner and cost us $50.00 a month. The flooring throughout the apartment reminded me of my encounter with the old tile floors at the American Consulate in Rotterdam. The tile had a good bit of white paint splattered on it and, to get the apartment ready for move-in, I decided to give it a thorough cleaning. I took steel wool and scrubbed the entire floor by hand, discovering that, after many layers of wax had been removed, the floor was brown with white speckles on it. The paint I saw was the white speckles in the tile design.

I thought that, while we were on our honeymoon, Trudy's car would be safer in the General Electric parking lot where a 24-hour guard was on duty, rather than leaving it on the street in front of our apartment. Trudy had a 1949 Plymouth, which she had bought as a college senior from her Daddy's sister, Aunt Mary. It was a good-running car. When we came back from our honeymoon, we picked up the car in the GE parking lot and went home. Several days later, Trudy said that there was a fishy smell around the car, and we thought that someone had thrown some fish on the street or something like that. I went to the car and examined the surrounding pavement, checking for any sign of rotting fish. I did not see anything, and we forgot about the incident.

Meanwhile, in the fall, GE decided to have a Family Day. Every employee was invited to bring his or her family to the parking lot of the plant, where all sorts of games were set up for the children and adults to have a good time. Along with the good food and drinks that were provided, it was a fun day for all. As Trudy and I walked up to the first booth, where there were three balls to knock off six cans roughly fifteen feet away, I said to Trudy in a loud voice, "Hey, daughter of a professional baseball pitcher, show your stuff."

The man manning the booth gave her three balls, and with the first pitch, she knocked off every one of the cans, at which she turned to me and gave me the remaining two balls and said, "Now, you try!" Having opened my big mouth again, I had to try, and promptly missed.

* * * *

We were soon befriended by Jim and Doris Sides. Jim worked in the tool crib at GE and had taken me around Hickory when I first arrived. Naturally, I introduced Trudy to Jim's wife, Doris, and the girls liked each other's company, so we began to visit back and forth. The Friday night movies at their house, with Pepsi and popcorn, were great. They have remained our good friends all these years.

I was so well received in the maintenance department that my boss went to the program administrator and asked him to keep me six more months after the assigned six months were over. Along with all the other tasks that I performed, I built a clock that showed the number of man-hours the people in the factory had worked since the last lost-time-accident. I made it out of wood; it was driven by a small motor running at a slow speed, showing the man-hours as they were elapsing.

One night in January 1965, Trudy and I went to nearby Gastonia to hear the Boston Pops Orchestra, which was touring the country. We went in Trudy's car and, on the way down to Gastonia, we got a flat tire. Obviously, I had to change the tire before we proceeded but, to get to the wheel's lug nuts, one had to take the hubcap off the wheel. When I took the hubcap off, a bunch of dried-up fish fell out! The guys at work had put fish in Trudy's hubcaps while we were on our honeymoon. We had never figured out from where the fishy smell came, until five months later when the fish had completely dried.

* * * *

We enjoyed living in Hickory but, all too soon, the second year of the training program was completed, and we were getting ready to go to our next (and last) assignment. Where to? We did not know, but I had a feeling that it was going to be somewhere up north. The news came about two weeks before we had to move that we were to report to Johnson City, New York.

The General Electric Company plant in Johnson City made electronic equipment for military aircraft. We made flight controls such as gyroscopes, which were the hearts of the automatic pilot systems on Air Force jets. My first assignment was as an Advance Manufacturing Engineer. We designed machines with which the operators in the plant would manufacture the products. It was highly technical and it gave me tremendous insight into the tolerances with which one must work in order to achieve an end product that is reliable under adverse conditions.

We worked on flight controls for the F111, a highly-advanced fighter-bomber. The press had reported that the F111 was a "piece of junk," that it was not reliable, and other such comments. It was hard for me to believe because I knew the kind of quality we engineered into the plane's components. In retrospect, the F111 has been an unbelievably good and reliable airplane, considering the fact that, more than forty years later, it is still flying and performing exactly as it was designed.

✳   ✳   ✳   ✳

Trudy had applied for a teacher's position in Binghamton, Vestal, and Johnson City, called the Tri-Cities. She had decided on the job closest to our apartment in Binghamton, and was going to teach third grade at Theodore Roosevelt Elementary School. The custom at the start of the school year was that the children would go to their last year's class and that teacher would walk the class to the next grade for the coming school year. Trudy had to get used to all the Polish and Ukrainian names of the children and to their manner of speech. Needless to say, the children had to get used to her very distinct Georgia accent. Later in the school year, their second grade teacher, with whom Trudy had become friendly, confessed that, in warning to her former second graders, she had told the students, "Your next teacher is a very nice and smart lady. However, you must really pay attention to what she says because she is from the south and speaks differently; you may have difficulty understanding her if you don't pay attention."

Well, it doesn't take too much to deduct that that scenario worked both ways! When the first day of school at Theodore Roosevelt began, Trudy decided that it would be a good idea to start the third grade class by having the children write a short story about what they had done during the summer vacation. "If you have any problem with the spelling of a word ask me, and I will write it on the blackboard," Trudy said to the class.

One of the requests was, "How do you spell *fear*?" What could that child have experienced? Trudy thought. She proceeded to write on the blackboard "fear".

"No, like World's *Fear*!"

That year the World's Fair was in New York City, and the child had been there with her family. "This is going to be an interesting year," Trudy thought.

❋ ❋ ❋ ❋

One of my colleagues was Bill Sweet, a fantastic human being who had fought in the European Theatre of World War II. I called Bill my "Liberator" because it was people such as Bill who had defeated the Germans and made us free again. Bill and Maisie Sweet, his wife, had a large number of acres on which Bill had built his house in Greene, New York. Bill had been in the Army as a very young Lieutenant Colonel. He would not say too much about his war experiences but, when he had a drink too many, he would get his service pistol out and say that he regretted threatening to shoot one of his own American GIs with the damned thing. His direct order to the GI was to stop laying out new markers to signal the Army Air Corps where to start strafing the German troops. The Army Air Corps had ignored an earlier marker, and Americans were strafing American troops. Some boys wanted to realign the markers, even though they knew that that would expose additional American troops to an even greater danger. Bill had been successful controlling his troops, but could not get over the fact that he had had to threaten his own man with certain bodily harm.

Trudy and I would go visit Bill and Maisie on Saturday afternoons and, on one particular Saturday when we drove up to the farm, I heard shooting. We went to the back of the house and saw Bill with a few other men shooting at clay pigeons. I had never seen that, nor had I ever seen a shotgun in my life.

"Hey, Dutchman, you want to shoot some?" Bill asked.

"I've never seen a shotgun, let alone shot one, but let me try."

"Where is the sight on this thing?" I asked, remembering my Lee Enfield of the Dutch Army.

"You don't use a sight; just look over the barrel and shoot."

"Tell me when you're ready." Bill slung the clay pigeon in the air, and I hit it on the first shot.

"You've never shot a shotgun — hey, I hear you" was the doubtful response. On the bench where the ammunition was placed was one lead slug.

"What's that for?" I asked

"Oh, that's for deer hunting."

"May I use it?"

"No, don't use that; use a cartridge with shot; that's what you use for clay pigeons."

"I'd like to try it anyhow, may I?"

"All right, go ahead." They threw the clay pigeon in the air and, about six feet before it hit the ground, I hit it with the deer slug. Boy, this was fun! The guys were making fun of me because they did not believe that these two shots were my first ever with a shotgun. Trudy observed it all and said quietly under her breath, "Stop while you're ahead." However, I was having too much fun at this game and proceeded for the rest of the afternoon, with the result being that I could not have hit the side of a barn if I had tried.

* * * *

Our winter in Binghamton, New York, was a very snowy one. It seemed that we were getting twelve inches of snow each Thursday afternoon, and it was not very difficult for us to think that we would rather move to an area of the country where the weather was a little milder. Even if General Electric was sending their young engineers all over the country during their training period, it appeared that most of the guys would go back to the area where they grew up. As far as we were concerned, the South was still the place to go.

Another funny thing was that, when we went to the supermarket to buy our week's groceries, the checker, an older lady, would quiz Trudy about whether she was sure that she had selected this or that over some other brand. Trudy used to comment and say that these people are so interesting and caring. I told her, "Yes, they are nice, but realize that the lady at the supermarket wants to hear you talk because she likes your accent."

My second assignment in Binghamton was as a foreman in the shop. I had thirty-eight people doing grinding and precision lapping. It was precision work of the first order, and it is still mind-boggling to me that I had people working in my group who lapped to a zero finish. That means that the bore of a hole in a piece of high grade steel was polished to a mirror-like finish and had no high nor low places over the length of the bore, which could be four inches deep. The so-called high and low spots were measured in millionths of an inch! One absent-minded moment and an operator could ruin a servo block that had accumulated $3,500.00 worth of labor before it came to my department. Needless to say, it took a special individual with a great deal of patience and craftsmanship to be able to do that kind of work.

The entry kind of job in my department was the de-burring bench. I had one man who came to me repeatedly and asked me to let him start in the lapping area. I did not think that he had the kind of temperament that it took to do that kind of work. He kept on literally begging me to give him a chance. I finally relented and told him that I would give him a week to start on some "easy" parts, then assess if there was a future for him in that particular kind of work. The week went by, he scrapped a few pieces, and a couple of other parts were corrected in time by a co-worker. The scrapped pieces were not too expensive, but still, after a week, I called him in my cubicle and told him what I thought. He again assured me that he could do it, saying that all I had to do was give him one more week. "Well, what the heck," I thought, and said, "All right, this is the last chance. If it does not work out, you go back to the de-burring bench." I did not spend too much time checking on him, but it became apparent that he was not fitted for the job. On Friday, I got too involved with something else, and after the employees had gone home, I thought, well, Monday is time enough to have my talk with him. Monday morning came and my man did not show up for work. In Binghamton, it was customary for the foreman to check on his employees who were absent, so at about ten o'clock I called his home, and the phone was answered by his irate wife, who accused me of being the cause of her husband's having had a heart attack. It scared the living daylights out of me. I hung up the phone and started looking for my manager. Mr. Wilson, a man of about sixty years old who was a friendly, strict kind of manager, was conducting an important meeting. I called him out of the meeting, and Mr. Wilson said, "Not now, Bob, later."

"This cannot wait sir!"

Mr. Wilson came out and asked, "What's the matter?"

172

I told him what the wife of my employee had told me after I had given her husband two weeks to prove himself.

"Then you were right," Mr. Wilson said to me.

"What, sir?"

"You were right that he wasn't suited for the job; tell the plant doctor to check him out."

Whether I was right or wrong was the last thing about which I was concerned. I was thinking I had caused someone a serious illness, and that was one thing for which I was not quite ready. As it turned out, the man was all right, but had reacted to the stress of doing something beyond his capabilities in a manner that caused his wife to think that he had had a heart attack.

＊　＊　＊　＊

My group of thirty-eight was an interesting mixture of people. The youngest was perhaps 30 years old and the oldest most likely around 57. One man gave me trouble every way he could. There were two who tried to be super nice to me. The latter actually told me things that the others were planning to do behind my back. I did not like the tattle-tales, but could not help listening to them and surreptitiously undermining the possible outcome of the schemers. My "trouble-maker" was eligible for his raise of a few cents per hour because he had been in the department at the same pay level for the prescribed six months. It was sort of an automatic raise, with which I did not agree. After some thought, I figured that I would perhaps motivate him if I postponed his raise.

I called him into my cubicle, and before I could open my mouth he said, "Oh, I am going to get my raise."

"No, you're not. I believe that I would be doing your colleagues an injustice if I gave you an automatic raise," I answered.

He appeared not to care. It bothered me, but I stuck to my guns and waited to see if anything would change. The change, if there was any, was difficult for me to detect.

A new machine had been ordered for my area. It was called a crush grinder; it was going to be the first one in our plant. In a few weeks, a service engineer would instruct one of my operators as to how to operate the machine. I was trying to figure out whom I could pull off the machine for which he had been originally trained. Having not made a decision, I thought I would take care of that when the machine was installed. The next morning, I got a call from personnel saying that they had a man in the lobby who was applying for a job as a grinder. Personnel said, "We did not want to hire him because he only has an eighth-grade education."

I thought I'd see what kind of a person this was so I said, "I'll be right out to see him." The man was nicely dressed and was very pleasant. I talked with him and asked him about his education. He told me that his father had died when he was fourteen and that he had had to go to work to support his family. After I had informed him that GE would not want him because he did not have a high school education, I thought about my new crush grinder and told him that, if he wanted to try really hard, I would have him trained on the new machine. He was very happy that I was willing to give him a chance. As it turned out, he became one of my better operators.

When spring arrived, I was approaching the end of my three-year training period and would now start to interview within the General Electric Company for a permanent position. Trudy and I decided that I would interview for a number of southern locations only. I visited three General Electric manufacturing locations and received offers for fulltime positions in each location — Salem, Virginia; Hendersonville, North Carolina; and Rome, Georgia. I chose Rome because it is seventy miles from Atlanta, close to where Trudy had lived all her life before our marriage.

When it was time for me to finish my work as a foreman in Binghamton and move to Rome, it was time to say goodbye to all my people. I went to everybody's work station and said goodbye and exchanged a few words with each one of them. As I approached the man whose raise I had stopped, my mind was racing a hundred miles an hour as to what was appropriate for me to say to him — "I could skip him altogether; no, I could not do that; it's been nice to know you, no, that's an outright lie" — and my mind went on and on trying to come up with a reasonable comment to make. When I was two work stations away from him, he stopped his machine, walked over to me, and stuck out his hand. He said: "No hard feelings, Bob; good luck on your new endeavor." I could have hugged the guy — he made me feel so good, and I had a feeling that he must have sensed my relief. Again and again, at times when I dread that the worst may happen, somehow it works its way out differently, and all my worries are in vain.

19

Permanent Position

We transferred to Rome, Georgia, in July, after Trudy had finished her year in the Binghamton School system. The Rome GE plant was starting an eleven-million-dollar expansion and needed advanced manufacturing engineers to design the manufacturing equipment for the expansion, in order to bring the Medium Power Transformer Department ahead of the competition with modern manufacturing facilities.

The transformers that were being built were large ones, even though the department was called the "Medium Transformer Department." The overall dimensions were roughly 20 feet long, 12 feet high, and 6 feet wide, and they could weigh 100 tons completely assembled. It was considered an old business because they had been building transformers for the last fifty years and had not really had any major changes; even the assembly process had not undergone any substantial changes. After some time, I understood the product and the manner in which it was assembled, and started thinking if there were any ways that I could change the method of assembly.

One day, by chance, I received a flyer about a different kind of hydraulic cylinder. Most often, hydraulic cylinders are constructed in such a manner that the housing is stationary and a piston is either extended out of the housing or retracted into the housing. A small shop in Xenia, Ohio, had developed a differential hydraulic cylinder. It was the housing that moved up and down over a stationary piston, which consisted of two cylinders of different diameters welded together along their longitudinal axis. Due to the fact that the housing moved over the piston, the assembly had to be twice the length of the working stroke of the housing. So if one wanted to lift a load ten feet, the apparatus to accomplish that had to be twenty feet tall. I looked at the flyer and, all of a sudden, saw an application that could be adapted for the transformer assembly area.

To build a transformer, you have to have a laminated iron core (to direct the magnetic field) and coils of wire (to transform the voltage from a high potential to a low potential). The core is built up from sheets of transformer steel; these are laminations that are about .03 inches thick and have a total width of a transformer leg, or yoke, of 24 inches. To get to the top of a ten-foot-tall transformer core, the Rome operators had to build a masonry scaffolding in order to disassemble the top yoke, which involved taking 800 pieces of the laminations out of the top of the core. Those laminations could be six feet long and the total weight of those laminations of the yoke could be, in some cases, as much as 10,000 pounds. Once the 10,000 pounds of laminations were out of the top of the core, the operators would tear down the scaffolding and, with the help of a crane, lower three big transformer coils over the legs of the transformer core. Then they had to build the scaffolding once again to enable them to reinsert the 10,000 pounds of steel laminations, and then move the scaffolding one more time to allow the operators to make the electrical wiring connections.

My Workstations, 1968

It took a long time for the operators to get ready to do the actual task of building a transformer. I realized that if I could do away with the masonry scaffolding and replace it with a sturdy workstation, the operator would have a comfortable working position for being moved up and down hydraulically; thus I could reduce the labor time tremendously, save money, and become more competitive in the market. I sketched my differential cylinder design. It would be mounted on rails in the factory floor, allowing it to run electrically back and forth and up and down by means of the hydraulic cylinder system.

My boss's boss, a mechanical engineer educated at Duke, thought that the idea could possibly be successful. He decided that I should make a presentation to a group of managers who were responsible for the work done on the factory floor. Well, my idea got shot down almost before I started to explain how it would work. It was the typical attitude of, "We have done it for years this way. Who are you, brand new in our business, to tell us how to do it differently?" I was terribly disappointed, and did not know for a moment how to get my idea sold to the people who could either approve it or outright scrap it. I decided to go around to all the individuals who had nixed my idea at the first meeting. This time I sat down with them, one on one, and, lo and behold, they listened, and each gave me his idea of "the one little thing" that would make it work. Suggestions included a bracket here, a backstop one inch higher there, a counterweight at that spot, and so on. The basic idea and design had not changed one iota, but I had everybody's ideas incorporated, and that sold it at the next meeting.

I found a vendor who was going to build my design of the workstation, and I was given the authority to have two platforms of one set built to see if my idea would work. Several months later, I received a call and was told that the first workstation was ready for my inspection. I went to Birmingham, Alabama, and saw my creation for the first time. Even though I knew every gusset and bracket on the workstation, the first view I had of it was overwhelming. The unit was 20 feet wide, 20 feet tall, and ten feet deep. I tried it out, and we ran into a few glitches, but those were resolved before I authorized the vendor to ship the unit.

✳ ✳ ✳ ✳

Even though I had worked at four different GE locations, all of which had labor unions, the Rome plant was a "different animal" all together. They had a very strong union, and it did not take a whole lot to get a grievance filed against you if you did something that an exempt salaried employee was not allowed to do. Picking up a piece of trash would take work away from the janitor, etc. I knew it and dealt with it accordingly. All the hourly employees who were organized were members of the IUE, International Union of Electrical Workers.

When the plant expansion had started, the contractors who were building the new addition to the existing facilities were required to be union members even though they did not belong to the IUE. The erectors were represented by the iron workers union, the fitters by their union, the electrical workers by theirs, and so on. The union members have you believe that they are a "brotherhood" among themselves, but that is seldom the situation. When my platforms were shipped to the Rome plant, I was introduced to the way a union worked.

A fifty-foot-long tractor-trailer carried both of my platforms in a knocked-down state. I told the driver to drive right into the plant, since my equipment was the first to arrive in the empty building, a big manufacturing space. The truck arrived at 8:15 a.m., and I was about to call for a forklift truck to help me unload the platforms.

As soon as the foreman of the pipe fitters (who was not a General Electric employee, but a contractor working in the building addition) saw the load, he noticed the hydraulic tubing and cylinders and said, "My men have to unload this."

The foreman of the millwrights, again not a GE employee, had a different opinion because there was a lot of steel on the truck that had to be reassembled, so he demanded to be the one in charge of the unloading.

"Not so fast," said the foreman of the electrical union. "I see many electrical cables, switches, and breakers, so this is obviously my people's kind of work."

It is hard to imagine, but this discussion went on until 3 o'clock in the afternoon among these non-GE workers. The truck driver, most likely a Teamster member himself, said that he wanted to go back to Birmingham, and he was contemplating leaving the trailer in our plant.

Well, the disputing parties decided to go to the cafeteria to have a cup of coffee and continue their discussion as to

180

how to unload the trailer and not violate each other's rules or have a slugfest on the factory floor. Since each platform was neatly stacked on the truck bed, the entire load could be picked up with two forklift trucks, one on each side of the trailer. As soon as the contractors left for the cafeteria, I asked two of our forklift truck operators to lift the load just a half inch from the trailer's bed and leave the load at that height in the plant. "Leave your forklift trucks unattended and wait for me to give you further instructions," was my order to the forklift truck operators. When the three foremen came back from their coffee break, they wanted to have "a little talk" with me. I told them, with a straight face, that all I had done was let the truck driver go home. The entire load was still five feet above the factory floor supported by two forklift trucks. They finally saw the ridiculous sense of the argument, and told me that I had gotten away with something but I had better not try it again! The forklift trucks lowered the platforms to the floor, and everyone went back to work after almost a day of haggling.

After a week or so, I had the workstation assembled and operating on the floor. The plant manager, Mr. Law, came by as I was finishing the last little details, and he said to me, "Bob, can you imagine how it is going to look when you have five of these sets assembled and installed on the floor lined up like soldiers standing to attention?" Guess what — I had no problem getting money for seven more sets afterwards, making a total of eight. The best thing, totally unexpected, was still to happen.

Once the first five sets were installed and working, everybody realized what a tremendous time savings the installations would yield, so the Manager of Manufacturing, who was three reporting levels above me, decided to reap the savings as soon as possible. In those days, in the union environment, task time was calculated with a stopwatch and a very lengthy assessment as to how long that certain task would take. Once the time was agreed upon by both management and the union, that time could only be changed if there was a change in the process. This process had to be followed for each model of transformer, hence that would take a lot of time before all the agreed-upon times would be established. The time study for the workstations was going to take weeks, and the Manager of Manufacturing agreed with my estimate of a time reduction of at least 60%. Thus, to shorten the process, the Manager of Manufacturing decided that, starting the following Monday, the hourly operators would have the advantage of having the new workstations on which to work, but all allotted time standards were going to be cut by 40% until the official time study had been completed, and the new time standard would be the one that was going to be used from then on.

Of course, the union was not going to go along with that idea, and declared a one-day strike each week as long as that edict was in force. General Electric, not to be outdone, penalized the workers for participating in an "illegal" strike, with an additional penalty day each week as long as the strike lasted. Thus, hourly people worked three days a week, and the salaried employees who were qualified worked in the factory the other days.

In addition to designing the workstations, I had the responsibility for a number of other processes on the factory floor. During the strike, problems arose almost like clockwork; the automatic operations usually went haywire about two to three hours after the last shift left, right before the two-day strike began. For example, the operators would place very small pieces of paper between certain contacts and, as an engineer, you would spend hours trying to find out what had been messed with. My solution was simple: about three hours prior to the start of that week's strike, before the operator of a critical operation left, I started to talk with him and stuck with him no matter what he did. Once I did that, I had no more problems while the strike was in full swing for that particular week. This routine went on for more than eight or nine weeks.

The "Strike-Breaker" that saved a life

Neither the union nor GE was going to give in. On one Tuesday morning, an operator, getting ready to take out the transformer yoke laminations, forgot to take a bolt out of a beam that held together the laminations of the core and, basically, the entire transformer. The 100-ton crane lifted the beam from the assembly but, since one bolt had been overlooked, the crane pulled the entire yoke, with a weight of 10,000 pounds of laminations, over on the platform. The operator standing on the platform, about eight feet from the factory floor, was bumped out of the way by the falling steel, but because the platform was five feet wide, he was pushed to the back of the platform with 10,000 pounds of steel at his feet. If the old way of assembling power transformers had still been the practice, the employee would have been killed. I got a call to come and look what happened. My platform bowed about six inches, and the operator, white as a sheet, came to me and said, "If it had not been for this damned workstation, I would have been killed."

My boss's boss came over and, with a grin on his face, said, "Bob, I told you that you over-designed this thing." It certainly made me very happy that the workstation had withstood that kind of unexpected test. The most remarkable thing was that the incident caused the strike to end.

✳ ✳ ✳ ✳

Being back in the South gave us an opportunity to be better informed as to what was going on at Virginia Tech. Of course, I was interested in football and basketball at VPI, so Trudy and I went back to Blacksburg a few times and enjoyed a few games. There was a VPI alumni club in Atlanta that we attended whenever possible. One time we saw Casey Jones, my classmate and German Club friend, and his wife Maggi. Casey was studying at the veterinary school in nearby Athens, Georgia.

One of my colleagues at the Rome, Georgia, plant had a PE certificate hanging in his office. A graduate engineer from an accredited university can take a two-part national engineering exam and, if he passes successfully, he is entitled to be called a Professional Engineer. The PE behind one's name entitles one to design and certify work that is used by the general public. The PE can also testify as an expert witness in court cases. I remember that, during our senior year at VPI, we were eligible to take the first part of the national exam, the EIT (Engineer in Training) exam. However, I had enough trouble trying to graduate, so I did not sign up for the exam at that time. I figured that if I could be so lucky as to get an engineering degree, I'd be more than happy. Seeing the PE certificate on the office wall, I could not resist expressing my admiration for anyone who was a Professional Engineer and said so to my colleague.

"Oh, Bob, there is nothing to that. I went to Georgia Tech, and you, as a Virginia Tech graduate, should have no problem taking it."

Darn, there it was again! I dearly despised comments such as that. I could not let that one just roll off my back, so I went to my desk and called Georgia Tech, seventy miles down the road in Atlanta, Georgia, and inquired if they taught any refresher courses. Of course, Georgia Tech did and, next thing I knew, I was going to Atlanta twice a week at night to take ten basic engineering courses. I had no idea how much fun that would be. We went through Chemistry, Physics, Math, Strength of Materials, Thermodynamics, and other courses in record time. What amazed me so much was the fact that some courses, which I had not studied in more than five years, came back to me quickly. I had no idea that I had not only learned it at VPI, but had also retained it as well, so it was a real confidence builder.

Several months later, I took an eight-hour E.I.T. exam in one of the state conference rooms in downtown Atlanta, with about 200 other aspiring Professional Engineers and Land Surveyors. The room was divided in two, and the exam was open book. I walked in with two suitcases full of all the books I could possibly need. The Land Surveyor candidates, who were sitting in one part of the room, brought their electric calculators that made a racket that was almost deafening. I was in that torture chamber for eight hours and, when Trudy's Dad picked me up, I knew I had just wasted a nice day, and there was no way in the world that I could have passed that exam. Well, I had tried, and that was one thing I did not have to worry about any longer.

Months went by, and I did not hear the results. Finally, I decided that I was going to call the Georgia Office of Professional Engineers and Land Surveyors. A nice-sounding lady answered the phone and told me that it would take a long

185

time to grade the exam because it was a national exam that had to be sent to New York. She said that she would check and see if anything had come and, as I was being put on hold, I was thinking that I should know one way or the other pretty soon.

A little later, she was back on the phone and said, "Mr. van Luyn, you have passed the exam."

I could not believe my ears! I said, "Probably by the skin of my teeth."

She told me that my score was 78, which she considered very good, and added that it looked like about 60% of the Georgia Tech seniors had failed the exam.

"As a matter of fact, you did very well," she concluded.

Six months later, I passed the PE exam (another eight-hour test), which I did not think was as hard as the EIT. I framed my certificate, and my colleague said, after seeing it on my office wall, "I told you that you could do it! Congratulations."

* * * *

Mamma and Pappa had been saying that they would like to come to visit us; even though we had some well-reasoned reservations, we told them that we would love to have them come. The reason for our apprehension was the fact that Pappa had broken his back while visiting Thea, who lived in a very small old town called Broek in Waterland, north of Amsterdam. The house that Thea and Gerard were renting then was very old, well over 200 years. When Thea was away at work in Amsterdam, Mamma had decided to do the ironing for her. After Mamma had finished, she told Pappa to put the ironing board on the second floor. The staircase was very steep in the old house, and Pappa, suffering from Parkinson's disease, lost his balance, fell backwards, and broke his back. Pappa spent four weeks in bed, enduring agonizing pain without the doctor having taken an x-ray. Finally, the diagnosis established that Pappa had broken his back, and he was fitted for a steel brace that he had to wear for the rest of his life. Obviously, Trudy and I were concerned as to how well Pappa would travel all the way from Holland to the U.S., but when I saw him smiling as he disembarked from the airplane in Atlanta, all my worries were gone, and we were happy to have them with us. In about seven weeks, we would celebrate Christmas together in Rome, Georgia. Little did we know, it was not Pappa whom we should have been worried about.

Two weeks after my parents arrived, Mamma became ill and Trudy took her to our family physician, Doctor Harold Robinson. Since Pappa had his medical problems, we had decided that, if anything were to happen, we would put Pappa and Mamma on the plane back to Holland. In Holland, socialized medicine would take care of any medical expenses, with no charge to the patient. Trudy called me at work and told me that she and Mamma were on their way to the hospital and that I should come right away and meet them there.

As I entered the room where Mamma was, I met Dr. Boyce Brice, a general surgeon, who told me that he had found an obstruction in her abdomen and had to operate. Mamma could not speak English, and did not understand what was happening, so I could freely discuss our situation without Mamma being embarrassed or frightened.

"Doctor, we will put her on a plane back to Holland."

"There is no time for that; I need her permission to operate tonight, or she will not make it to tomorrow." This was something we had not expected.

I turned to Mamma and said, "Mamma, the doctor has to take out your appendix."

"Thanks be to God. I thought I had cancer!" was her response.

"Sir, you had better tell her." Dr Brice urged me on.

"I just did, doctor, I told her that you were going to take her appendix out."

"Well, that's as good as anything, I think. While I am at it, I will do that, too."

Mamma was operated on during the middle of the night, and the operation lasted one hour and forty-five minutes. I was allowed in the recovery room because they could not figure out what she was saying. All she wanted to know was what time it was, and she insisted that I would do better to go home and get some sleep.

"You're going to the football game tomorrow." She was referring to the game that Trudy's dad and I were going to see. Georgia Tech was playing Notre Dame, and we had been looking forward to that Saturday.

"Mamma, the game is not until Saturday."

"Did you say that it was 2:30 a.m.?"

"Yes, ma'am, I did."

"Well, then, it is Friday morning right now and tomorrow it's Saturday." Boy, there sure wasn't anything mentally wrong with Mamma! Obviously, the game was no longer important.

When Dr. Brice finished the surgery, he told me what had happened to Mamma. Mamma had diverticulitis, which had caused her colon to rupture, causing peritonitis. In addition, she developed a kidney infection, pneumonia, and congestive heart failure while she was in the hospital.

She was seriously ill, and it was only then that we found out that Mamma had had some problems before she left for the States and had gone to the doctor. She had been admitted to the hospital and had undergone a D&C, after which the surgeon told her, "Send me a card from America!"

Mamma's recovery was very "stormy," as Dr. Brice put it; she was in the hospital for four weeks with massive infections, and had to undergo a second case of surgery to alleviate some adhesions and an abscess. After four weeks, we had her back in our house, rather weak, but definitely on the mend.

When I took a look at the insurance certificate that my parents had taken out before they left Holland, I read that it said (in the small print) that this policy was invalid if the insured was 70 years of age or older. Mamma had just celebrated her seventieth birthday in September, so that was a real setback. Trudy had been working in the Rome City School System and had done very well teaching music. We had been saving so that we could build our dream house, and had a tidy sum accumulated. We had started out with my college debt when we got married, and now, four years later, we were debt free and had about $3,500.00 in the bank, so we were doing OK. After the hospital and the doctor's bills were paid, we were out of money, but were convinced that we had just saved two lives. Pappa was so dependent on Mamma that we were certain that he would not have lasted long if Mamma had passed away.

One night in the hospital, Doctor Robinson, our general physician, who visited Mamma every night, and who never charged us one single penny for his care and counsel, asked me, "Bob, what is it with this lady? She is supposed to be dead and still she keeps on fighting and is winning the battle!"

I said, "Doctor, you are the physician, but I believe that, beside the excellent care here, it is the medicine you are giving her that her system has never experienced. She is responding outstandingly because her system is not 'immune' to its power."

"That must be it," Doctor Robinson responded. In Holland, antibiotics were not given as readily as in America, especially not for minor ailments like sore throats, earaches, etc.

The management of the General Electric Company really showed what they were made of. Ben Rouse, my boss, asked me repeatedly how we were doing financially. Rome is a small town, and people will talk. They had heard that Mamma had no insurance. I told him that we were doing OK. After Ben's third inquiry, I started to get worried and asked Trudy what she thought about my asking for a loan, just to let them know that things were getting tight. I figured if we just kept going and telling people we had saved enough to weather the storm, they might not think that I needed a raise the next time around! So I told Ben that I would try to ask for a loan from the company, and he said that he would start the proper paperwork for it.

About a week later, Ben asked me to go with him to personnel and sign the papers for the money. We went to the office, and I was about to sign the paper when I read the word "Grant" in the text. I looked at Ben, and he had a big grin on his face and said, "Go ahead, sign it!" I could not believe my eyes! Trudy and I received $600 as a gift! I went to the plant manager and thanked him. He told me that management was proud of Trudy and me for taking care of, and not complaining about, a situation over which we had no control.

One more good side effect came out of this very bad experience. Since Pappa had a broken back and could not stay at the hospital for any length of time, it fell upon Trudy and me to keep Mamma company. Since I could only be at the hospital for so many hours each day, Trudy, the trouper that she is, taught music for half the day, and would then come to the hospital and relieve me, staying with Mamma — many times through the night. Because of her prolonged stays with Mamma, Trudy quickly learned some Dutch so that she could translate for the doctors and nurses when instructions were given.

We were fortunate that Mama and Papa Florrid were not so far away. Their support, as well as that of our other relatives, colleagues and neighbors, kept us going, both while Mamma was in the hospital and as she recuperated at home. At the end of January, Mamma was well enough to travel back to Holland. A strange thing happened as they boarded the plane. In those days one walked on the tarmac at the airport and boarded via the staircase that was part of the plane. That day, as soon as the passengers were on board, a coffin was loaded into the cargo hold via a conveyor belt. I could not help but think how close we had been to sending

Mamma back to Holland in that manner. We were relieved and so grateful for all the help we had received from so many kind people, because things could have been so much different.

✳ ✳ ✳ ✳

Later that spring, I came home and Trudy was in a kind of slump.

"What's the matter, Trudy?" I asked

"Well, I've received this letter from Emory University in which they tell me that, starting next year, I will begin to lose my credits towards my master's degree."

"Well, let's discuss what we are going to do about it," I replied.

Trudy responded with a fair amount of aggravation in her voice, "There you go again. That's not as easy as you may think."

She first thought of going to West Georgia College in Carrolton, closer to Rome, but would have had to start over. We discussed it, and I suggested that she go to Atlanta, have a conference with her course advisor, and be prepared to go back to school during the summer.

"You want me out of the house."

"No, of course not. I suggest that you go, take an overload of courses during a summer session, and stay in the graduate dorm without a car." My thinking was that, if she had transportation available, the temptation to go around Atlanta, her hometown, would be there. I did not want her to stay at her parents' home (which would have been cheaper) because I knew Trudy: she would be helping her parents often, which would take away time from her studying. "Plan not to have any Saturday classes, so I will pick you up late Friday afternoon and take you back Sunday evening."

After discussing her situation with her course advisor, Trudy arranged her schedule as we'd hoped. She got all A's, and made such an impression on her professors that she was

191

allowed to take other courses as independent study and submit her work weekly without having to attend classes during the fall and winter quarters. During the spring quarter, she had to attend one weekly seminar, and she worked on her thesis. Trudy had just been promoted to music coordinator in the Rome City Schools, and had seven music teachers reporting to her. Among the seven were three band directors. Her thesis was on the music background of public school classroom teachers and their ability to follow through on lessons given by the music specialists. She constructed a well-thought-out survey and distributed it throughout the Rome City Schools. Since she was the coordinator, she had 100% response in return questionnaires. Then the effort began.

She had projected to herself what a certain outcome would be, but she could not, of course, "lead to" it in her survey questions, even though she thought it to be true. My engineering training came in handy when helping Trudy sift through and interpret the results of the survey. That June, 1969, Trudy proudly graduated from Emory University with a Master's Degree in Education. I wanted her to go on and get her Ph.D., but Trudy decided that she had had enough of the academic world, and decided to call it quits. I knew she could do it, but she drew the line, and this was one time I could not persuade her differently.

20

The Family Grows

By now, Trudy and I had been married for almost five years, and we were starting to realize that pregnancy did not seem to be in the cards for us. We explored the thought of adoption and, after some serious discussions, we decided that we would go to Social Services and fill out an application for adoption.

We went through a number of interviews, and had to give a tremendous amount of background information so that the agency could properly match us to a child that had a similar heritage. It included details like family physical characteristics, our general health, hobbies and aptitudes, and even the likes and dislikes of each of our own grandparents! The wait seemed to be going on forever and, of course, it was complicated by the fact that Trudy and I had agreed to ask for a baby girl, an infant if possible.

One Sunday, we were in Atlanta visiting Trudy's parents when Trudy's first cousin and her husband came by with their recently adopted baby girl. The child had just changed from a formula diet to whole milk, and it so happened that she got sick and spit up on the living room sofa. The amount of mucus could not have filled a soup spoon; however, the feeling it caused in my system almost had me join in the effort, but with a much larger volume. I thought perhaps I should rethink this idea of adopting a child if that's what they are doing and it causes that kind of reaction in me. Pretty soon, I had forgotten about the incident and proceeded to call the office of Social Services regularly to find out what our status was relative to becoming adoptive parents.

* * * *

At the plant, there was a club of which exempt salaried employees could be members. It was called the Management Club, or something like it. I was elected president and, as soon I took office, the consensus was that the club was not what it used to be and that perhaps we ought to dissolve it. I did not mind dissolving it, but it was not going to happen while I was president. We had monthly meetings, and would look for members who would organize and decide the topic of the next month's meeting.

My first monthly meeting was the usual dinner meeting, and I had invited the Chief of Police of Rome to be our after-dinner speaker. I thought that the fact that he was going to talk about pornography in Rome would attract a good crowd. On the day of the meeting, I counted fifteen commitments of members to attend. I was about to die! I had the Chief of Police coming and only fifteen people showing up! It was going to be a disaster. As a courtesy, I went to the plant manager, Russ Morris, and asked him if he was going to attend. He said, "No, Bob, I can't because our divisional Vice-President is coming to town." I asked him if he would bring the VP to the meeting. He said that he would check and let me know later that day. Well, I did not expect too much but, to my surprise, Russ called me half an hour later and said the VP would attend. I made a mad dash through all the offices and the factory, asking if people would attend, and when they said no, I told them that the VP would certainly miss them. By the time I went home, I was riding high as a kite because my attendees list had swelled to 86!

I told Trudy what had happened and remarked that I'd say something upon opening the meeting like, "Welcome faithful members and bootlickers." Trudy advised me not to do anything like that! I went to the meeting feeling pretty good. As I opened the meeting, I quickly scanned the gathering and noticed that Russ Morris, the plant manager, was sitting to the right of me in the meeting hall and the VP was in the hall to my left. I decided not to look at them as I addressed the group so that I would not be accused of playing to the big wheels.

"The first order of business is to find a volunteer who wants to chair our next month's meeting," I stated. "Since the next meeting is our annual Atlanta Braves meeting and, since the Braves are presently 6-and-0, it should not be hard to find a chairman for the trip."

"Seven-and-one!" shouted Joe Helie, the manager of personnel.

"Isn't that nice, Joe Helie just volunteered," I responded, with the result that the whole gathering laughed that I had just stuck it to the manager of personnel, and he was not about to debate it with me in the presence of a company Vice-President. I felt that I had my audience with me, and things were looking up. I introduced the Chief of Police and, as I sat down, I realized that I had not welcomed the VP. I had tried so hard not to look his way that I had completely forgotten to introduce him. The vice-president of the club, Buddy Carver, slipped me a note of which I anticipated the contents.

"Do you want me to introduce the VP?"

I wrote back, "No, thanks, I'll do it." The entire presentation escaped me completely because I was feverishly trying to figure out how to recoup my blunder.

When the Chief sat down, I got up and thanked him, and said, "I can imagine that you may ask yourself what the exempt salaried people do at GE. Well, we get paid to make many assumptions every day. If we make 100 correct assumptions, we do our job well; however, if we make one wrong assumption, we immediately get rapped on our knuckles. For example, tonight our club's vice president told me that I had not introduced our company Vice-President. Well, my assumption was that *'Good wine does not need any praise!'* Even though that is correct, I should have welcomed our Divisional Vice President."

Afterwards Russ came to me with a big grin on his face and said, "Good wine, heh?" Ouch, I got out of that embarrassing moment halfway decently.

※　※　※　※

Work went on and, on one occasion, I was working with James Kinney, an engineer in the development lab, and saw his inventor's medal. "Bob, the kind of work you do could yield you an invention," he said. I told him that my workstations could be patented; however, General Electric would have no way to enforce the patent since they would not have access to a competitor's factory after we had shown them all the details of our design. "We need a new type of leak detector," he said. "Why don't you come up with something new and better."

"That's easily said. But how?" I thought.

I went to the stockroom and took out a pressure gauge, the kind that is installed on top of each of the transformers. I placed the pressure gauge in the middle of my desk, and every time I sat down, I had that gauge staring me in the face.

A power transformer is installed outside in a field away from where people would be working. When the transformer is in normal operation, it cycles every 24 hours. During the day the demand for electric power is high, which heats up the transformer and the cooling oil in it. There is a gaseous space, in this case filled with nitrogen, above the oil level to act as a reservoir for expansion. The transformer is sealed off from the outside atmosphere so that, during the day, the pressure has a positive value. Since the demand for electric power at night is low, the transformer cools down, and the pressure of the nitrogen goes to zero and then to a negative value. The next day the cycle repeats itself and so on.

If there is a very small leak in the space above oil level, the pressure will push out the dry nitrogen during the day and, during the night, the negative pressure will suck in the moist outside air. If this were only to happen a dozen times, it probably would not have any adverse effect on the performance of the transformer but, if this were to go on month after month, a sufficient amount of moist air would result in a great deal of condensation, thereby allowing water to be sucked into the unit, eventually causing the dielectric strength of the transformer oil to degrade and the transformer to fail. At regular intervals, a service operator would check the transformer and, if the gauge indicated a neutral pressure, the operator would assume that the transformer was cycling and had just gone from negative to positive pressure (or from positive to negative pressure). There was a yellow plastic lever, that the guys called the "banana peel," that was supposed to warn the operator that something was wrong, but everyone thought that it was not that reliable. I needed to come up with something that did not, in itself, cause a leak, but would tell the operator checking the transformer that the neutral pressure had been present for more than 24 hours.

Every time I returned to my desk, there was that pressure gauge looking at me. One morning, while getting ready for work, I went to the bathroom to brush my teeth after breakfast. Trudy had beaten me to the electric toothbrush. The thing was a few years old, and the rechargeable battery was at the end of its useful life. It "petered out," and I resorted to the old-fashioned regular toothbrush. A light went on in my mind; I had found a way to design my leak detector around a characteristic that is inherent in a rechargeable battery. That is, it works fine if one keeps recharging the

197

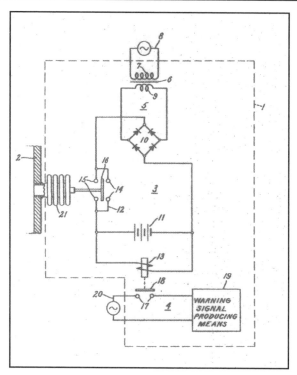

A diagram of Patent #3,731,295 (May 1, 1973)

unit; however, it will take the battery a predetermined time to discharge completely. I could take that simple phenomenon and use it to my advantage. I drew up a simple full-wave rectifier circuit that would change the alternating current to direct current, making it possible to charge the battery. A special switch would charge the battery only when the pressure was positive or negative and, at the same time, keep the warning signal closed. As the transformer cycled through zero pressure, the switch would be kept in closed position, but now would be powered by the battery, which would be discharged, if only for a short period of time.

Sizing the rechargeable battery in such a way that it would be totally drained in 24 hours was the key to the sensing of a deviation from normal operation. If the pressure stayed neutral (signifying ambient pressure) for more than 24 hours, a leak had to be present in the transformer, and my invention would then cause an alarm to be sent to a control office, warning the operator to make a thorough check.

The patent attorney liked the idea and began filing the patent. I did receive a patent and was given $125.00 as an award recognizing my accomplishment. My thought was that to be awarded with a patent that was registered at the U.S. Patent office was sufficient, and the $125.00 for the effort was secondary. Unfortunately, I was transferred before the invention was implemented, so I really don't know if U.S. Patent Number 3,731,295 was ever used on power transformers.

❋   ❋   ❋   ❋

We had worked for four years in Rome, Georgia, and we liked the area, the work, and the people we had met. I was in the Lions Club (serving then as vice-president), Trudy was in the Rome Junior Service League, and we both sang in the First Presbyterian Church choir. In short, we had a good life with the two of us and, for a young couple, we were on our way to becoming "a successful American family."

While waiting to hear about the adoption from Social Services, we began looking for a house that we could afford to buy. One Sunday morning, I was scanning the real estate section and found a house for sale on our street. Excitedly, I called Trudy, who was doing something else somewhere in the house. "I wonder which one it is," Trudy said. We decided to call first thing the next morning to find out its location on our street. To our surprise, our own house, which we had been renting for the past four years, was the one for sale. We needed four thousand dollars to take over the old loan, and we borrowed that amount from Trudy's parents. This was following a tradition of their family, since Mama Florrid's parents had done the same for them.

Then, we began fixing up the place to our liking. I converted one room into a small library and music room, and bought carpet from one of the mills in Rome, which they offered for sale by the pound. Rome is smack in the middle of the carpet industry in the U.S., so there was a place that sold mill ends. Once one knew which type of carpet one wanted, it was just a matter of time to get enough remnants of the same number and size to redo an entire house at a very low price. Next, we had the bathroom retiled, painted the house, and fixed up the outside. The biggest thing that I undertook was the central air conditioning of the small, very cozy, house.

On May 4, 1970, I was contemplating whether I should hook up the central air conditioning unit that I had installed. Everything was ready to go; all I had to do was hook up the pre-charged copper line that ran from the inside charged heat exchanger to the pre-charged compressor outside. I had never done it, so I wanted to talk with an air conditioning mechanic at work one more time before I proceeded.

The phone rang. It was the social worker calling. "Mr. van Luyn, this is Dolores with Social Services — we have a baby girl for you."

I was so nervous that I asked her to hold on one moment so that she could talk to Trudy. I went outside and was pacing in the front yard nervously. My neighbor came out and said to me, "Bob, did you hear? The National Guard just killed three students at Kent State."

I was so nervous that what happened elsewhere in the country did not interest me in the slightest, and the only response I could muster was, "I don't give a damn." I went in the house and asked Trudy what we were supposed to do. We were not supposed to tell anyone what we were going to do so that the anonymity of the birth mother would be respected. We were told to go to a motel in Dalton, Georgia, and meet the social workers there who would have our baby girl. "Our own girl should not move into a house without central air conditioning," was my immediate thought, and minutes later, I found myself crawling under the house hooking up the air conditioning components without the benefit of a last minute bit of reassurance or advice from the pro at work.

The next day, the fifth of May, I took a personal day off without telling my boss what the reason was. Our baby girl was three days old. We went to the motel and were told by the receptionist to what room we should report. As I stood in front of the door, I turned around and asked Trudy, "Do you want to go through with this?" Trudy said "Yes," so I knocked on the door. A lady opened the door, and there was Nancy Ann van Luyn!

We looked at her, and as we marveled at that lovely little girl, she lifted her head as if she were saying, "Hi, how are you?" I was the first one to pick her up, and she was truly a beautiful baby. We were told that there was a trial period of one year, and that if upon inspection Social Services deemed it necessary, they would take Nancy Ann from us. To our surprise we were told that it worked both ways, meaning that if we decided that it would not work out for us we would be able to give Nancy Ann back to Social Services.

All that remained was to pay for the motel room, and we were on our way in our two-door 1966 Chevy. I drove extra carefully and took every corner with great care because we were transporting precious cargo that day. As we got home, Trudy had the formula ready for Nancy, and I was allowed to feed her. She drank her entire bottle and I burped her. I held her in my arms and, all of a sudden, she spat up all over me — from my neck down to my shirt and on my pants and shoes. I said, "Trudy, she is sick!" Trudy laughed and said that I had not burped her correctly. I gave Nancy to Trudy and made a beeline for the bathroom. I took off all my clothes and stepped in the shower and, as I was showering, I realized something all of a sudden and hollered at Trudy.

"Trudy! Trudy, I did not care!"

Trudy came running. "What's the matter?"

"I did not care that she spat on me." Then I realized that I had never told her about my feelings a year earlier, when her cousin's baby upchucked a little on the Florrids' sofa in Atlanta.

It is absolutely impossible to explain how the transformation happens, but it happened. Nancy became our child instantly, and there was nothing in this world that could change that. It was funny — the first couple of weeks when she made even the slightest sound in the middle of the night, both of us would wake up instantly and swing our legs out of the bed in unison to find out what the matter was. After a couple of weeks, we decided to take turns.

＊　＊　＊　＊

We were in Rome for five years and I had gotten active in Lions International, progressing from "Tail Twister" to vice president and, subsequently, to club president, after which I became a Zone Chairman and Deputy District Governor. As a Zone Chairman, I organized a Zone meeting that five area clubs attended. For the keynote speaker, I chose a former Georgia District Governor who, a year earlier, had run an unsuccessful race for the Georgia gubernatorial seat. I believe he had come in seventh out of a group of eight, but seemed to be a nice man and could have a promising career in state government.

I wrote that past District Governor of Lions International, and asked if he would like to be my keynote speaker. I got a letter back with the agreement that he would be very glad to come to my meeting. It was signed Jimmy Carter. The meeting went fine, and I told him that I had heard that he grew peanuts and that I had never seen a peanut plant. "Come to Plains and I will show you all the peanuts you want to see," he offered.

Time went on, and we got busy with other things. Trudy was singing in various churches and was active in the Rome Junior Service League. Then, an incident happened in the plant that gave my career a new direction. Bill Harrison, the Georgia Tech engineer who, unbeknownst to him, had "challenged" me to get my PE license, had designed a very nice system for the factory's transformer core area. There was one piece of equipment that transferred spools of core steel from one station to the next. It was well thought-out; however, it had one flaw — it was powered by a three-phase electric motor. A three-phase motor will be at its maximum rotational speed practically instantly. The rolls of steel were very heavy and, as soon as the switch was turned to the "on" position, the drive motor was at top speed, with the result that the roll of steel would just about fall off the transfer equipment.

The union realized that if the system was implemented, the normal time to do the task would be reduced significantly, and that would mean the workers would have to do more work in less time. With the inability to start the device gradually, the union could legitimately nix the transfer equipment and slow down the process. I did not like the fact that Bill was about to scrap the piece of equipment, and I said that I could probably find a way to rig the equipment and make it work. I had worked enough with motors at de Hoop NV to know that one method was to drop the starting voltage of all three phases, which would reduce the starting jolt — not a very good way to fix the problem, but it would soften the startup jolt if done properly. I sized the resistors needed and took three, switching them in a stepping mode that showed that, although it was not perfect, it could be operated safely.

The union did not want to hear of it. I discussed it with them, and everyone agreed that, if I would work as an hourly employee for one week operating the unit, then everyone could decide once and for all if the system was workable. I started on the first shift, and all went well. After a while, the guys ignored me, and I became one of the group.

The manager of Manufacturing Engineering came on Wednesday and observed what I was doing. He told me,

"Bob, as you are working here on the floor, I want you to observe what is going on and write it up each evening when your day's work is done. When you finish, I want you to send me a report on what is going on on the floor, any nonsense or anything out of the ordinary." Since he was two reporting levels above me, I did what I was told. On Friday, it was very hot. The guys were throwing water at each other and threw water on the core steel. The steel, when wet, would rust and had to be cleaned so I put that in my notes. Big mistake!

The following Tuesday, I started to work as an engineer again. As I opened a door that would let me on the factory floor, I heard one whistle, and the entire shop stopped working. I thought it was strange, but had a feeling that it was caused by my presence. I left the floor immediately and entered from a different area. The same thing happened. Now there was no doubt what was happening. I knew that something had happened that caused me to be singled out. I went to the manager's office and told him what was happening. I had to demonstrate it for him, so he preceded me by a minute or so and, when I entered, sure enough, work stopped again. He told me to stay in my office and not to enter the factory floor again. Now the guys in the office were getting annoyed. They felt that management should not give in to the union, which was telling management that Bob van Luyn was no longer tolerated on the factory floor. My colleagues felt that management should let them know, in no uncertain terms, that their actions were totally unacceptable.

I found out later that the manager had told shop management what went on that hot Friday, and the manager of shop operations had called in the respective foreman and told him to be aware as to what was happening in his area. And that is how the hourly workers found out *what I had done!* I did not realize it at the time, because it all settled down, but I had become a liability and somehow had to be taken out of the picture. However, the transfer system for rolls of core steel, which I had modified, proved to be working, so that part of my effort was successful.

✻ ✻ ✻ ✻

One morning, I went in early to meet some contractors who were working in the plant. I entered the plant area from the side, and there, in the darkness of the early morning, was no one else but Jimmy Carter. Jimmy was again running for governor. Since Jimmy had helped me as a speaker for my Lions Zone meeting, I felt that I owed him something.

"Jimmy, I'm Bob van Luyn. If you need any help let me know; I still appreciate your helping with my Lions Club meeting."

I gave him my card and went to work. A couple of days later Jimmy called me.

"Bob, can you pick me up at the airport? I have a campaign speech to make at the Holiday Inn."

Before I knew it, I was the designated driver for fellow Lion Jimmy Carter. Trudy's parents were excited because their son-in-law had finally seen the light and was supporting a Democrat. It was "Bob" and "Jimmy" back and forth, and I must say that I liked being in his company and chatting about this and that. One evening, after I had picked him up again at the local airport, Jimmy said that we were to go to a pipe fitters union meeting. The union did not have any members in the General Electric plant, but I just about died. Can you imagine me sitting at the head table with the president of the local pipe fitters union? In my mind's eye, I could see a picture with Jimmy, the union president, and me on the front page of the *Rome News Tribune*. Of course, nothing of that sort happened, but I had some very uncomfortable hours during that meeting. Jimmy was elected governor, and Trudy and I were invited to the Gubernatorial Inaugural Ball of 1971.

The incident with our plant union in the summer definitely had its repercussions and, on December 17, 1970, the manager of Manufacturing Engineering called me into his office to tell me that the eleven-million-dollar expansion was just about complete and that there was no longer any need for six Advance Manufacturing Engineers. He added that, by the following November, there would be a reduction in the organization and, if I wanted to, I could explore possibilities within the General Electric Company for a position with another department at a different location. Whether or not intended that way, I took from it that I would be considered surplus and had better find somewhere else to work within the company.

We had one hour for lunch in Rome. Trudy and Nancy and I lived close enough to the plant that I could go home for lunch and be back in plenty of time. That day, I told Trudy that we were moving, and I started to update my resumé. I had two resumés, one to be used within GE and one outside the company. I was not going to take any chances on being out of work, even if I knew that I would be safe for at least a year. I figured that, once the word got out, there would be more engineers from our group looking for a position with the company, so I had better get started. When I came back to my desk that same afternoon, I had both resumés ready for reproduction.

My boss walked into my office, saw what I was doing, and asked, "What's happening?"

I replied, "Your boss told me what's going to happen, and I thought I'd better do something about it."

"Not for at least a year!" was the amazed response.

I did not care what he thought; his boss had given me the go-ahead to look for a position within GE, and I was not about to waste a minute. I spent the rest of December calling GE plants for a position. I decided that Trudy and I were happy in the South, so I limited my search to companies no farther west than Alabama, and no farther north than Washington, D.C. There were a large number of GE manufacturing plants in that area and, once I had exhausted that entire area, I would expand my search to other parts of the country. Of course, everyone to whom I talked told me that they were not making any decisions until the following year.

Then, by the end of January 1971, I was getting requests to interview at the various places. It was rather strange; I had not realized how really "small" this big GE Company was. I got calls from Erie, Pennsylvania; Flint and Detroit, Michigan; and all sorts of places where I had not even applied. Somehow, the word had gotten out and people were talking to each other.

One call from Detroit was interesting. A manager of marketing called me, and the following dialogue ensued over the phone:

"Bob van Luyn, is that you?"

"Yes, sir, this is he."

"I would like for you to meet me in Detroit. I want to discuss a position with you here at the GE office."

"Sir, I did not apply for a position."

"That does not matter."

"Well, sir, to be honest, I heard yesterday on the news that Detroit had one murder a day."

"Oh, things are not that bad."

"No, sir, I don't think that I'll be interested."

"Have you ever flown in a 747?"

"No, sir, I have not."

"Why don't you take an early 747 out of Atlanta tomorrow morning, have lunch with me, and I will have you back in Rome, Georgia before the evening news?"

I just could not go somewhere on the company's expense account, knowing that it was just a visit and that I would not take the job if it were offered. Since I had no idea what that person had in mind for me, I thanked him and hung up. January went by, and work was interesting but my heart was not in it any longer because I realized that my days in Rome were numbered. I received an interview request from Erie, Pennsylvania. The engineers with me on the training program would refer to Erie as "Dreary Erie, the mistake on the lake!" I had never been there and was not particularly interested in the location, but there were a number of divisions there. There was GE Locomotives (where the large diesel locomotives were built, as well as DC Motors and Generators) and a new start-up program called "Rapid Transit."

My boss, knowing that I was looking for a job, kept tabs on me, and I realized that I could not outright refuse to go on interview trips just because I didn't like the location. He could put his foot down if I were not to try to land a job, so I thought it best to go to Erie and see what would happen. In February, I was there on my first visit and, sixty days later, when they had invited me again, they had built a brand-new large building, in which the new product was going to be built. So I traveled to Erie again and went to the DC Motor and Generator Department. The manager of Quality Control interviewed me and, after seven minutes, told me that he had his mind made up about me and was going to tell me what *he* was like. The fact that I was not terribly interested did not help the situation any; besides, I was not too impressed with his demeanor.

"Let me tell you about me," he began. "I worked my way through college."

"So did I."

"Yes, but I did it the hard way."

"Oh, you did not speak English, either?"

"No, I did it at night."

And it went on like that. He gave me a plant tour and said that I should meet the Manager of Manufacturing, but I did not have enough time because I was supposed to be at Rapid Transit before lunchtime. "Well, promise me that you will come back later this afternoon and let me introduce you to the Manager of Manufacturing." I told him that I would do so, and took a taxi to what turned out to be an old A&P grocery store that had been converted into a temporary office space. Inside, people were feverishly working to put a manufacturing plant together. They were placing orders as I was being interviewed, and I made the comment that there must have been a tremendous effort writing specs and assessing multiple bids, etc. They informed me that they were in such a hurry that they just did not have any time to do that kind of thing!

The afternoon went by, and I took a taxi back to DC Motors and Generators and saw the QC manager as I had promised. It was about 5:30 and he said that we were going to the Manager of Manufacturing. He opened the door of a very spacious old-looking office with a desk and a few chairs in it, and a big burly guy was behind the desk talking on the phone. The man had a flattop and looked like a drill sergeant; momentarily, my mind went back to Ossendrecht and the incident with the boot camp sergeant who did not like my putting my hands in my own civilian pockets. The QC manager literally pushed me forward in the office as if it were the lion's den, hollered at the man behind the desk on the phone, saying, "This is the guy I spoke with you about," and quickly closed the door behind him as he left the room.

I walked to the desk, and the man motioned for me to sit down. Framed newspaper clippings, reporting strike news about the department with photographs that looked like the man behind the desk, were hung on the wall. The conversation on the phone continued:

"John, I'll be damned if I will ever spend one more penny with that son of a bitch of a cheat."

"No, don't you doubt that one damned minute."

The manager of Manufacturing slammed the phone in the cradle, instantly picked it up again, and dialed another number. "Where is George?" he asked briskly; he gave his name, and then he turned to me and said, "I hate those goddamned secretaries who shield their bosses." He ranted and raved for a few more minutes, which gave me time to think that this was not the kind of environment where I wanted to make a living. He again slammed the phone in the cradle and turned to me, saying, "What the hell do you want?"

"I want to be a manager."

"Why?"

"Because I'm getting too goddamned old if I don't." I was all of thirty-seven years old at the time.

For the first time, I noticed a glimmer in his eyes, and from then on we had a somewhat normal conversation that was interspersed with a few salty remarks. I sensed that this was going to be a high pressure job that in itself would be interesting, but I had experienced my share of bulls-in-the-woods and I was not looking for one more just to add excitement to my life.

We parted, and I went back to the Erie airport, where a TV in the airport bar was showing the local news. The news was informing its listeners that the weather had just broken the all-time record of total snow accumulation for the year. As I was waiting for my flight, enjoying a beer, the public address system called out my name and asked me to come to the desk. All I could think of was that Trudy had called to tell me that there was something wrong with Nancy, who was a little more than nine months old. I asked the bartender, a nice lady, if I could leave my bag with her, and I ran to the desk to which I had been summoned. As I picked up the phone, the voice identified itself as the manager of personnel and stated something to the effect that the DC Motor and Generator Department, a gang of young tigers, thought that I was a perfect fit for the organization. He proceeded to inform me that the offer came with a more than 30 percent raise! I could not believe what I heard. The voice told me that he would follow up the offer with a telegram the next morning to my boss. I hung up the phone, excited and, at the same time, relieved that there was nothing wrong at home, and went back to the bar to finish my beer and pick up my bag. The bartender asked if there was something wrong, and I told her that I had just been offered a fantastic promotion, upon which she said, "Well, we will have to celebrate!" and tapped me another beer, while insisting that she pay for it because she had "a little leeway for special occasions." I gave her a big tip as I left for my flight back to Atlanta, where I was picked up by Trudy, who had decided to go to her parents' house and pick me up when I arrived at the airport.

Even though I was still rather excited, I knew that Trudy would not be too happy about the possibility of moving to Erie. I didn't think that I would accept the offer, but I had to consider it, keeping in mind that it could be the only viable offer from GE. When I came back to the office, the telegram had already arrived with the expression of "the gang of young tigers" repeated verbatim in it, making my boss very unhappy.

I got the feeling that he was disgusted with the raise that the Erie people had offered me, and that he was a bit jealous. I continued to send out resumés because I had a little time to make up my mind, as far as Erie was concerned. I was getting a nibble from Portsmouth, Virginia, where GE was manufacturing color televisions. The manager in the manufacturing department was very much interested in me and was about to extend an invitation to me to come and visit them, when he asked me for my boss's telephone number. I had a funny feeling about the request, so I just casually walked by my boss's office right after I hung up the phone and, sure enough, the phone rang in his office. From what I heard him saying, there was no doubt in my mind that he was talking to the Portsmouth manager. He proceeded to run me into the ground. Later that afternoon, I got a call with a phony reason for why they were no longer able to offer me a position.

Even later that afternoon, as I was walking down the hall, I saw my friend Ruby Curry coming out of her office in Personnel. She asked me how things were going and I told her what had happened. She got very perturbed and went back into her office, where she picked up the telephone and called George Sakash in Wilmington, North Carolina. George had worked a number of years in the laboratory in Rome and had moved to Wilmington when he was offered a promotion there.

The following day, I received a request to visit the Nuclear Fuel Department in Wilmington, North Carolina. Little did I know that we would stay in the Wilmington area until I retired from General Electric. Situations such as these remind me of what Sir Winston Churchill said after the Battle of Britain. It went something like this: "The Battle of Britain was a blessing in disguise; the only thing I wish was that it had not been disguised so well."

I had gone through some anxious months and was more than ready to see if I could land a position that I would really enjoy, especially if it was in a place that Trudy would not mind moving to. I figured that the prefix "North" in "North Carolina" might still be a slight concern for my southern belle!

✳ ✳ ✳ ✳

In the State of Georgia, the rules stated that adoptive parents would be considered "provisional" parents until the court had made the adoption final, exactly one year after the child was taken into the new family. For us, that would be May 5th, and I was about to be transferred by the GE company. Fortunately, after six months, Dolores, of Social Services, had told us that, because things were going so well between the three of us, they had waived the requirement and we could have our lawyer, Robert Royal, prepare the papers. We went to Mr. Royal's office, and he had a court document that stated our name, but he went so far as telling us that he could not read "the following information" because it contained the name and address of the birth mother. Mr. Royal left the document open on his desk, saying that he had to find something in the other room. I looked at Trudy, and Trudy looked back at me.

I asked, "You want me to look?"

Trudy answered, "No, let's leave it alone."

On the twelfth of February 1971, Trudy and I were in the Georgia State District Court, in downtown Rome, with Judge

Robert Scoggins presiding in his office. The judge said that there are two occasions in a judge's line of work where all parties part happily afterwards: adoption and naturalization. Well, my only two occasions in court have been for those two situations, and I often think of Judge Scoggins' words.

The routine that followed, as the judge spoke to us, was that a clerk would go out in the hall of the Courthouse and call for the birth mother. I believe the clerk must have gone out into the hall, perhaps called the birth mother's name softly, and then told the judge that no one was there to claim our Nancy Ann. So we celebrated the fact that the adoption was final and that no one could take Nancy Ann from us.

I traveled to Wilmington for an interview and was introduced to the Nuclear Fuel Business. The thought of nuclear, meaning radioactive, was an interesting thing but, at the same time, somewhat frightening. The interview went well. I noticed that the "PE" following my name and the fact that I had a patent did not hurt my chances of getting an offer one bit. Less than a week later, I had an offer and happily accepted it.

21

Move to North Carolina

The Nuclear Fuel Department was liberal with their transfer allowance. Trudy and I were invited to come to Wilmington for one week to do some house hunting, and GE sent us the local paper to help us get acquainted with the area. We stayed at the Hilton and were given a rental car. A realtor showed us all over town but, during the first two days, we saw only houses that did not suit us or were too expensive for our budget. I felt that, since the company was paying for our stay at the Hilton, I should put the pressure on myself to be successful in our search; so I decided that we'd go at it alone and start looking for a house without a realtor.

I knew that I was going to be an Advance Manufacturing Engineer, and that I would probably be called at night once I was fully assigned to my area of responsibility. I suggested to Trudy that we drive circles around the plant and look for a place close to work that we could buy. Little did I know that the plant was backed up to the North Cape Fear River, and it was impossible to make circles around the plant.

On our way to the plant, we noticed a street in Castle Hayne, a suburb of Wilmington in which the GE plant is located. The street's name was Holland Drive. We both started to laugh, and I drove up the street and looked around, just for the fun of it. About a half mile up the street, there was a house being built with two "For Sale" signs on it, one belonging to a realtor and the other one belonging to the builder. We looked around, and, since there was no one there, we went into the house. I went up into the attic to check the wiring. In those days, copper was expensive and there were some houses being built with aluminum wire in them. My experience with aluminum wire in the transformer business told me to stay away from houses with aluminum wiring. Everything checked out OK, so we went to the back-yard and happened to meet the neighbor, who quickly revealed that he had sold the half acre on which our house was being built for three thousand dollars. We went to a nearby shopping center to use the pay phone and called the builder.

His wife answered the phone and said, "Mr. van Luyn?"

I could not believe my ears! We had been in town for only three days, and some stranger knew my name and recognized my voice?

"Mr. Sakash told me that you were looking for a house," she said, "so I thought that you had talked with him and were trying to get in touch with me."

We made an appointment with the builder, Tony Dombroski and, after meeting him, we decided that we were dealing with an honest man when he said that $25,750 was a fair price for the house since he had paid $3,000 for the land. We found out later that Tony was one of the best builders in the area. Trudy picked out the carpet and had a dish-washer added to the kitchen, and we were told that the house would be ready May 1. Thursday was spent at the bank, and we had Friday left to do some sightseeing.

Castle Hayne was a small town. It so happened that there had been a number of Dutch and Slovakian people settling there because of the fertile soil, which attracted bulb growers, flower growers, nursery people, and truck farmers. The family who had built the first house on our street was that of a cabinetmaker from Utrecht, Holland, and they had named the street. Had it not been for that street name, we would not have found the house as quickly as we did.

Before going house hunting in Wilmington, I had talked with a welder in the tank shop at work in Rome who also happened to be a part-time realtor. General Electric would pay the realtor's fee when someone was being transferred, so I thought a fellow employee would be as good a choice as anyone to sell our house. We had decided to try to sell our house in Rome for $16,750 and see what would happen. Before we left to go to Wilmington for house hunting, the realtor had left a "For Sale" sign for us to put in the front yard. We had left it in the carport because we did not want to sell until we were sure of what date we were going to leave.

On Friday afternoon, as we were happily flying back to Atlanta, I said to Trudy, "Do you realize that we own two houses?"

Trudy, who has a way to bring me quickly down to earth, answered, "Yes, and two mortgages to pay!"

When we were back in Rome Saturday morning, the realtor called and asked me to put the "For Sale" sign out. I did, and the next call from him came Monday morning before I went to work: "Bob, take the sign down. I've sold the house." That was quick, and we could not believe it. There was one more call that blew us completely away; the request came to us from the prospective buyers asking if we could please raise our price $1,000 more so that they could get a down payment for the purchase of our house. Of course, we did not mind it at all and were all too happy to sell the house that we had owned for less than two years. In addition, General Electric gave all transfers an allowance for "curtain money," which was based on the selling price of the previously-owned house.

✳   ✳   ✳   ✳

I started work in Wilmington at the beginning of April, and stayed at the Holiday Inn for a month until the house was finished. Every two weeks, I was given a trip back to Rome, all expenses paid. The weekend after the movers loaded our household goods in a large moving truck, we stayed with Trudy's parents in Atlanta and, while there, we all celebrated Nancy's first birthday.

It did not take too long to get acclimated and completely involved in my work and, pretty soon, I understood the process of changing UF_6 gas (Uraniumhexafluoride) to UO_2 (Uraniumdioxide) pellets. It was very interesting, and the rules were totally different from other manufacturing norms because one had to be constantly alert in order to avoid getting too close to creating a critical mass.

The first responsibility I had was in the pellet area. The UO_2 pellets came into that area after they were sintered and were to be ground to a certain diameter. The pellets were about half an inch long and approximately half an inch in diameter. I was the engineer in charge of the processes and the welding of the zirconium fuel rods. It was very interesting and extremely precise work. The shop ran on three shifts, five days a week, and I was called out of bed many a night because of a problem on the factory floor. There was no union in Wilmington, and it was a delight to work there. If there was a problem, we would have the hourly people join in an effort to eliminate an aggravation in a certain process or any other problem that we had on the factory floor. An operator might make a suggestion in a certain situation and, with my training and experience, I could readily see if such an approach would not work; however, I would take the time to explain, in detail, why I did not think that it would work. By doing so, I was forced to think of all the factors of a certain situation. Because of that interplay of ideas, the two of us would come up with a fix. It was such a delight to try to do the right thing and not constantly "fight" with hourly workers because they thought we would make them work harder in less time allotted.

Work was fun, and things were going well at home. In that spring of 1971, Nancy started to walk. Also, she made her first trip to Holland to see her Dutch *Opa* and *Oma*.

Nancy's First Trip to Holland (1971)

✳   ✳   ✳   ✳

In those days, there were not so many commercials on TV so, when you decided to watch a football game, you always saw and heard the band play the national anthem, as well as the half-time activities. I watched my fair share of football games and, unbeknownst to me, Nancy was watching, too. One summer evening, when Nancy was two years old, a band from the Army was going to give a concert at the

Wilmington open-air amphitheatre. I thought this was a good opportunity to see how Nancy would like the concert; plus, if it did not work out, I could easily leave without disturbing any of the other people at the concert. The band members, in full dress uniforms, took their places; the conductor came on the stage and took a bow to welcoming applause. The band members stood up and began to play the national anthem. Nancy then proceeded to embarrass me by yelling out: "Football, football!"

The rules in Georgia were such that, once approved as an adoptive parent, the mother could not work outside the home any longer. Trudy and I had already decided that it made more sense to continue to live on one salary and to bring up our daughter the best we could, rather than let a stranger bring her up in the most formative years. Nancy proved to be a smart little girl and caught on to things very rapidly, so we decided to request a second baby. Since Trudy had always regretted not having had a sister, we thought that it would be good for Nancy to have one. The North Carolina adoption system did not seem to run as smoothly as the Georgia system, so I came up with a brilliant idea.

Since I was on good speaking terms with the Governor of Georgia, Jimmy Carter, I decided to write three letters to outstanding people in Georgia whom I had met during my years in Lions International there. I informed each of the three that I was going to write a letter to Jimmy, and asked if they could please "prime the pump on behalf of us." A week or so later, I wrote Jimmy Carter and told him that we wanted Nancy to have a sister from Georgia, because she had been adopted in Georgia, and they would have the paperwork on file to assist them in matching the children. It just could not miss. I had practically died sitting at a union meeting in Rome, Georgia, as Jimmy Carter's chauffeur, and had driven him all over the place; I just knew he would come through for us. Two weeks later, we got a letter from the office of the Governor of Georgia. In Jimmy's well-known green ink, the letter opened with, "Dear Mr. and Mrs. van

219

Luyn." That was all I needed to read; I knew that he was going to say no. He surely had forgotten what I had done for him, because I was "Mr. van Luyn, " instead of "Bob," the person he would ask to pick him up at the airport.

By the time all that had happened, we went back to the local social services department of North Carolina. They were starting to make noises that we were getting too old for adoption. Nancy did not get a sister, but it wasn't because Trudy and I had not tried.

Trudy had accepted a volunteer job as choir director in Bethany Presbyterian Church, where we were members at the time. Every Wednesday, on choir practice night, I was the one who would put Nancy to bed without having Trudy to tuck Nancy in one more time. I thought that I had the routine down rather well. I would think up a story to tell her, and then we would play "relax your toenails, your foot, your ankle, etc." She usually was so relaxed that I could quietly sneak out of the bedroom with Nancy being sound asleep.

One Wednesday night, I was somewhere in the routine of "relaxing" her arm or elbow, when she suddenly sat up straight in bed.

"Daddy, when I die, will I go to heaven?"

"Yes, Nancy, you will go to heaven."

"Will Mamma go to heaven when she dies?"

"Yes, Mamma will go to heaven when she dies."

"Will you go to heaven when you die?"

My mind raced and contemplated the correct answer, and I decided I might as well go the whole way. "Yes, I will go to heaven when I die."

"Will my tricycle go to heaven when I die?"

"No, your tricycle won't go to heaven when you die."

"Will the driveway go to heaven when I die.?"

"No, the driveway will not go to heaven when you die."

"Call Jesus, and tell him that we're not coming!"

"As soon as you're asleep, I will call Jesus."

"No, I won't go to sleep until you call Jesus."

I went to the phone, put my finger on the button, and "dialed" Jesus.

"Hello, Jesus. Nancy, Trudy, and Bob are not coming to heaven when we die."

Nancy was satisfied, and we had solved one more crisis in her young life.

* * * *

I worked with a number of GE's foreign visitors and would invite them to our house for dinner. Having lived on the other side of the Atlantic Ocean, I had a good feel for what foreigners liked, and what they would like to know about the U.S. The usual custom in the States was to take them to the best restaurant in the area or to the local country club. I thought it would be more interesting for them to be invited into our home. When we worked in Rome, Georgia, I had brought home five Italians from "Italtrafo" and several Canadians from our Canadian GE, so I continued the practice in Wilmington. I would call Trudy and ask, "Can I invite one Japanese?" or "three Canadians?" or whomever I had worked with that day. Then we would have a nice time at our house, after a delicious meal Trudy had prepared for us.

A funny situation developed with Mr. Sadoyuki Omori from JNF, Japan Nuclear Fuel. I called Trudy one particular afternoon and asked her if it was OK for me to bring a Japanese engineer home for dinner.

She said, "What about a roast for supper?"

I replied, "Surely sounds good to me."

Mr. Omori came, and his English was very limited. To help the conversation along, Trudy, having been a music teacher for many years in the elementary schools, asked if there were many children in Japan who learned to play the violin with the method developed by Suzuki, the Japanese master. Mr. Omori nodded vigorously and confirmed that it was happening there and kept saying that the "steak" was very good. We had a nice time and forgot about the visit.

Three months later, unbeknownst to me, Mr. Omori was in the plant for a very brief visit, and I happened to see him in the parking lot just as I was getting in my car to go home. Mr. Omori came to me and said, "Mr. Roonesan, I have velly small plesent." He called me Roonsan because he pronounced the "L" as an "R," and added the honorific "san" after my name, ignoring the "van." He gave me a small cardboard box that contained a perfectly crafted miniature violin with bow. I was flabbergasted. I could not believe my eyes. I protested and said that it was too much, but he would not hear of it. Obviously Mr. Omori had misunderstood Trudy's question at the dinner table big time. When I came home Nancy wanted to have the "toy," and Trudy assured her that she would be able to play on it when we had found a teacher in Wilmington. At that time, Trudy was not successful but, by the time Nancy was five years old, Trudy had found a Suzuki-method teacher who had moved to Wilmington, and Nancy started taking violin lessons the Suzuki way. Several months later, Trudy was told by the violin teacher that Nancy had outgrown Mr. Omori's one-tenth-size violin and needed a quarter-size. Since it did not take Nancy too long to outgrow her first violin, I suggested that, on our next trip to Atlanta, Trudy should check into renting a violin of a quarter size. Sure enough, Trudy was successful and Nancy progressed nicely on her quarter-size violin. Mr. Omori was coming back to the plant from Japan, and we told Nancy that Daddy would invite Mr. Omori again, so that she could play for him after dinner and show him how well she was doing.

Mr. Omori was much impressed with Nancy's performance of "Twinkle, twinkle little star...," but he had an expression of puzzlement. In broken English, he said, "That is not the violin that I brought for her the last time." I was more than happy to explain. Mr. Omori smiled approvingly and praised Nancy on her nice way of playing.

Three months later, Mr. Omori had to be back at the plant and showed up with a quarter-size violin. This was getting embarrassing! We did not know what to do, but Mr. Omori did not want any explanation, and it was for Nancy to keep. Afterwards, I told Trudy that we would make sure that, when Nancy was ready for the half size, we would buy it and stop this routine. Later Mr. Omori came back and Nancy played again for him, but we assured him that this violin was bought by us.

※　※　※　※

During the summer of 1973, Trudy, Nancy, and I went back to Holland for a three-week vacation. Pappa and Mamma had moved from the Malvastraat, where I grew up, into an assisted living home. It was a seven-story building, called Oldenoord, with all the amenities one could wish. The care was fantastic, and the food was very good. Pappa's retirement check was not large enough to cover the cost, so the city of Rotterdam made up the difference (and even gave them some spending money to boot!). In 1973, while the care of the elderly was still first rate, the three of us were even allowed to stay in the guest rooms there and take our meals with Mamma and Pappa, which Mamma and Pappa paid for as thanks for our help when Mamma was so sick during their visit to Georgia. I could not understand how this type of care was possible in Rotterdam but not in our rich America. When the Rotterdam city council decided that they could no longer afford such luxuries for their senior citizens, the entire care package was realigned and had no resemblance to what it had been earlier. The realignment happened after Mamma passed away in 1986; I was glad that my parents were the lucky recipients of the good care while it lasted.

On a side note, Warm Hearth Village in Blacksburg, Virginia, is a copy of the way an old-age home in Rotterdam used to be. It was planned and built by Wybe Kroontje, the

223

Dutch agronomy professor at VPI. Wybe, who had lived in Holland throughout World War II, had avoided capture by the German occupiers, and had never had to work in Germany as a slave laborer. He and his wife Marietje felt that they owed such a tremendous debt to America for helping to liberate their countrymen, that they made it their life's goal to have a care center in America for the elderly of all economic levels.

✳   ✳   ✳   ✳

Work went on and I enjoyed it very much. We used written instructions for the operators to follow as they were doing their work. These instructions were called Standard Operating Procedures (SOPs). To grind the UO_2 sintered pellets on a centerless grinder, the operator had an instruction that was sixty-three typewritten pages long. Somewhere, hidden in the middle, were vital and specific measurements to which the pellets had to be ground under exactly spelled-out conditions. The operator would "memorize" the specifics, often guessing if he was not quite sure about a certain tolerance. It was just too cumbersome to go through sixty-three pages trying to locate the specific instruction, so they would be "pretty sure" that they knew what needed to be done. In addition, engineers were reluctant to improve or change the process because the paperwork routine was so cumbersome. The result, of course, was that mistakes were made unintentionally, and it forced me to consider thinking about changing the way that things were done.

The SOP had five distinct parts to it, all intertwined in one long and cumbersome document that was the real cause of most production errors. I set out to separate the intertwined parts and to create a new document that contained the five needed items.

The five parts were:

1. Equipment Description and its Operating Procedure

2. Method Sheet (how the manufacturing engineer designed the sequence to be followed)
3. Equipment Parameters (used to produce an acceptable product)
4. Quality Control Requirements (establishing control limits for the end product)
5. Nuclear Safety Sheet (the controls that had to be followed to avoid any nuclear accidents. In the business, these accidents are referred to as "excursions.")

It made sense that the equipment description would never change, so I decided to get a small 3-ring binder for those papers. The Method Sheet for performing the task was written in short concise sentences and indicated as: step #1, step #2, step #3, etc. A number of pages would follow, depending on the length of the sequence. It was also placed in the binder. My decision was to start each line of the Method Sheet with a verb so that the instruction would be brief and concise. The tolerances from the Manufacturing Engineer and the Quality Control Engineer were each to be on one

The PROD System and its designer,
next to a nuclear fuel bundle.

single sheet, and the Nuclear Safety Sheet was on one sheet also. I had a cabinetmaker make a board with three picture frames for the sheets and one pocket for the three-ring binder. The three single sheets were different colors, and I made my presentation to management, calling it the PROD System (Production Requirements Operator Documents).

Having met resistance to my idea of radically changing the method of working with the new workstations in Rome, Georgia, I should have been smart enough to anticipate that Wilmington would also have a large crop of naysayers. I was ridiculed, and lots of managers made fun of the acronym I had devised, but I stuck to my guns. Lo and behold, again, with one minor change made by the plant manager and some suggestions by the building manager, Gene Lees, the new way was accepted. The plant manager Stu Miller wanted my board to be "zingy." He suggested that it should be made of clear molded acrylic, which I wanted, but had thought to be too expensive. The cabinetmaker charged me $35 for a nicely-made board, and I knew the acrylic would be more than that by far. Stu told me to "do it for $15," which I knew was ridiculous, but I was not about to argue, and immediately placed an order for the first hundred PROD boards at $110 each.

The nice thing about the PROD System was that individual sheets could now be changed or modified independent of the other four items of the same operation. The PROD for a specific process had a number assigned to it, and its individual sheets had the number plus a letter assigned for the first (A) and the second (B), to indicate the revision of either the Quality Control, Manufacturing Engineering, or Nuclear Safety sheet. None of the engineers hesitated to update an instruction, and it was done quickly; each workstation had a PROD board close to where the operator would stand or sit. In the end, two Manufacturing Program trainees were assigned to me to revamp the entire instruction system for the plant.

22

Bosco Marengo, Italy

The Italians who had trained with us were ready to start their new nuclear fuel manufacturing plant, to be called *Fabricazione Nucleari*. I was asked to help with the start-up of the new plant, outside Bosco Marengo, a small town in Northern Italy, over the mountains from Genoa. I was all excited to go, and then reality set in. I knew that, once in Italy, I would not be Robert van Luyn, but the Engineer that General Electric sent to help them out. Realizing the theoretical training that European universities give to their engineers, I was rather apprehensive and was concerned about living up to their expectations. For two weeks, I studied every subject that I thought might be of help once I was in Italy. What surprised me more than anything, when I started working in Bosco Marengo, was the fact that the Italians had no trouble with the theory; it was the practical approach with which they had problems.

Things were different in Italy. The engineer who was in charge of the time standards in the plant was also the union shop steward and, at that time, there were no women working in the plant. My task was to teach the workers how to weld zirconium fuel rods. I had a devil of a time convincing not only the chief engineer, but also the equipment supplier, that the setup had to have gas flow meters as well as pressure gauges for both the argon and the helium gas. It took me a week-and-a-half to prove that we could not produce a good weld consistently if the setup were not done properly.

Finally, the setup was done according to our proven methods, the way it should be, and I was given the best welder in the plant. Of course, he did not speak English, and I did not speak Italian. After several days, I was not able to get good welds. I noticed that the operator was not following the prescribed method I had written down. I called over Mario Boccalari, the Chief Engineer. I told him the problem, and he spoke with the welder. The way I learned English in 1957 was to listen, but most of all to observe the facial expressions of the one talking, the body English, etc.

I said to Mario, "Do I understand correctly what he is saying?"

Mario laughed and said, "I don't know what you are understanding."

"I understand that he said that I should leave him alone, go away, and let him weld, and all will be OK."

"That's about right."

I convinced Mario that I did not want that person on that machine even if everyone thought that he was the best stick welder in the plant. I wanted to train a girl, but I was told quickly that girls were unreliable in a factory setting because they got "ill" once a month.

"Let me train the driver who picks up guests at the train station," I said.

"You're kidding!" he responded.

"No, I am not."

I got a distinct feeling that they were just going to agree with me but, the next day, the driver was assigned to me. I asked the driver if he was willing to learn a new task. He said that he was, and, in a week, we had a qualified welder, were making good welds, and I was able to go on to the next task at hand.

✳ ✳ ✳ ✳

The first time I was in Italy, I was there for six weeks, and I was getting anxious to get home. It was 1973, and the oil crisis was about to begin. I remembered the General Manager of Italtrafo, Julio Adobati, whom I had met in Rome, Georgia. Along with four of his engineers, Julio had been a guest at our house. I decided to give Julio Adobati a call, that is, if he was still in Rome, Italy. At that very moment, I learned to appreciate the telephone system in the USA. It took the plant's telephone operator quite some effort to contact Julio in Rome, but she finally made the connection, and Julio invited me to come for a weekend to Rome.

It so happened that the weekend that I decided to pick was the last weekend with lights on. After that, no public lights were to be used to light the streets, or anything else, in order to save energy in Italy. Julio picked me up at the train station, and a little man outfitted in a uniform complete with a cap tried to grab my attaché case. Julio nodded in approval to me, and it turned out to be Julio's chauffeur. I was given a king's tour of Rome in its full glory at night, with all the buildings lit up, perhaps even more than normal because this was the last lit-up night until the oil crisis was over. I felt so spoiled and missed Trudy so much because I knew that she would love the tour and would know a great deal more about what I saw, due to her liberal arts education.

As oil crisis restrictions went into effect, cars were allowed only limited driving during the weekend, and the government instituted an even/odd system. Cars with license plates ending with an even number were allowed to drive one weekend, and those with an odd number the next. Because of this, I was able easily to learn two new Italian words, *"Pari"* and *"Dispari"* (even and odd).

The next day, Julio took me on a whirlwind tour of Rome. We literally went everywhere. We went in the Basilica of Saint Peter, where I saw the *Pieta* for a second time (having already seen it in 1965 with Trudy at the World's Fair in

New York). Julio and I went onto the roof of Saint Peter's and even into the dome, where we really had to bend to the left because the curvature of the dome stopped one from walking upright. Then, we went through a passage to the Botticelli rooms in the Vatican museum and to the Sistine Chapel. Afterwards, Julio took me to all the famous fountains. My head was swimming because, in about five hours, I had seen more sights than I could possibly comprehend or remember.

I could not stop thinking of Trudy, who, with her liberal arts education and exposure to Italian opera, would have understood and remembered more than I could. The two of us must come back to this place; this was so magnificent that it should be enjoyed with your life's partner. Even though I had a wonderful time, and thought back on that weekend often, I was getting anxious to go home and see what was going on with my little family.

❊　❊　❊　❊

Back in Bosco Marengo, Mario Boccalari told me that there was a Federal Penitentiary in Alessandria, the same town in which my hotel was located, and that the inmates were building bicycles. The director of the bicycle shop, not an inmate, was a former world champion bicycle racer named Girardengo. The interesting thing about the bicycle, which had Girardengo's name on it, was the fact that it could be folded in half. They made full-size bicycles and child-size. Of course, I had to get one for Nancy. One evening after work, Mario took me to the penitentiary to get Nancy's bike. A guard led us into the jail where there were these enormous gates, for which he had the keys, separated by a distance of about fifteen feet. As he closed and locked the first gate behind us, he would skillfully swing the key ring in the air to catch the next key to open the second gate. The whole routine would have been funny had it not been for the awful feeling that came over me. I was just visiting, but I could not help feeling uncomfortable just being locked up in there. We met with Mr. Girardengo, and I paid him about $32 in American money and walked out, leaving the jail and that awful feeling behind me, with a brand new foldable bicycle for Nancy.

We had to work on Thanksgiving Day, which, of course, was a regular work day in Italy. Several engineers from the GE San Jose, California, office had come to Bosco Marengo, and so we decided that, even though we had been working all day on a holiday, we would have turkey. One of the guys checked around and found a restaurant that would serve us a turkey meal. Accompanied by some Italian wine, we had a typical American Thanksgiving meal. The slices of turkey we had were about the size of two slices of cold cuts, but it was turkey, and that made the day!

✳ ✳ ✳ ✳

I was supposed to return to the States on Monday, December 17, 1973, and had a plane ticket that would fly me from Milan to Rome and then to New York. I was supposed to switch planes in Rome in midmorning and fly into New York later that evening. Since I had worked during the Thanksgiving holidays, I thought it would be OK for me to leave work Friday afternoon, December 14, and fly to Amsterdam and visit Pappa and Mamma at Oldenoord in Rotterdam. It appeared that both my parents were in relatively good health. I had a nice visit in Rotterdam and, as it turned out, that was the last time I saw Pappa. All had seemed to be all right with the health of both my parents, but less than two months later, after a brief stay in the hospital, Pappa died on February 13, 1974. I later found out the reason for his stunted gait; he had been suffering from Parkinson's disease.

I left Amsterdam Sunday morning and missed my connection from New York to Wilmington that evening by ten minutes and had to stay in a New York hotel. I had a lot of luggage because I was carrying the fold-up bicycle for Nancy, along with my regular luggage. I remember the headlines in the newspaper that evening in the hotel: OJ Simpson had broken the all-time rushing record.

The next morning there was a tremendous ice storm in New York. I went to La Guardia Airport and was on and off five different airplanes before I finally caught a plane that was not cancelled. This flight took me to Atlanta, where I figured that I would be able to get back to Wilmington, since the ice storm seemed to have been local. I arrived in Wilmington around midnight, and our good friend, the cabinetmaker Jaap Bron, picked me up at the airport. When we arrived at home, Nancy was still waiting up for me. She was sure that the big cardboard box contained a present for her. Minutes later, she was trying to ride her bike in the den until well after midnight! The next morning, the news informed us that there had been a terrorist attack during the midmorning hours at the International Airport in Rome, Italy. I would have been right there had I not decided to go to Holland and visit Mamma and Pappa.

* * * *

The Italians must have been satisfied with my services because, in April 1974, I was requested to return to Bosco Marengo and stay for three weeks. I had learned to say *duecento-quatordici*, "two hundred fourteen." When I came back to my hotel, the desk clerk wanted to give me a different room, but I told him "No." He did not understand why I did not want to stay in a better room that cost the same as the other one. I told him that I did not want a different number written in my clothes because the laundry marked all my clothes with indelible ink, and I had learned to say "214," and that was good enough for me.

The oil crisis was still in full swing in Italy and, since I was going to be in Italy for the Easter holidays, I decided to take the company car and go to Nice, France, and spend Easter there because we were not allowed to drive in Italy due to the even/odd rule that was still in effect. Two Wilmington engineers decided to go with me; they also were working at the *Fabricazione Nucleari* plant, and we had ourselves a wonderful time in the French Riviera.

When I came back to the Wilmington plant from my second trip to Italy, the two trainees had done a wonderful job of getting a large number of operations in the plant on the PROD system. About a month later, on a Friday afternoon, Gene Lees, my boss's boss, called me over to his office and told me that the General Electric Nuclear Fuels overseas manager in San Jose wanted me to come to California and talk about a position he had in mind for me. Gene gave me the telephone number and I went back to my office and called the man. I asked him if he could he tell me over the telephone what the subject of the discussion was going to be. He told me that he was considering me as a candidate for a position as manager of Quality Control in the Bosco Marengo plant. It really thrilled me to be asked without even having tried to get the position. He told me that he wanted me in San Jose, the corporate headquarters for Nuclear Fuels, on Monday morning. I asked him if it was OK with him if I came on Tuesday, so that I would have a chance to discuss it with Trudy. The assignment would be for three years and, based on the reports he had received from the people in Bosco Marengo, he thought that I would be a very strong candidate. He agreed to have me call him on Monday and to let him know if I would come the next day to have the interview.

I went home sky high and told Trudy about what was going to happen if I were to call him Monday to see him the next day. Well, Trudy was not too sure about going to Italy for three years. I told her that we would find an apartment in Genoa on the Italian Riviera. Trudy did not show any excitement and basically did not want to go. I worked very hard to convince her. I said that it would be fun, and that I would get the best voice teacher in the country because Trudy was still singing and in excellent voice; I even promised to rent La Scala one evening so she could sing in the most famous music hall in the country. Trudy could not be persuaded. She gave me three reasons why: she did not want to leave our church; she did not want to lose the chance of adopting a second little girl, which of course would happen were we to leave the country; and, last, she did not want to leave her parents. I told her that her parents could come and visit us and stay for three months, which would give them a chance to see Italy and, in essence, see more of us than they were while living in Atlanta. Only later did I really appreciate the devotion that Trudy had towards her parents, but at the moment I could not see it.

❊ ❊ ❊ ❊

I must admit that, in considering the offer, my first experience in Italy on the very first day that I was there reverberated in my mind. I arrived in Genoa on a Saturday morning in late October 1973. I had been given the name and telephone number of an American manager at the *Fabricazione Nucleari* plant in Bosco Marengo, and I was to call him so that he could tell me how to get to the plant the following Monday.

I spoke with him, and he invited me for supper at his house. I rode the *funiculari* (cable car) to his apartment and was introduced to his wife. While we were talking about what was happening here and there, she asked me about my background. The fact that I was born and raised in Holland caused her to say that I must be fond of drinking gin. I told her that I indeed enjoyed a drink of gin-and-tonic, and that was all it took; she got up right away and fixed me a drink. We had two, maybe three, drinks, and she was feeling very free to talk with me, and started to complain that the Italians had stolen her good silver flatware, and she did not like the repairman who fixed her American refrigerator, and such problems were not making her all that happy.

We went to the dinner table and started to eat, and right during the meal my hostess passed out. She just keeled over and her husband caught her, and said, "Oh, Mama," and took her to their bedroom. There I was, what was I going to do? Get up and go back to my hotel? Continue with my meal? It was awful for me, and I could not imagine how he was feeling. After a good while, he came back to the dinner table, and we just talked business. I could not wait to get out of that apartment and, soon after dinner, I excused myself, stating that the jet lag was catching up with me.

That whole incident flashed through my mind as I was trying to convince Trudy to go with Nancy and me to Italy. In Trudy's case, as a "teetotaler," I did not think that the booze would get her if we went, but I had to admit she did not have that initial desire. It just was not there and, since this was not a situation where I would either take the offer or lose my job, it would be foolish to go to San Jose and then say no to the job offer. So the following morning, with a heavy heart, I called the San Jose office and told the overseas manager that I was not interested in the position.

23

A Manager's Position

Since everything had worked out so well with the PROD system in the plant, and since I had had an excellent response from management in Italy, I was interviewed for a unit manager's job in Bundle Production. In April 1975, I became the manager of Bundle Production; my unit was 75 employees strong. I had three foremen and a couple of specialists working in my group.

On the very first morning, in my new position as manager, I walked into my office and sat down at my desk. The phone rang, and I picked up the receiver; on the other end was one of my foremen. He said, "Bob, our newborn baby has just passed." Their baby girl had been born three days earlier. I had already been working with him for the past four years and knew him well. What an awful thing to happen; it immediately changed the atmosphere. Since he was a Vietnam veteran, his little girl was buried in the National Cemetery in Wilmington and, as his manager, I had the sad duty of representing GE at the funeral.

* * * *

At regular intervals, the NRC (Nuclear Regulatory Commission) would have an inspection in the plant. It was always a frightening type of inspection, since federal inspectors had the power to shut down the plant if regulations were not followed to the letter or if any other deviation was made inadvertently. Everyone in management was on pins and needles because we knew that, even though we had done nothing wrong, who was to say that something was not left out or something did not meet expectations?

The instructions I would give all the people in my unit were: be honest, tell the truth as you know it, answer all questions truthfully, and do not embellish your answer. After two or three days, the inspectors would give a verbal exit report, which was followed by an official written report later. Of course, that verbal report was the part during which we would find out what they had discovered during their inspection. As a manager, I would accompany them through my area while they were observing, and they would constantly be making notes in their notebooks. I was dying to see what they wrote down, but was sure to hear about it during the wrap-up meeting.

The inspectors were cordial and professional, but never uttered a word that was not related to the task at hand; to be more precise, they were quietly doing their task, and I did not get any idea if the inspection went well or was a total flop. During the three years that I was manager in the Bundle Assembly area, I never had a bad report, but that was not to say that I ever took an NRC inspection lightly.

One particular inspection stands out in my mind. The inspector discovered a small omission in the method sheet of a PROD that was at a workstation. He showed me what he had observed, and I went to my desk, made the change, had the change properly signed by the respective people, inserted it in the books throughout the building, and replaced the changed method sheet at the workstation. Twenty minutes later, I told the inspector what I had done. He was not convinced that the task had been completed. I invited him to

Some of the Bundle Assembly employees with their manager

check any book he wanted to check and, to his amazement, it had been done as I had told him. At that week's exit report, the inspector made a special comment about how good and workable the PROD system was and that he would suggest similar systems at other suppliers that he inspected.

✳ ✳ ✳ ✳

The operators in the Bundle Assembly Unit were a nice group of people, and I got along with them very well. Later that year, the General Electric Company divested itself of its interest in *Fabricazione Nucleari,* and the "American detachment" came back to the States. Had I accepted an offer for the job as manager of Quality Control, I would have been in limbo at that moment. GE took care of their people but, in hindsight, I was happy that I had taken the position as manager in the Bundle Assembly area.

238

During the three years that I spent in that area there were some interesting and sometimes funny incidents.

A day after the election in November 1976, when Jimmy Carter became president-elect, one of my operators came storming into my office and said that he had been discriminated against when he tried to vote. He said that it was high time that I, as his manager, do something about it. What piqued my attention was the fact that he was a white employee. He claimed he was so upset that he was unable to keep his mind on his work. I attempted to calm him down, and assured him that I would get those "so and so's" and would get with him as soon as I had something to report to him. I called the voter registration office in the county where he lived, identified myself, and asked to speak with the registrar. After a short check, it turned out that my employee had not voted for more than ten years and had not bothered to register again. I called him back into the office, explained the rules and the system to him, and told him to register so that he would not be faced with that problem in the future. I made it a point to remind him for the next few months by asking him if he had registered yet. Of course, it did not matter to him any longer, and so, after about four months, having reminded him once a month, I gave up.

The General Electric Company has plants in some locations where hourly and, in some cases, weekly salaried employees are represented by a labor union. If it so happens that there is a lack of work, employees are sent home for as little as four hours or as much as several days, without pay, with the instruction that they will be called when work is available. Since the Wilmington plant was non-union, we would bend over backwards to keep hourly employees working so that they could count on having a weekly paycheck that was at least the same as if no overtime was worked. Scheduling depends on many factors, especially in the final assembly area where work depends on everything that has preceded that function. On some days, we could not get the

239

correct combinations of fuel rods with which to assemble a fuel bundle, and we would realize that we would be out of work for at least one day.

Jim Herring, one of my foremen, came to me and told me that he had about eighteen people standing around doing nothing. I decided that the area could stand a little sprucing up, so I told Jim to get his crew some paint brushes and to start painting the factory columns and touching up some of the equipment. The factory columns were painted in a light beige color and, where there was a fire extinguisher attached to the column, a bright red band about 18" wide was painted around the column. This way, if any employee needed a fire extinguisher, all he or she had to do was look for a column with a red band.

One of my female operators, Dot, perhaps forty years old, was assigned to paint the red band on a particular column. I walked over and said, "Dot, what are you doing?"

"I'm painting, sir."

"Yes, I see that, but why are you painting it brown?"

"I'm painting it red!"

"I'm sorry, but that isn't red, that's brown."

"No, sir, that's red!"

"Who says that is red?"

"My foreman did." Now I noticed a twinkle in Dot's eyes.

"Jim, what color is Dot painting that band?"

"Red, sir."

To prove that he was right, Jim picked up the can, and it said "red" on the label. I pointed at a nuclear warning sign that was hanging in the area, knowing that purple is a difficult color for a color-blind person to see. I asked Jim to tell me what the color was of the nuclear warning sign, and he answered "green," so I realized that Jim could not distinguish between colors. Dot had had some fun with her foreman, knowing well and good that it would be corrected.

The funniest thing happened with one of my rod-loading operators, who wanted to leave the company but would like to return if the plan he had did not work out. The General Electric Company will give employees a leave of absence if the company decides that the employee is a valuable contributor and that the fact that they are absent, in most cases, for educational purposes improves their value to the company after they return. The nice thing about a leave of absence is that, in almost all of the cases, the job one vacates will be available upon return to full-time employment. In addition, insurance will continue to be carried for the employee during his/her absence.

This particular employee was a problem operator, but his wife was in the hospital, so I gave him a little slack to take care of his business. One day, he did not show up for work and I was unable to contact him. The next day he came in, and I asked him what had happened. He told me that he was with "this girl" and that she had needed to be taken to the hospital. I said that I understood that his wife was in the hospital.

"Yes, but this has nothing to do with it," he replied.

Well, I told him to get back to work and to be careful with his attendance. Two days later he came into my office.

"Boss, I need a leave of absence."

"You know that I have to fill out all the paperwork, so I need to know what you are going to do that warrants a leave of absence."

"I'm going to college," he said.

"That's commendable, but what will your major be?"

"Theology, sir."

With utter surprise in my voice, but misinterpreted by him as ignorance of the meaning of the word theology, I said, "Theology?"

"Yes, that is the study of the life of Jesus Christ."

"But how in the world is that going to benefit the General Electric Company?"

"Oh, this is a new major taught in Texas; it's Nuclear Theology."

It took all I had not to laugh in his face. "I will fill out the paperwork, and we will see if it gets approved; it will take a week or so."

The next day, he stuck his head in the door of my office and told me that the buddy who was going to drive him to Texas was leaving and that he was leaving with him. Of course, the application for a leave of absence went straight in the waste basket.

The real scare in my time as Manager of Bundle Production came when the NLRB (National Labor Relations Board) announced that there was going to be a vote by the hourly employees to decide if they wanted to be represented by a union. If the Wilmington employees voted yes for the union, they would get the right to strike and would have to pay union dues. Everyone was worried because one never knows how a vote will come out. Management had to be very careful because if anyone coerced employees in an effort to influence their votes, he or she would get into serious trouble with the NLRB.

Management had a few months to prepare themselves. The employees would not get any additional money if they voted to have a union because General Electric had made it a practice that, if the union who represented workers in other General Electric plants had obtained a contract with salary agreements, the non-union employees elsewhere would get it immediately.

I felt good about my hourly employees, but I could never be sure. One day, I happened to return some United Way forms to Jack Bergman, who was assigned to be the plant's liaison with the Wilmington United Way Board. Stu Miller, the plant manager at the time, was in Jack's office. Stu was a strange man; he would not say much and had all these peculiar manners. Things had to be "zingy" (jazzy), and he would come in your area, say two words and, after you answered him, there would be these weird silences that left one with an impression that was difficult to measure. Did he agree? Did he not understand? Or what?

As I left Jack's office, and was five feet out the door, I hear Stu saying, "You just saw the guy who's going to be the only manager in the plant with a 100 percent 'no' vote." That was a nice thing to overhear; however, I was not that sure about my fifty-plus hourly people. The vote was held, and the workers voted two-to-one against the union. Everybody was relieved, and we were very pleased with that outcome.

About a year after I became Manager of Bundle Production, Stu Miller was transferred to Schenectady, and we got a new General Manager. He was Randy Alkema. The moment I heard the name my mind said, "That is a Dutchman of Friesian heritage." Most Dutch names ending with an "a" are Friesian. Friesland is one of twelve Dutch provinces, and their people are known as strong, stout, honest, and independent. When Randy was introduced to me, I found out that his grandparents on both sides were Dutch.

One morning, I was driving to work; for some reason I drove Trudy's car, a VW Beetle. It so happened that I got a flat tire on the way to the plant, which was less than two miles from our home. I pulled over, stopped the car, and opened the hood. Just as I was about to take a very doubtful spare out of the front of the car, another car pulled over and no one less than Randy Alkema got out of his car and started to help change my tire. Of course, I was terribly embarrassed, and told him that I was doing OK, of which he did not want to hear anything. I worked as fast as I could while all the traffic to the plant was flying by us. After I had the spare back on the VW, Randy got in his car and wondered aloud if I would make it on my doubtful spare. I told him that I was all right and please to go on. Later at work, I really got teased a tremendous amount because everybody passing me had assumed that I had helped the top man in the plant with *his* flat tire and was trying to get a few points with him by helping him.

When Randy came to the Wilmington plant, he was given the usual plant tour. The only way that anyone could enter the controlled area was to put on rubber overshoes and don a white lab coat and a surgical cap. If someone wanted to touch anything, he or she had to put on a pair of rubber gloves. It was assumed that uranium dust was everywhere in the controlled area so, in order not to get shoes or clothing contaminated, we had to be careful. To put on rubber overshoes was somewhat of a hassle. Operators who were working there had decided on their own accord to use a pair of their own shoes and leave them in the area. When Randy observed it, he thought that it was not a fair thing to do to those employees and made a ruling that gave every person working in the controlled area a pair of shoes. That in itself sounded very thoughtful; however, every person not working in the controlled area started to gripe because they did not get a free pair of shoes. The result was that all the hourly employees received a pair of shoes whether or not they worked in the controlled area! I am sure that Randy learned quickly that one can have all the correct and well-meaning intentions in the world, but it is basically impossible to anticipate all the possible reactions when working with hundreds of people, let alone satisfy everyone.

Another time, Randy was escorting five VIPs through the plant. One of the visitors, who had obviously backed into a piece of equipment, had a big greasy smear on the back of his jacket. To clean nuclear fuel rods in my assembly area, we used gallons of acetone and I had plenty available. I walked up to Randy and asked him quietly if I should offer to clean the man's jacket with some acetone. Randy looked at me and said, in perfect Dutch, "Just leave that dumb ass alone." I almost died because I had no idea that he could speak Dutch. He later told me that his Dutch grandparents had taught him a few words and he had remembered a few phrases.

❋　❋　❋　❋

Nancy was one of those precocious children you read about. She taught herself to read and was a speed reader at that, outstripping both of her parents. When she was in the third grade, she eagerly joined the local Girl Scout troup as a Brownie. That started several years of enthusiastic participation in the Girl Scouts, with total involvement and persistence that only subsided when her shoulder sash was completely covered with every kind of merit badge.

✳   ✳   ✳   ✳

In 1978, I was promoted to manager of Production Control in the Nuclear Equipment Operation. The plant site had three separate buildings, in which the various components for a nuclear fuel reactor were being manufactured. I had worked for seven years in the nuclear fuel building. The two others were large buildings, one of which manufactured zirconium parts; the other was the equipment building, where mainly stainless steel components were manufactured. My new position was in the equipment building. Not only did I not know how the Control Rod Drives and all the other components were built, but I also had no idea what went into making one. Neither had I had much contact with the people in that building on a daily basis. I had to deal immediately with the problems that this brought along.

My unit of about 14 employees, weekly salaried and exempt salaried, were not too excited to work for a manager who did not know the product that was to be manufactured, and they were not about to stick out a helping hand to make it a little easier for him. Above all, they felt they were more qualified to fill the job than I was. Needless to say, I struggled a good bit for the first few months. One thing I knew how to do was straighten out the unit's payroll mess. There seemed to be no rhyme nor reason as to why specialists who had equal responsibilities were not in the same pay scale. I straightened out the irregularities and, slowly, I was more or less accepted.

Again, in even such a small group, I had the full spectrum of characters. At one end of the scale were several men who would do anything to please me. At the other were some who fought me just enough, but could never be accused of not pulling a full load. The latter knew that I realized this, but a big company with so-called "deep pockets" is an easy target for lawsuits, and it's not easy to fire someone even if his or her performance is marginal at best.

I remember one employee who would leave Biblical phrases on my desk if I had told him to do something with which he did not agree or if something was bothering him. Luckily, I was married to an "A" student from Agnes Scott. Trudy had taken Bible study there under Dr. Mary Boney Sheats, who, coincidentally, later became our Sunday School teacher at First Presbyterian Church in Wilmington. I would tell Trudy what had led to the situation that caused me to get a Biblically-inspired justification for a situation and Trudy, with her fantastic memory, would tell me where to look in the Bible in order for me to respond with an appropriate chapter and verse. After a few of those incidents, that too went away and I did not have to bother with that kind of situation.

❊   ❊   ❊   ❊

Trudy had not worked since we adopted Nancy, because the Georgia rule for new adoptive parents was that the mother would stay at home. After the probation period was over, we had weighed the pros and cons and had decided that we would rather miss Trudy's income as a teacher with a master's degree than to have Nancy be brought up by a sitter.

When Nancy was eight years old, the local school music supervisor learned that Trudy had been a music teacher and supervisor in the Rome, Georgia, city schools. We had earlier decided that Trudy, with her still-valid teaching certificate, would teach again when Nancy was ready to go to college. One night in October, when I came home, Trudy told me that she had been contacted by the music supervisor of the New Hanover County School System. One of their "itinerant" music teachers had moved away, and Trudy had been asked to help them out and fill that position. (Itinerant in this context means that they served more than one school).

"You know what we have decided," she said.

"Yes, that is true; however, realize that you will be ten years older if you wait until Nancy goes to college," I responded.

Trudy discussed the situation with the supervisor, and the decision was made that, when Nancy had finished fourth grade, she would transfer to one of the two schools where Trudy would be teaching. Trudy taught music for three years, and we put every penny in Elfun Tax-Exempt mutual funds. During the Jimmy Carter White House years, the return was more than twenty percent per year. The nest egg for Nancy's education got a significant boost, thanks to Trudy's efforts.

24

The Elfun Society

Since I had reached a certain level of pay and had been with the company for more then ten years, I became eligible for the Elfun Society. Top management were members of this exclusive group, and not too much was said about the organization. It wasn't a secret organization, but it was kind of "hush-hush" at that time, and all non-members knew that members had a tie tack with a little tree on it.

For many years top GE management had been getting together for recreation and fellowship on Association Island on Lake Ontario. In 1928 Gerard Swope, GE's third president, requested a small group to assemble a day early. Mr. Swope explained his idea for an independent society that would promote fellowship and spirit among GE management, with investment opportunities available to them. The name of the society was a contraction of the two words "Electric Fund," that is, Elfun. The group's members served as role models for the younger inductees. Members of the Elfun Society gradually widened their activities to include volunteer work in the communities where GE facilities were located. In 1981, Jack Welch became CEO of the General Electric Company. He recognized the benefits of the society's volunteer work, not only to the members and their communities but also to the reputation of the company as a whole, and he encouraged opening the membership to a broader base of GE employees.

When I was invited into the Elfun Society, its membership consisted of the top five percent of General Electric employees. Each GE location had an Elfun chapter. By the time I became a member, the Society was not only giving its members a chance to invest some of their savings in a number of mutual funds, but was also doing a great deal of community service in the locations in which their members lived and worked. When, on the eleventh of April 1979, Randy Alkema gave me my Elfun tie tack at the annual Tarheel Chapter initiation meeting, I had no idea that anything further was going to happen.

Randy was on various community committees, to which the plant manager was invited and which showed the community that GE was a good corporate citizen. One morning, Randy gave me a call and invited me to lunch. Obviously, I was very pleased to have him ask me to go to lunch with him. We went to a meeting with about twenty-five people who were the top management of all the companies in the Wilmington area: Du Pont, Corning, the two hospitals, chemical companies, etc. There was a brief presentation about "Keep America Clean," and Randy said that he had brought his man, who was going to organize a cleanup day in Wilmington.

"Oh, this was not a free lunch after all!" I was happy to be the chairman of the effort because I basically had the blessings of all the top men in industry in the area. Ten big companies assigned captains who reported to me and, after I had set a date, I had our facilities people order and deliver a fifty-foot trash container to an area we had picked in one of the not-so-desirable areas of town, where littering was rampant.

On a sunny Saturday morning, seventy people from all the big employers in town stuffed that trash container to the top. We had the local TV come out, and the reporter interviewed me. We had made a big splash in the community. I had a colleague take some photographs of me while the local TV was interviewing me. I took a print of that photograph and sent it to Fairfield to have it published in *Under the Elm*, the official Elfun magazine. Randy was very pleased with "my performance"; the truth of the matter was that I could not have failed with the kind of backing I had received.

Having headed up the project with a great deal of success, I received the "New Elfun of the Year" Award. Hence, I became more and more involved in the local Elfun Tarheel Chapter. After a few years, having gone through the various chairs, I was elected the chapter vice-chairman. The following September, I was invited to the National Fall Meeting of the Elfun Society. The meeting was in Rye, New York, and I met Jack Welch for the first time at a cocktail party preceding dinner at the Fairfield General Electric headquarters. Jack is an impressive man who makes you feel comfortable with his sharp and penetrating eyes, but you could sense right away that he did not like someone being phony.

Mr. Welch spoke about an incident that he had experienced with the top management of the Dutch electronics company, Philips. Jack and a high official at Philips had verbally agreed on a mutual decision and had concluded the agreement with a handshake. Less than a week later, Philips called Jack and told him that the deal was off.

"How about the handshake?" was Jack's response.

They replied, "We have decided differently," and Jack said that he had lost faith in the Philips Company.

Bryan Rowe, the President of GE Aircraft Engines and a British native, was standing next to us when I looked at Jack and said, "You've got to watch out for those Europeans. Bryan knows because he, too, like me, was born and raised in Europe." We had a laugh, and Jack asked from where in Europe I came. "Holland," I said. "Oh, I see, you know firsthand," Jack quipped. I did not realize then that I would have the pleasure of meeting Jack many more times and would have several meals with him.

* * * *

Since the Nuclear Fuel business had been flat, to put it mildly, for a number of years, a decision was made to have the Aircraft Engines Division use part of the Wilmington plant's space as a satellite manufacturing operation to their assembly plants in Lynn, Massachusetts, and Evendale, Ohio. I saw an opportunity for a promotion, so I applied for a position in that division. I did not have to sell the house nor move the family; all it amounted to was that my desk would be in a different area of the plant.

* * * *

Since Nancy had an unquenchable thirst for books, Trudy and Nancy frequented the local public library on a weekly basis. One thing led to another, and Trudy found herself being part of the group of citizens who were trying to help the library get a better building. She joined the New Hanover Friends of the Public Library and was asked to serve on its board. She filled several jobs over a period of time and, later, served as president of the organization. She was also appointed by the Board of County Commissioners as the first secretary of the newly-formed Library Advisory Board that superceded the old cumbersome Board of Trustees.

Then the real work began because the Friends of the Library group was a strong supporter of moving the library's collection from its cramped location in the Armory to a three-story department store vacated by Belk's in the downtown area of Wilmington. A great deal of money was needed but, with the help of a visionary County Manager, Dan Eller, and the persistence of the Friends of the Public Library, the city councilmen and county commissioners relented. They approved the renovation of the old building and, with the help of a local architect, the city obtained a beautiful library.

Meanwhile, on several occasions, we made trips to Blacksburg. The reunions and football games there were

initially the motivators to consider moving there. Casey and
Maggi Jones were living in Christiansburg, near Blacksburg,
where Casey had his veterinary practice. They were our
gracious hosts on such visits. More and more, we started to
appreciate the small towns in the hills of western Virginia.

25

GE Aircraft Engines

My next job was as manager of Farm Out and Inventory with GE's Aircraft Engines Department. GE's Aircraft Engines, out of Lynn, Massachusetts, and Evendale, Ohio, was booming. Management was looking for a site where they could start a satellite plant to manufacture Rotating Parts for large and small jet engines. The decision was made to take over a part of the already-existing Wilmington plant, add buildings, and produce Shafts, Spools, Discs, and Casings in Wilmington. The hourly workforce would come from the Nuclear division, which made Wilmington lay-off proof. If there was more work at Nuclear, operators would transfer from Aircraft Engines and vice-versa.

The salaried workforce basically came from Wilmington; Lynn, Massachusetts; and Evendale, Ohio. For me to go to Aircraft Engines was a promotion; however, it quickly became apparent that the hiring manager had had someone else in mind for the job, but was told by the Aircraft Engines plant manager to hire me. To say the least, that is a bad start with which to begin a new position. It took me twice as long to settle into the new position, with constant backbiting by a number of colleagues. I found out that the people who came to Wilmington from the Lynn plant were cliquish and did not trust the Wilmington people as much as they trusted the Evendale people. It took a few years for the Lynn people to realize that the southern engineers were not after their jobs and that they could hold their own professionally.

I stayed in that job for about two years and then moved to another position in the Wilmington plant with Aircraft Engines. I became the staff engineer for the plant and was in charge of the investment budget, controlling millions of dollars. I had the function of writing specifications to purchase equipment with which to operate the plant. I would write a specification for a VTL (Vertical Turret Lathe), then I would send out the specs to the various equipment manufacturers for quotes, make up a spread sheet, select the best machine for our needs, and present it to the plant manager. My recommendations, based on sound engineering principles, were seldom, if ever, overruled. The next step was placing the order. While negotiating the price, I would say, "Well, I would like fourteen of those at $750,000 apiece. What can you do for me?" One can only imagine what would happen when one had that kind of leverage.

Chuck Chadwell, then the plant manager, would ask me, "How are you doing, Bob? Are you getting along with your vendors?"

Of course, I would say, "I'm doing great, and I have no problems with any of my vendors."

Chuck said something that always stuck with me, "Just ask yourself how many of those friends you will have when you don't control those purse strings any longer." If you let the nice complimentary talk of your vendors go to your head, it is not very difficult to get in lots of trouble.

Needless to say, when I went to "run off," meaning when I would go to verify that the machine met my specs and was performing as it was supposed to, I was treated as if I was the president of the company. The vendors would take me to the best places in town to eat. A typical runoff would take three days. Although this sounds like fun, it too gets old after a while, and you would rather be left alone. There was lots of traveling in that job, and it took me to Germany several times, as well as places throughout the U.S.

When I got to be Staff Engineer in Facilities Engineering of Aircraft Engines, having to write the specs and being in charge of all the major equipment purchases for Wilmington, I kept in mind a well-known fact of company life — in industry, it does not matter if one has purchased hundreds of millions of dollars worth of manufacturing equipment for the plant; if one machine does not perform as promised, all previous effort goes out the window. "Don't tell me what you have done for me, tell me what you are going to do for me!" I was lucky. I never had a machine that I had approved come to Wilmington and turn out to be a failure.

That year, the national campaign for the presidential election was in full swing, and the Republican candidate, Ronald Reagan, was coming to Wilmington. I decided to go to his speech outside the Cotton Exchange, an area that was located at the site of several old cotton warehouses that had been tastefully converted into an attractive, small shopping center. I took some pictures and decided to stand at the rope line and see if I could shake Ronald Reagan's hand. After the speech was over, Ronald walked over to the rope line and started shaking hands. Lo and behold, he grabbed my hand! The only difference was that he thought that it was someone else's hand! Well, I was not going to let that happen, so I held on to his hand long enough for him to realize that I was the owner of the hand. He smiled, understanding the situation, and I was thrilled to death that I had shaken the hand of perhaps a future president of this great country.

* * * *

When Nancy started junior high school, Trudy resigned from being a music teacher, once again becoming a full-time homemaker. She had turned down a request from Wilmington College (later UNCW) to teach music education to future classroom teachers because she was not looking for additional work experiences. As it soon turned out, it was a smart and timely decision.

In 1985, both of Trudy's parents had been diagnosed with cancer, and Trudy flew to Atlanta several times to help out as much as she could. We soon realized that this could not be sustained over a long period of time. Since both of them had successfully undergone treatment and were stable, we started thinking about their future care. Within a year, a house three doors up the street from us was put up for sale, and the Florrids decided to leave their beloved Atlanta and move to Castle Hayne, North Carolina. They were welcomed royally by the Holland Drive neighbors and by the members of the Wrightsboro United Methodist Church. When Pappa Florrid's cancer recurred, those neighbors and friends became support for all of us.

In Holland, things were not going too well either. Mamma had been a widow for thirteen years, enjoying the friends she and Pappa had made in Oldenoord. Her sight was bad, but she never admitted it. For all practical purposes, she was blind. She pretended to watch TV, but in reality she was just listening to the sound. After a bout with the flu, she peacefully passed away in February 1986. Trudy and I went to Holland for the funeral, and it was bitterly cold. Nancy had written a poem for *Oma* in the middle of the night after we had received the sad news, and I read it at Mamma's service. We were again grateful to Doctor Boyce Brice of Rome, Georgia, for the extra nineteen years of life he had helped Mamma enjoy.

For the Florrids, having moved to Castle Hayne, the most important thing was the fact that they were now able to enjoy, in person, the successes that Nancy attained during her junior and senior years at Laney High School. Nancy had lettered twelve times in junior high school but then had "lost her grip" because she lettered only eleven times in high school! Sports were especially big at Laney High School because Michael Jordan had graduated from there. When

Michael became a professional basketball player, he gave the Laney boys' and girls' teams shoes and other outfits. To top it all off, Michael started a scholarship at Laney High School for a graduating boy and girl who had participated in school sports while making good grades and planning to go to college. In 1988, her senior year, Nancy was the proud first recipient of the Michael Jordan Award, worth $2,500. This was a special pleasure for her granddaddy, Richard Florrid, the former Georgia Tech championship baseball pitcher.

We had talked with Nancy over the years about going to college. In her senior year at Laney she started her search for a college to attend, and we traveled to a number of them, both in-state and out-of-state. Nancy applied to about six. After receiving their replies and doing some further investigation, Nancy chose Furman University in Greenville, South Carolina.

Nancy was pleased to be chosen to give the prayer at Laney's graduation ceremonies. Papa Florrid's cancer had returned, and he was too ill to attend but eagerly enjoyed Mama Florrid's description of it. The Florrids flabbergasted us all by offering to buy Nancy a new car for her trips back and forth to Furman University.

✳ ✳ ✳ ✳

Sadness came to our family when Papa Florrid died in the summer of 1988. Trudy's mother came to live with us and, at our insistence, kept her house up the street — just in case she got tired of her son-in-law. This also turned out to be a good place for out-of-town guests to stay. The enormous loss in all our lives, combined with Nancy's going off to college, were major changes for our family. Fortunately, Mama Florrid was well enough to travel with us several times to see Nancy at Furman University and to go to Atlanta to see old friends. We also added another member to our family, Cora Leonard, the multi-talented sitter who stayed with Mama Florrid when Trudy and I went to football games.

She cooked like a dream, played the piano, and especially excelled at "Jeopardy." She and Mama Florrid became fast friends.

On Nancy's first return home from Furman, after a few weeks of classes, she told us that her major would be political science. I just about died, and I uttered my dissatisfaction with her choice because I questioned what she would do with that major, unless she went for a Ph.D. in that field. Her comment was, "Dad, I know what I am doing; just stick with me."

At one of the Wilmington Elfun meetings, Bryan Rowe, president of GE's Aircraft Engines Business, who had emigrated from England, was our keynote speaker. Don Ratliff, a friend of mine, reminded Bryan that I used to be as European as he. Bryan and I found out that we had arrived in the U.S. in the same year. Later in his speech, Bryan was talking about this great country of ours and all the unbelievable opportunities that are available to all of us. He said, "Take, for instance, Bob van Luyn; he came to America in April of 1957. I did, too; however, I came in January. He came by boat, and I came by plane; that's why I am in my position and he is in his."

＊　＊　＊　＊

Writing specifications for the purchase of machines led to new experiences for me. I remember the first time that I was sent to check and accept a machine for GE. Harry Spenner, my boss, was a good man, but a no-nonsense type of guy — direct to the point, gruff, and appearing to be impatient. At about a quarter-of-four one afternoon, he called me into his office and said, "I want you to go to deVlieg tomorrow, run off this machining center, and bring back a good machine. We are paying $475,000 for it, so it better be good."

"What in the world are you telling me to do?" I thought. I had no idea what they had ordered, nor what it was supposed to do. Many other questions spun through my mind. I was not about to tell him that I did not know what he wanted me to do because, if I gave him the slightest feeling that I was not up to the job, I knew I would lose the chance to do something new. I told him that I would do the job, then went immediately to my office and called an old friend whom I had met years before, who was in charge of purchasing all the equipment for the Steam Turbine Department in Schenectady, New York.

I called Earl Troup, a smart engineer who had many years of experience in that type of work, and told him what my situation was. I asked, "Earl, what am I going to do? What's the best approach?" After picking Earl's brain for about an hour on the phone, I was equipped with plenty of notes with which I was able to go to deVlieg and at least give the impression that I knew what I was supposed to do. Earl told me to be sure to check the main bearings on the spindle. "The spindle should not have more run-out than .00005 of an inch," Earl stated. If assemblers were not able to attain this measurement, they would over-tighten the spindle at the bearings, which then would cause the bearings to run hot.

I arrived at the de Vlieg Company in Royal Oak, Michigan, the next day before lunch, and I made a cursory inspection of the machine. It was the first time I had seen it, and at last I got a look at what I was supposed to approve for shipment. An operator was put at my disposal and was going to run the machine for me. I let him start the machine, and I suddenly recalled the way I felt when the NRC inspectors were checking my Bundle Assembly Area. They did not say much but, boy, did they take notes. The less I said at de Vlieg, the smaller the chance that they would realize that I was sent to do a job I was not sure I was capable of doing. The operator worked the various functions with the machine, and I took notes.

At the end of the day, the engineering manager asked me what I wanted them to do the next day. I told them that I was interested in how the machine would perform if I were to take the temperatures of the two main bearings of the main spindle. "I would appreciate it if you would place two thermocouples at these two places and provide two digital temperature meters so that I can take some readings." They looked somewhat puzzled, but agreed to have the setup ready for me the next morning at 8 o'clock.

The next morning, I recorded the starting temperature before the machine started to run and decided arbitrarily to take readings every ten minutes. As could be expected, the temperature increased and, after about an hour, the rear bearing attained a steady temperature, but the front bearing temperature continued to rise a few degrees for every time interval. Nobody was alarmed; however, this went on for over an hour-and-a-half. By then, everybody in the plant was worrying, walking around the machine, and talking to each other with comments like, "Do this," and "Has so-and-so corrected this earlier deviation?" All along I was taking notes and recording readings. By not saying anything but just listening, I overheard a number of points that I would check on later in the day. Finally, someone noticed that an external cooling machine, which was supposed to supply cooling water to the front bearing, was malfunctioning. The result was that the front bearing temperature was continuing to increase. (In the Wilmington plant I would just hook up the cooling loop to the factory cooling water system and not need a special cooling unit).

Everyone was smiling and relieved that there was not a major problem with the machine. I calmly went to work on checking the other features of the machine. I gave the electrical wiring and components a thorough check, which was right down my alley. During my wrap-up meeting, I arranged the shipping to Wilmington and flew home that night. Once back at my desk, I called Earl in Schenectady and told him what had happened. I wrote my report with computer-generated graphs of the temperature excursion, and I became the plant's equipment runoff specialist.

As I went along in the job, I became a great deal better prepared because I was writing the specs; hence, I knew what was specified, and I was steadily learning more about the numerically-controlled machining capabilities. In hindsight, the inspectors of the NRC had taught me a tactic of which I was not aware at the moment, but which had gotten me out of that very sticky situation many years later.

The tolerances with which aircraft engine parts are manufactured are very tight. We were measuring dimensions plus or minus one-half-a-tenth-of-a-thousandth of an inch. Considering that a human hair on the average is .003 inch, we were splitting that hair sixty times! A little trick we would play on guests when we would take them on a plant tour was to ask one person to help me. Someone would volunteer, and I would ask the person to look at his or her left or right thumbnail, study it very closely, and remind me of that fact at the end of the tour. The tour would last about forty-five minutes, after which we would go back to the conference room, have cookies and Coca-Cola, and answer any questions that our guests would have.

This is when my "assistant" would say, "What about my right thumbnail?"

I'd reply, "Look at it closely again and you will notice that it has grown an amount that is equal to the amount of tolerance to which we work here."

I would end with telling people that General Electric did not want to have any of their engines fail, because good engines would need spare parts at a later date and the sale of those spare parts would keep the company in the profit margin.

✳   ✳   ✳   ✳

By some coincidence, the Wilmington City Council had decided to have a foreign city as its "Sister City," and they had chosen Doncaster, England. That was interesting because that was where, in 1945, my group of Rotterdam boys arrived before going to the Woodlands camp. Around 1992, the Wilmington City Council invited the Doncaster Town Council to visit Wilmington. I decided to go to one of the high schools, where the visitors were meeting after a tour of the school.

When the meeting broke up, I singled out one gentleman and said, "I hope that we in Wilmington are as hospitable to your group as your town and people were to my friends and me in 1945. We were your guests for two months, recovering our health after the German occupation of Holland." With those words, I showed him the newspaper photo of me holding a small suitcase on my head as we arrived in Doncaster. Needless to say, the Doncaster delegates were very pleased to have me contact them.

About a year later, the group returned to Wilmington as guests during the annual Azalea Festival. I was contacted by John Chapman, the councilman to whom I had shown my paper clipping from 1945. After the first visit to Wilmington, when he got back home to Doncaster, he had looked up the specific newspaper. He brought me a printout of the microfiche that had the article that had accompanied the picture. Unbelievable as it may sound, there were my words (somewhat mis-translated) printed in the paper, complaining about the heat and refusing to take off my sweater. I could not read English in 1945, so I did not know then what was printed with the photograph about us, but was now reading it for the first time (see pages 264–5). The Doncaster delegation invited Trudy and me to become part of the tour, and we were treated by the Wilmington City Council as if we were part of the group.

✳   ✳   ✳   ✳

Since I had been elected chairman of the Wilmington Tarheel Chapter of the Elfun Society, I had gone to two national meetings. I had met Bill Zint, a retired GE engineer from Mebane, North Carolina, who was the Elfun board member representing senior Elfuns. Retired GE employees who were members of the Elfun Society would become Senior Elfuns and continue to do volunteer work in the community in which they lived. Their representative served on the administrative committee that met in Fairfield six or so times each year.

The Elfun Society organization was divided into several regions or territories that were represented by Territorial Administrators. They would report to the office in Fairfield and relay information to the chapters. The position of Territorial Administrator rotated through the area chapters with a term of two years. The Wilmington Tarheel Chapter was part of the territory that included all the chapters in North and South Carolina. The administrator for our territory had just been elected. He was from the Palmetto Chapter at the plant in Florence, South Carolina, where GE manufactured super-cooled magnets for the GE CT scanners. Five months after the person accepted the job as Territorial Administrator, he resigned from GE and the position was open.

Who would be asked to fill the unexpired term? During a meeting in Fairfield, Bill Zint suggested that Robert van Luyn would be the right person for the job. I received the call and was asked if I was interested. I replied, "Yes, I surely am interested if my boss, Bob Workman, will allow me to do the work in addition to my regular job!"

I went to Bob; he thought that it was an honor that I had been asked and said that I should accept the job. I knew that the time remaining on the term was eighteen months and that the Tarheel Chapter, in its turn, would be asked to elect the next Territorial Administrator. If I was successful in the remaining eighteen months of my term and did a good job, there was no telling if I might possibly get my own term for two more years. After I completed the eighteen months, I decided to run for secretary of the International Elfun Society, which then would also pretty well cement my reappointment to the Elfun Board as the Tarheel Chapter's Territorial from *The Doncaster Chronicle*

From the Horrors of Belsen to Doncaster

Dutch visitors from Southern Holland and the Rotterdam areas, some of whom only escaped the horrors of the Belsen gas chambers by a matter of minutes, arrived in Doncaster by special train from London last Sunday, accompanied by doctors, supervisors, and priests.

The party, numbering 147, mainly consisted of children from six to 14 years of age. They are billeted in the mining trainees' hostels at Woodlands and Warms-worth, where they will remain for about two months before taking up private billets.

They are receiving medical attention under the supervision of Dr. Van der Wilk, chief Medical Officer to the Dutch Government's committee who travelled with the party.

Most of them are suffering from malnutrition, and their digestive systems have to be built up afresh. They are on a simple scientific diet, the recipes for the dishes being prepared by Mr. H.S. Davies, the area superintendent for the hostels.

"They are overjoyed by their reception and cannot understand all this kindness," said Mr. Davies. "Many of them have cried with joy."

The Rev. M.H.F. Witteveen, the Protestant pastor at the Woodlands hostel, said, "We cannot thank the English people too much. We love the English as much as we hate the Germans. I think it is a great thing that after all the children have been through they can still love people and respect something which is their own. I have just seen a small boy," he went on, "walking about in the broiling hot sun dressed in a thick woollen pullover and complaining of the heat. Growing tired of his complaints I asked him why

Thursday August 2, 1945
Dutch Children Cry for Joy

he did not take off his pullover. He plucked at it fondly and said, 'Oh I can't take this off. The English have given it to me. I want to look beautiful.'"

On Monday most of the children received new clothing. All of them let the supply room smiling, with looks of wonderment in their eyes. Some, overcome by emotion, shed tears.

Mr. A. F. Boeft, the Dutch principal of the hostel, told of the Belsen horrors. "Some of the children have been in Belsen," he said. "Had the Russians been an hour later in liberating them those children would not be here. Some are Jews and would have been in the gas chambers. People who were taken to the chambers were given a piece of soap and a towel and led off in a line, and nothing more was heard of them. Shortly before my liberation, the Germans telephoned my home and told me

to report to their headquarters. I knew what that meant. That was the German way of working. I would report and nothing more would be heard of me, so I escaped and hid in a nearby farm."

After being issued with their clothing, among which were two pairs of boots or shoes, the children took them to their dormitories, where some of the girls were trying them on delightedly. A small girl had photographs of her parents pinned above her bed.

The scene at the Woodlands hostel is a busy one. Dutch nurses walk along the broad white drive to and from the sick bay, followed by strings of children, some of whom have curly fair hair in contrast to the close-cropped, almost naked heads of others. Blood tests are taken and innoculations done. The children's education is to be continued under Dutch authorities.

Administrator. After that, I would have one more year on the committee, so I started letting some selected people know that I was interested in running for Vice-President. Thus I was planning, but a few things had to happen to have it all come to fruition.

* * * *

During the spring of my year as secretary, the then-president of the Elfun Society, Bob Clark from Louisville, Kentucky, looked across the meeting room in Fairfield and said, "Bob, would you take on this project of an affinity credit card, set up some rules, and see what you can do with it? It probably won't amount to anything, but look at it if you would." Of course, I accepted, not really knowing what was involved. The Elfun Society would get half of one percent of all charges put on the affinity credit card by the Elfun members. The committee members received a card, and we started using it. No one on the committee gave it any thought that 35,000 Elfun members were going to be offered a Gold Elfun Credit Card and that this could really amount to some serious benefits.

In June, Bob Clark called me from LaGuardia Airport on his way back to Louisville and, with a bit of urgency in his voice, said, "Bob, this credit card thing is taking off, and we have already received more than twenty thousand dollars. Get a few people together and go to Fairfield and make up your rules as to how we are going to distribute the money." I quickly scheduled a meeting for the following day and asked Jim Grimes, from the Salem, Virginia, plant, to meet me at LaGuardia, and we drove to Fairfield.

We met with Phyllis McGrath, the administrator of the GE Fund controlling all of the millions of dollars that GE gives to educational and other benevolent organizations, and Dave Warshaw, who at that time was working for Joyce Hergenhan, Vice President, reporting to Jack Welch. We made the rules about how the chapters could get "Sharing the Gold" money. The basic way for an Elfun chapter to receive an award was as follows: the chapter had to come up with the project and supply the manpower, and the "Sharing the Gold" committee would supply the money.

At the Fall Meeting in Stanford, Connecticut, I was given a slot in the evening program and, after dinner, I unveiled the "Sharing the Gold" program to all the Elfun Chapter Chairmen and Vice-Chairmen from the U.S., Canada, Japan, and the UK. We had about fifty-three chapters at that time. This was the introduction of a new program, and at that moment we had more than $70,000. I announced that each chapter chairman could submit a project the following day to our committee of three; if we approved the project, he would go home with a $1,000 check for their chapter project.

Of course, each chapter came up with a project, and one can only imagine who was the most-liked and popular guy at the meeting! I had the pleasure of calling each chairman to the front of the meeting and giving him a check for $1000 — some secretary! When the fiscal year, which ran from July 1 until June 30, ended, it just so happened that I was elected Vice-President of the Global Elfun Society. At that time, we had about 35,000 regular members and about 17,000 senior members.

* * * *

During these years, Nancy was studying hard at Furman, but also enjoying the many benefits of college life. She was selected to join a sorority, which meant a lot to her, and she enjoyed the friendships and activities it offered. She also joined a Bible study group and volunteered for several university-sponsored service organizations. She put her whole heart into everything she did.

Nancy's visits back home were full of stories of professors, friends, and the full gamut of college life. We were able to visit her at Furman at various times, and Mama Florrid enjoyed going with us to see Nancy and Furman's beautiful campus on the outskirts of Greenville, South Carolina.

Between her sophomore and junior years, Nancy had a summer internship with the District Attorney's office in Marietta, Georgia, near Atlanta. (This was made especially interesting by the fact that the District Attorney had prosecuted a case that had been featured in a television motion picture that we had all seen.) Nancy did various jobs in the office and got a look at the day-to-day operations of this aspect of law enforcement.

When we visited Nancy in Marietta, she surprised us with tickets for a stage show at Atlanta's Fox Theater featuring Lewis Grizzard, humor columnist with the *Atlanta Journal-Constitution* newspaper and one of Trudy's favorite writers. The three of us had a great time in Atlanta.

Nancy's future plans included the possibility of teaching political science, but tended more and more to the study of law. Between her junior and senior years, her interest received a boost from an internship, along with fellow students, in Washington, D.C., with the public defender's office. Some of her experiences were with juvenile offenders but, although this revealed a very raw side of life, none of it dampened her enthusiasm.

When Nancy was at home at the beginning of her senior year, she approached me with a request. She said she had enough credits to graduate from Furman early, or she could wait until spring to graduate and take advantage of an opportunity for a study trip abroad. I knew right away which choice she favored! The study abroad, led by two Furman professors, included "The Travels of Paul," in Italy and Greece, and "The Politics of East Africa," in Kenya and Tanzania.

After much discussion about what was involved in such a trip, including the considerable expense, I agreed. That was far from the case with Trudy, especially when she found out what immunizations Nancy would need before taking the trip. Malaria and cholera were not even the most serious diseases for which vaccinations would be required! Trudy finally acquiesced, and set up appointments with the health department to get the shots Nancy needed.

Nancy learned a lot during the study trip, not least of which was the reinforcement of her realization that the United States was a country with so many more advantages than other nations. She was touched by the people she met in Kenya and Tanzania and their many acute personal needs. She truly came home with a different outlook on life.

After visiting and applying to several law schools, Nancy chose the University of Richmond's T.C. Williams School of Law. "See, Dad, I knew what I was planning to do!" was Nancy's comment to me when she received her acceptance letter. Her choice of a major had been justified!

Nancy graduated from Furman University in 1992, with good grades and a long list of student and community activities on her resumé. When Trudy, Mama Florrid, and I attended her graduation, we were looking forward to having her home for the summer. Nancy took a summer job and, of course, the prospect of law school loomed large in all our plans.

During that summer, Nancy met Bruce Oglesby, and they started to date. Born in Texas, Bruce had moved to Wilmington from Panama City, Florida, where he had worked in the resort industry. He and Nancy shared many common interests, especially their love for the beach.

26

Wrapping It Up

There was a strong effort coming from headquarters pushing the idea that the Aircraft Engines Division in Wilmington had to start its own environmental effort, rather than depending on the Nuclear Division's staff. My boss asked me if I was interested in filling the need and, since I was starting to look for the day that I would retire, I thought, "I could learn all there is to learn in this field and, then, when I retire, I could become a consultant." I was sent to all sorts of courses so that I could be the Wilmington trainer and make everyone aware of the importance of the strict regulations that were promulgated almost daily. The federal government sent out reams of paper in which the laws were spelled out. If there had ever been a moment in my life when I thought I would seriously take up the official at my naturalization ceremony on her expectation that someday I would be a congressman, it left me after I read all these laws. Congress was writing these laws, and I had a devil of a time keeping up with the changes.

I attended a number of large conferences dedicated to the field of environmental protection, along with engineers from all over the U.S. and Canada. We were invited to bring our spouses with us and, while we were attending long lectures from eight in the morning until five in the afternoon, our wives would be relaxing or shopping. During the lectures, we were given cautionary instructions of how certain things had to be done and the ramifications that would follow if not followed to the letter. At night, fantastic dinners were given, along with lots of entertainment. The next day, it would be back to the grindstone. I found all of this information very interesting. Ninety-nine percent of the lecturers were lawyers and, as could be expected, were quite knowledgeable about the hundreds of environmental laws.

One engineer from the audience asked, "Will the General Electric Company defend me, since I am the environmental engineer in charge of enforcing rules in my plant, if someone, during the graveyard shift, illegally dumps a five-gallon can of oil into a storm drain?"

The lawyer stood on the stage and thought for perhaps twenty seconds, which seemed to last several minutes, before he answered, "The General Electric Company *may* not defend you!"

That answer did it for me. I told Trudy I was going to get out of this line of business. It was entirely too risky.

✳   ✳   ✳   ✳

Nancy's first year in law school was, as traditionally predicted, a tough one, but she and Bruce continued to date, one or the other driving the four hours between Richmond and Wilmington. We were fascinated by her recounting of some of the complicated cases she was studying. When Trudy and I visited in Richmond, we enjoyed meeting her law school friends and joining them at a popular local restaurant, Potter's Pub.

In the spring of 1993, Elfun Society elections were held, and the most unbelievable thing happened — I was elected president of the organization! I received a call from Fairfield asking if I could be in Fairfield because CEO Jack Welch

271

wanted to have lunch with me. Of course, there was a hole in my schedule! I left Sunday night so that Ray Mathieu, our Elfun Society Executive Secretary, could meet with me and inform me of the latest happenings. I spent all that Monday listening to facts and reading material that would prepare me for the meeting with General Electric's CEO. I stayed at the guest house, which is a marvelous hotel on the corporate headquarters' grounds but, because of all the excitement, I could not fall asleep that night. At four in the morning, I finally dozed off, only to have the alarm go off at six o'clock. Needless to say, I was a little punchy.

Again, I had lots of paperwork to read and, during the middle of the morning, I started to feel sleepy. "Holy mackerel, that's all I need! Fall asleep at lunch!" That was just one more thing to worry about. Things went well during the luncheon, and my assessment of Jack from earlier meetings was correct — he was direct, had penetrating eyes, and could see through a situation instantly. I could not help but think how far I had gotten since the boat had moored in Hoboken, thirty-six years earlier. Jack asked me what was going to be done with my regular job while I was president. I told him that I could handle both, which seemed to meet with his approval.

Back in Wilmington, I was planning what I was going to do to smooth the workings of the international organization. The other officers made up a terrific staff to help me. Ray Mathieu, the Executive Secretary of the Elfun Society and editor of *Under The Elm*, held it all together nicely. I traveled a lot and went to England, Puerto Rico, Mexico, and many places in the U.S., representing the Elfun Society.

✽   ✽   ✽   ✽

Over a period of several years, Trudy and I had decided that we would leave Wilmington after I retired; she referred to the move as an attempt to get away from the "Three H's:" heat, humidity, and hurricanes. But where did we want to move? We had often gone back to Blacksburg for German Club events, class reunions, and football games. The German Club of Virginia Tech was thriving, and we were surprised to learn that a number of classmates had retired and returned to Blacksburg. I knew what I would like, but I thought that it should be Trudy who would make the choice. I asked her where she would like to go. Her answer came without hesitation, "Atlanta. That is, if it were still like I knew it when I grew up there." Well, of course, Atlanta had changed, and Trudy did not think that it had changed for the better. Therefore, she said, "Let's see if we can find a place in Blacksburg."

Casey Jones, my VPI classmate, has his veterinary practice in Blacksburg, and had been helping look for a place. For five years, Casey had sent information and had taken videos of possible pieces of property; but, when we went to look, nothing, for one reason or another, seemed to fit or meet our expectations.

One weekend we were in Blacksburg visiting and had, again, been unsuccessful in finding something. I was beginning to get frustrated with it all and, just when I was ready to forget about the idea of finding a place in Blacksburg, Trudy calmly said, "Let's look in the local newspaper." Five minutes later, she found the "For Sale by Owner" section of the classifieds. There we found exactly what we were looking for. We had found the spot Casey and I had been trying to find for the past five years.

Subsequently, we bought the property, which turned out to be 7.98 acres large. It was at the edge of Blacksburg, with all the benefits the town offered, yet we still had that feeling of being way out in the country. Trudy and I talked with "my American brother," Carlton Abbott, an outstanding and well-respected architect in Virginia for many years, and we told him that we wanted the outside of the house to look like a farmhouse in Holland. Carlton was reluctant because his office was so busy with the design of many projects, among which would probably be the redesign of the Jamestown

Park. (The National Park Service was getting plans together for the 400th anniversary of the three ships that landed in Virginia and established Jamestown.) After going through some Dutch books that I had provided him, Carlton made the concept design, which he then passed on to John Dreiling. John was an architect who had worked for Carlton but had since started his own business in Roanoke, with his wife Helene.

* * * *

On March 31, 1995, I closed my desk for the last time at GE, and left with five big boxes of paperwork that I thought I could not live without. I had completed thirty-two years of a wonderful career with the General Electric Company, the greatest company in the world. In April I was elected to serve as Vice-President Seniors in the Elfun Society, and I looked forward to continuing that enjoyable association with other GE employees and retirees.

Mama Florrid, who had been living with us for seven years, began having serious health problems that Trudy, even with Cora's help, could not handle on a long-term basis, so we moved her to a retirement and health care center. Cora continued to help by visiting her one day a week, allowing Trudy to continue her volunteer work at the library. Fortunately, there was a piano in the dining room at the center, so Cora could continue to play for Mama Florrid's enjoyment.

That summer, Nancy took advantage of another opportunity to study abroad and, with several of her fellow law students, spent a summer session at Cambridge University near London, England. Since there were no Friday classes, Nancy and her friends spent weekends traveling and taking advantage of cheap student airline tickets to fly to Scotland, Ireland, and Spain. We were concerned when she said they were going to Pamplona for the running of the bulls, but she assured us that she would find a safe vantage point. She was never fainthearted!

Retirement Dinner
at GE Corporate Headquarters in Fairfield, Connecticut.
(The guys made me eat a tulip bulb,
which I roasted over a candle.)

I used some frequent flyer miles to fly Trudy to England to meet Nancy after her courses were finished. Trudy was entranced with Cambridge, and she and Nancy took in shows and did sightseeing in London before flying home together. My frequent flyer miles entitled them to fly business class, and they were appropriately spoiled! Meanwhile, Bruce had wired flowers to Nancy at Cambridge, and the seriousness of their courtship was confirmed. Nancy returned to Richmond for her final year of law school.

275

Our excitement over planning the building of a house in Blacksburg had to be put on the "back burner" when something unexpected happened. Trudy and I met Carlton Abbott in Blacksburg so that he could "walk" the property with us to find the best orientation for placing the house. While there, I fell down a slippery embankment and broke my left ankle in four places. We returned to Wilmington for surgery, followed by twelve weeks of recuperation. While Trudy continued to see her mother every day at the nursing home, I was forced to spend those weeks in my easy chair. The O.J. Simpson trial and the programs on the History Channel kept me occupied. I was not bored, but we did miss all the opportunities to go to Blacksburg to continue our building plans. (And we missed all the football games that fall!)

✳ ✳ ✳ ✳

Christmas of 1995 was very different for our family. Mama Florrid came home from the nursing home to spend Christmas Eve and Christmas Day with us, and Bruce was a frequent guest while Nancy was home from law school. Bruce and Mama Florrid "hit it off" and she enjoyed his attention and kindness to her. To top off the season, Nancy and Bruce became engaged near the end of the year.

Even though my ankle had healed completely, we decided to put the house in Blacksburg on hold for two reasons. Our Dutch friends, Dick and Aja de Boer, had planned to come to see us about the same time that I broke my ankle, so we had postponed their trip until the spring of 1996. Even more important was the fact that Nancy wanted to plan the wedding for one week after her graduation from law school! Talk about a busy time — retirement was far from restful!

On May 11, Nancy graduated from T.C. Williams School of Law and, on May 18, she and Bruce Oglesby were married at Wilmington's First Presbyterian Church. It seemed to be almost too much of a good thing to celebrate all these important events in such a short span of time; however, Nancy had every detail carefully worked out so that her aunt and uncle could come from Holland for both her graduation and her wedding. So Thea and Gerard came, took part in the festivities, and enjoyed meeting Mama Florrid and Bruce's family. They were especially glad to renew their acquaintance with the Brons and the Groots, whom they had met on previous trips. These close friends, who had emigrated from Holland after the war, still spoke Dutch, which made Thea and Gerard's visit even more enjoyable.

The wedding party consisted of Nancy's and Bruce's good friends, as well as Bruce's family. The Brons' son, Johnny, was a soloist, and our Dutch friends from Castle Hayne were among the wedding guests. It was very much like a reunion because, besides Thea and Gerard and Bruce's family and friends from Florida, the wedding guests included Trudy's cousins from both sides of her family, her two close high school friends from Atlanta, and our group of fellow VPI classmates and German Club buddies. Mama Florrid especially enjoyed seeing all the family members and having Cora Leonard as a fellow guest.

To add to all the excitement of graduation and the wedding, Bruce had decided to move to Richmond and become the owner of the law students' favorite hangout, Potter's Pub, whose owners were retiring. His prior experience in the resort business in Panama City gave him confidence in making it a success. That July, Nancy took the bar exam and, in October, received the good news that she had passed it on her first attempt!

Meanwhile, we had resumed planning the house in Blacksburg; the plans that John Dreiling had completed eventually allowed us to start the actual building on January 2, 1997. We were pleased that we would be moving closer to Richmond, where Nancy and Bruce were living.

✳   ✳   ✳   ✳

The Elfun Society sent me to England again, and I was there for a meeting for about a week. While there, I had a day off in the middle of the meeting, so I decided to go to Retford, in Nottinghamshire, to see if I could find any of my friends from 1945. Before leaving Blacksburg for London, I had gone on the Web and had tried to contact someone who was working at the Retford newspaper, not realizing that Retford did not have a newspaper. The computer reply referred to a newspaper in Worksop, Nottinghamshire. I remembered that town, so I contacted the paper through the Web and got a response from the Deputy Editor of the paper, Stephen Booth. I told Stephen that I was one of the Dutch refugees who had stayed in Retford, and that I wanted to meet some of my former friends while I was in England. Stephen e-mailed me back and told me that he was responsible for a weekly supplement paper for Retford and would be glad to put in a request for me to get in touch with Kenneth Stimson and John Cartwright.

Stephen and I zeroed in on the day when I could take the three-hour train ride from London's King's Cross Station to Retford. Stephen e-mailed me back and informed me that the Brits, too, had made progress, and the train ride would now only take an hour and forty minutes. I invited Stephen to let me take him to lunch when I came to Retford. Stephen thanked me, but could not take me up on the invitation because he had a speaking engagement about a novel he had just written and, as he said, "It seems to have taken off."

I went to Retford, walked around, and tried to get my bearings so I could recall all the places that I had visited. I went to the house of Mr. and Mrs. Jessie Bingham at 66 Spital Hill and stood in front of the house reminiscing.

Two ladies who appeared to be of my age walked by, and I approached them.

"Excuse me, madam, I know that you are not old enough to remember this, but I am one of the Dutch refugee children who spent two months at Mr. and Mrs. Bingham's. I wonder if any of my friends are still living in Retford?"

Both ladies loved what I asked. They did remember, and we started to recall names.

"Amy Smith, you ask? Well, she still lives in her house right there across the street."

I was told that Amy's married name was Osborn and that she had become a widow less than a year before. I walked over to Amy's house, and when I rang the bell, Amy looked through the window and asked, "Yes, can I help you?"

I said, "Amy Smith, do you remember Robert van Luijn, who lived with Mrs. Bingham?"

"Get in here!" was her response. I went in, and we talked for a few hours and went back over all the many things we had done. Afterwards, we went to the local pub where Mr. Bingham had done a little waitering in the evenings after he had had supper, and we recalled more interesting moments from long ago.

On the way back to the Retford railroad station, I picked up the weekly newspaper, and right there was a notice in which I asked for people to contact me if they remembered me. Stephen Booth had gotten my request in the paper, but it was too late for any further contacts at this time.

As I got back to the States, I started to get responses from England and, before I knew it, I was writing to five former friends. I kept in touch with Stephen Booth and, indeed, his novel had taken off. It was called *Black Dog* and was the beginning of a very successful career in writing. Soon after *Black Dog* was published in England, it was published in the U.S., and Stephen told me that he was invited to a big conference in Washington. D.C. I invited him to stay with us in Blacksburg for a few days, and I arranged a few book-signing sessions for him in Virginia. I showed him some various places of interest in Virginia, such as Monticello in Charlottesville, and took him to Richmond for a couple of days, where he had a book signing. On the way back to Dulles airport, we stopped at Luray Caverns, and I believe that I gave him just a little taste of Virginia.

Since the initial contact was made with my friends in Retford, Nottinghamshire, Trudy and I have since visited

The van Luyn/Oglesby family:
Berkeley with Bruce and Mackenzie with Nancy,
grandparents Trudy and Dutch in the background.

them twice, and some have reciprocated by visiting us here in Blacksburg, Virginia. To my surprise, all of my childhood friends were now white-haired! (Then again, so am I.)

* * * *

After passing the bar exam in 1996, Nancy had her own law practice for a few months. Then an opportunity to become an Assistant Commonwealth's Attorney in Chesterfield County, Virginia, presented itself and, from sixty-four applicants, Nancy was chosen for the job! After gaining valuable experience in that office and establishing herself as a respected prosecutor, she is now Deputy Commonwealth's Attorney in Goochland County, in the Richmond Metro area.

In August 1997, we moved to our new home in Blacksburg and moved Mama Florrid to Heritage Hall Nursing

Home near us. When she passed away in 1999, Trudy and I realized that, like many of our age group, we were now the "older generation," and it is a strange feeling to be without parents.

To our delight, since we moved to Blacksburg in 1997, a number of other classmates and German Club members have moved back to the Blacksburg area, adding to the camaraderie of our group.

Life in Blacksburg has been wonderful for Trudy and me. We have our close group of friends from college days, and have made friends at church and in the community. We both frequently say that we made the right decision to move here. What really makes it fantastic is that we have two beautiful, smart, sweet granddaughters: Mackenzie, who was born in 1999, and Berkeley, who was born nineteen months later in 2000. We're fortunate that Richmond is only three-and-a-half hours away.

Retirement has been just fantastic! Every day, I literally have to tell myself that it was not a dream and that this really is my wonderful life. I enjoy working in my woodworking shop and playing electrician for my friends if they have a little task along those lines. Trudy and I have been blessed with good health and have done a good bit of traveling, although that was not our initial plan, since I had a healthy dose of traveling while working. Nowadays, however, we have the time to take in the details of the places we visit.

27

Conclusion

Over the years, I have often thought how it could have been possible to have so many things fall into place. One could say, "Well, you worked hard for it." However, I don't feel like I've worked any harder than anyone else with whom I associated. Was it luck? Being in the right place at the right time? Or any of the other clichés that could probably apply?

I think it was America and the wonderful spirit of its people that made it all possible. I have thought up a story over the years that may illustrate, in my opinion and experience, the differing mentalities of the Dutch and the American people. Picture a young man pushing a cart up a slight incline in the winter, with a small amount of ice in spots on the road. There is a house on the side of the road, and people are watching from behind the curtains. In Holland, the young man slips and falls, the Dutch people see it happen, but the man gets up and tries again. He falls again, and now, the people behind the curtains start to laugh. Seeing him fall for a third time, they decide that he is an idiot because he doesn't know that ice is slick. However, take the same situation, only this time in the United States. The second time the man falls, Americans say, "Lord, he is determined." After the third time, they look at each other and say, "Let's give him a hand." And they do!

One time, I heard the young son of a minister say, "Coincidences are when God creates a miracle and wants to be anonymous." I surely have been given more than a fair share of coincidences in my life. To America, the people in this book, and the hundreds of people I neglected to mention, I owe you an unfathomable debt. Thank you.

28

Epilogue

I finished writing this book in the middle of January 2007. It was then that Trudy took up the unenviable task of spotting the grammatical mistakes and pointing them out to me.

On January 28, we got a call from Thea's neighbors, the Zonnevelds, who told us that Thea had suffered a massive stroke and was in the hospital in Amsterdam. The doctors did not think that Thea would survive more than twenty-four hours. I called the doctor in charge and was referred to the nurse on duty, who informed me that everything was being done to make Thea comfortable, but that the end was near. As predicted, we received a call the next day, telling us that Thea had passed away peacefully, never having regained consciousness.

The neighbors, Heidi and René Zonneveld, were as good to Thea and Gerard as they are to their own parents. The Zonnevelds offered to assist us in taking care of the funeral arrangements and suggested that we come to Holland later that week. After the service, the mammoth task was ahead of us to get all of Thea's belongings in order. To our consternation, there were boxes and boxes of paperwork that we had to examine individually to be certain that we would not throw away a needed insurance policy or something similar. Luckily, Trudy had learned Dutch well enough to be able to go through the paperwork with me, which made the effort a great deal easier.

After all was done, Trudy and I selected some items as keepsakes, packed them in our suitcases, and returned to Blacksburg. Some weeks later, I started going through some photograph albums that we had brought back and, among several, there was one that was an early album of Thea's, from when she was a teenager. To my utter surprise, there was a picture with the caption, *"Zijn eerste stap in't zand"* ("His first step in the sand"). Having been almost fifty years in America, I could not remember if I had ever seen the photo of me at the beach but, if I had, it had to have been more than fifty years back. Here was visible confirmation of my memory: the photo showed me walking in beach sand.

From Thea's album: "Zijn eerste stap in't zand"
"His first step in the sand."

April 23, 2007, was the 50th anniversary of my coming to America, and we figured it was a milestone that should be celebrated. For months, Trudy and I had planned what we were going to do. We wanted to have the party at the German Club Manor, so to fit into its schedule, we picked Thursday, May 3, as the date. Invitations were sent to eighty-eight friends and relatives, of whom sixty-five were able to come to the Blacksburg party. Most of them had helped me through my early years in America. I jokingly thanked them for not having me deported! Gale Abbott Roberts represented the Abbott family. During the weekend she handed me a folder. She told me that she had gone through some old papers after Mamma Abbott had died and had discovered the letters I had written to the Abbotts while I was a student at VPI. Gale was as surprised as I was that Mamma Abbott had saved my letters. After everyone had left, I decided to go through the folder and read the letters. I have decided to include a couple, unedited, in this book.

Blacksburg November 3, 1958

My Dear Mamma and Pappa Abbott and Gale

*Many thanks for your nice letter which I re-
ceived last week, it was so good to hear from you
all again. My grades are ok I got an average in
Algebra of 93, English 76, Introduction Engineering 84, Drawing 80 But I got not such nice grades
in the two hard courses, Chemistry D and Western
Civilization a D, no excuse the subjects are hard but
I got a good chance to make up for it I will try
hard.*

*The blue letter is my third theme, this is a
rough copy of my original for which I had a B.
Last week the first time I got a B for a theme I am
so glad with it and can't believe it.*

*As you know I am an official member of the
famous !! VPI Glee Club, we have meetings twice a
week in the afternoon and are working for December because we are going to sing the Messiah with
the Girls Choir from Radford, I enjoy it so much
and have made there, I mean in our Glee Club, a
lot of friends. I'd love to come home for a week-*

end but it is a drive of about 7 hours and I am not able to leave before 12 o'clock in the Saterday afternoon, I only have one class Saterday but it is in Chemistry and I don't want to miss any of that course, and at the other hand I won't work when I am in Yorktown than I say the heck with the books, now don't misunderstand me I am not constant with my nose in the books but at least I do something. I am counting the days for thanksgiving and than one more week and the quarter exams starts.

Mrs Abbott I am, honest I hate too but I have too, a little mad with you; we did not make a deal that you would fix my camera anyhow thank you very much for it. I don't think that it was necessary to send it up.

And now a question, does Gale knows my weak spots?? I ask that because lately I use her present from Holland quiet frequent, I mean the ash-tray it started with some packs given as a sample well I could not throw the cigarettes away so I smoked them and so every now and than I buy a pack.

Can you please send Busters address because I want to drop him a line and don't know his address.

Well this is all for now till you write again thanks for the letter I am so greateful to have such good friends as you all be good and God Bless you

Love

Bob

✳ ✳ ✳ ✳

The following is my third theme, written during the fall quarter of my freshman year at VPI. I copied it in a letter to the Abbotts on the thin blue paper that, at that time, was sold as air-mail stationery. I used that type of paper to send letters to Holland via air mail. I copied the theme on "air-mail paper" so that the letter would not cost me an extra stamp of four cents to send.

Beautiful Holland

Early in the morning, just after sunrise, a market gardner pushes his boat through a circular canal. The only sound which disturbs this peaceful morning are the splashes of the pushing pole in the water and the click clack of hs wooden shoes as he walks back and forth over the boat.

The landscape, which moves slowly by as he pushes his boat, is entirely different on the right side than it is on the left. On his right can be seen a straight green line of grass which borders a dike. This dike protects the land — which is called the polder — on the left side of the canal. The polder

289

looks like a painter's pallette, with colors ranging from the fresh green of the grass to the deep, dark black of the fertile soil. Proud turning windmills dot the landscape at regular intervals along the canal. These windmills are a necessity in Holland, for they pump the water out of the circular canal, over the dike.

The water in the circular canal is drain water out of many ditches in the polder. There is no need for fences because the ditches devide the property of each gardener as well as drain the land.

Looking at the products piled high on his boat, the market gardner thinks of how much was necessary to obtain this amount of vegetables. He is confident that the price at the market will be good for he knows that he is early in the season with his products and the chance that too many other gardeners are at the market is not too great.

About two miles ahead he sees a green steeple of the church and knows that it is in the little town where the market is. The church steeple is plated with bronze and through the years the salty western sea winds have changed its dark brassy color into a mild green.

Although he has made the trip over and over again, the gardener absorbs the beauty of the country on each trip; a beauty which is unique and has his own personality. For this is his country; a country which had made itself independent by the efforts of its hard working people through the years.

The market gardener is born and raised as a farmer and knows no other life, and after he has taught his sons how to work the soil, they will take his place when he dies. There is no question of seeking a different means of livelihood, which may lead to a better way of living for his sons, for it is the custom that has been this way down through the years. But, I am proud of Holland and although the people there are not as open as the Americans I will never forget it.

✳   ✳   ✳   ✳

Blacksburg May 28, 1959

My dear Mamma and Pappa Abbott and Gale

I am sorry that I have waited so long with thanking you for writing me and giving me the information about the common glory job. I have accepted the job and will start there June 23.

Life realy is getting busy the last days here; coming Tuesday the exams will start and I will have four exams of which two are three and two are a two hour exams. I am, however, very lucky because I will have one every day.

I will be home Sunday afternoon or night on June 7. And honest I am looking forward for it. June the 6th Lester will marry and he has asked me if I want to be an usher. I realy am glad with it because he has, just as I have many friends here on campus and I considder it as an honor that he ask me for it.

I have had a nice experience again which shows why America is such a great country and that it is such because of its people.. Last week my math prof said, "Mr van Luijn where are you from?" I first made him think I was an American by saying "From Yorktown, sir." But he did not believe that 'cause he said that he recognized an accent. Well I told him that I was from Holland and as you can understand he asked some more questions. He said " You will come back for summerschool, don't you?" I told him that I had to work to make it possible to come back in September. Next day after class he told me to come to his office. I went and let me tell you that I had the hardest time refusing money from him. Because he said, "You can't tell me that you don't need any, I know it 'cause I've been a student myself." I only was able to leave his office after I had prommised that if I were in trouble, I would not hesitate letting him know. I won't do it but I just want to show you all how wonderful all the people here in the States are. Just immagine a prof in Holland, Boy, he would never do a thing like this.

I will end this letter with a few lines out of the song which I love so much

This is my country,
Land of my choice....

Love + see you all soon
Bob

Reading this, forty-eight years later, reinforces my conviction that I should continue to learn, speak, and write the English language better. Reading George Will's highbrow use of the English language, in his regular columns of the daily newspaper, continues to challenge my knowledge and comprehension of the English language. At the same time, the letters and the theme show me how far I have come since 1957. Regardless, the sentiment is still the same:

This is my country,
land of my choice.

Bob
"Dutch"
Robert